LICK

A LIP SMACKIN' BOOK

YOUR

FOR EVERY HOME COOK

PLATE

JULIE ALBERT & LISA GNAT

photography by **RYAN SZULC**

illustrations by **BEN WISEMAN**

appetite
by RANDOM HOUSE

For our parents Larry and Judy,
the best thing since sliced bread.

Appetite by Random House® is a registered trademark of Penguin Random House LLC.

Library and Archives of Canada Cataloguing in Publication is available upon request.

ISBN: 978-0-147-52988-6
eBook ISBN: 978-0-449-01698-5

Book design by CS Richardson
Printed and bound in China

Published in Canada by Appetite by Random House®,
a division of Penguin Random House Canada Limited

www.penguinrandomhouse.ca

10 9 8 7 6 5 4 3 2 1

appetite
by RANDOM HOUSE | Penguin
Random
House

"You like me, you really like me."

Sally Field

Praise for
LICK YOUR PLATE

"I've always had a fantasy about sisters . . . cooking for me. Lisa and Julie make it come true. Like so many men, there's only one room in my house where I know what I'm doing. And it's not the kitchen. Thank goodness these ladies can show me how amazing the kitchen can be (and how much more valuable it is than the room I'm better in). This is a fun, readable book with great, doable recipes—delicious, easy, largely no-muss, no-fuss—for real food, the kind mom said would put hair on my chest (she left out the section of meals that put hair on your head). If I weren't married, I would marry these women. It would be illegal in most places and I'd go to prison, but the food would be more than worth it. I love to eat. I love great food. I love these girls. I ate this book." **Jason Alexander, actor**

"These sisters know how to bring family and friends together with great food." **Jon Bon Jovi, musician**

"There is nothing better than the joy of the table: totally delicious, fresh food, shared with family and friends. For Julie and Lisa it is a true passion, and you can see their passion in this book—it's irresistible!" **Heather Reisman, founder, chair and CEO of Indigo**

"Julie and Lisa are sisters whose love for food, family and fun comes through in this out-of-this-world cookbook." **Chris Hadfield, astronaut**

"*Lick Your Plate* is the ultimate kitchen companion for the modern home cook. Loaded with drool-worthy dishes, and just the right amount of encouragement, it makes cooking for your family a rowdy, revelatory adventure!" **Gail Simmons, food critic, television host and cookbook author**

"Julie and Lisa know exactly what it takes to keep your family healthy, happy and well fed. This beautiful book is packed with real world recipes, loaded with big bright flavors, and crammed with the wisdom that can only be earned as a true family cook!" **Chef Michael Smith**

"An amazing resource for easy (and absolutely crave-able) nibbles, bites and meals. You'll always find this on my kitchen shelf!" **Meghan Markle, actor and founder of thetig.com**

"Julie and Lisa make me laugh, cook and eat. Their new book is a recipe for a delicious life." **Geraldo Rivera, television personality**

"*Lick Your Plate* is the ultimate cooking companion: a warm and witty collection of easy, tasty recipes that will leave the whole family asking for more." **Tori Avey, founder of toriavey.com**

"These two talented sisters make cooking humorous and just downright fun! With their always clever and delicious recipes, I can't help but keep coming back for more." **Elisha Cuthbert, actor**

CONTENTS

> "I'll have what she's having."
> Woman in restaurant, *When Harry Met Sally . . .*

[INTRODUCTION]

No need to covet; you can have what she's having—a party in your mouth. With the turn of a page (or in this case, 289 pages), you'll find a road map for dishing up delectable, doable and crowd-pleasing eats.

    Lick Your Plate is your new best friend in the kitchen, your go-to for 160 easy-to-follow, foolproof and delicious recipes. With a focus on hearty-yet-healthy food and readily available ingredients, you won't be asked to make a three-day meat sauce, haul out the deep-fryer or go on a wild-goose chase for juniper berries. What *Lick Your Plate* will do is save you time with invaluable tips and set you up for success with an arsenal of inspiring, guaranteed-great recipes that will take you through breakfast, lunch and dinner.

    Why should you trust us? We're sisters (and not the how-do-you-solve-a-problem-like-Maria variety, but the give-me-back-my-sweater kind) who love working and cooking up fun together. From Lisa's Easy-Bake Oven days, she has been experimenting in the kitchen, developing her bionic palate and our original recipes, while Julie hasn't stopped writing since she banged out her first chain letter on her IBM Selectric I typewriter. Together, with Lisa firmly planted at the stove and Julie at her laptop, we're a sister act whose goal is to bring easy eats and laughs to your table.

    With six teenagers between us, we understand time crunches, insatiable appetites and picky palates. We create cookbooks (*Bite Me, Bite Me Too* and now, *Lick Your Plate*) that speak to home cooks of all levels—real people with strong appetites to combine food, family, friends and fun. So get ready, because in no time, you're going to have everyone licking their plates.

    With you every step (and stir and whisk) of the way,

Julie & Lisa

To make the most of *Lick Your Plate*, keep your eyes peeled for these symbols:

LICKETY SPLIT
Meals under
30 minutes

BRAIN FOOD
Tips & trivia

SIDE PLATE
Recipe pairings

CHANGE IT UP
Swapping out
ingredients

SHORT CUT
Time-saving tricks

LET'S DO LUNCH
How to use leftovers

NO FORK REQUIRED

Pesto Chicken & Caprese Lettuce Wraps | 4

Caramelized Onion, White Cheddar & Arugula Pizza | 7

Mac & Cheese Cups with Buttery Bacon Crumble | 8

Apple, Fig Jam & Brie Grilled Cheese Bites | 11

Fresh Tomato & Whipped Feta Polenta Crisps | 12

Lime Chipotle Hummus with Spiced Pita Chips | 13

Grilled Shrimp & Guacamole Mini Tostadas | 14

Quick & Easy Beef Enchilada Nachos | 16

Easy Teriyaki Cocktail Meatballs | 17

Thai Turkey Sliders with Peanut Slaw | 18

Maple Sriracha Baked Chicken Wings | 20

Golden Edamame Dumplings | 21

Tofu Salad Rolls with Miso Dipping Sauce | 24

MAKES 12–16 lettuce wraps
PREP   10 minutes
       (+20 minute marinade)
COOK   15 minutes

. . . .

MARINADE

¼ cup fresh lemon juice
2 tbsp olive oil
½ tsp dried Italian herbs
½ tsp kosher salt
½ tsp freshly ground black
   pepper

4 boneless skinless chicken
   breasts

PESTO

2 cups fresh basil leaves, loosely
   packed
¼ cup ground almonds
½ small garlic clove, minced
1 tsp kosher salt
½ cup olive oil
½ cup freshly grated Parmesan
   cheese
1 tbsp fresh lemon juice

1½ cups cherry tomatoes, halved
1 cup mini bocconcini cheese
12–16 Boston (or Bibb) lettuce
       leaves or romaine leaves

Fresh basil, for garnish

I can be pretty helpful in the kitchen, but Lisa never lets me give her a hand. In fact, she's so territorial, I can't even wash her dishes. Despite her closed kitchen, I'm still going to give her a hand—a rousing round of applause for this healthy and delicious recipe, a lettuce wrap filled with juicy grilled pesto chicken, cherry tomatoes and creamy bocconcini cheese. Each bite of this hand-held wrap bursts with the fresh flavors of basil, almond and Parmesan pesto, along with the makings of a fork-free Caprese salad. Standing O, sister: you've got us eating out of your (actually, our) hands.

PESTO CHICKEN & CAPRESE LETTUCE WRAPS

1. FOR THE MARINADE, in a large bowl, whisk lemon juice, olive oil, Italian herbs, salt and pepper. Add chicken to marinade and marinate 20 minutes on the counter or refrigerate for longer marinating.

2. WHILE THE CHICKEN MARINATES, prepare the pesto. For the pesto, place the basil, almonds, garlic and salt in a food processor. Process 10 seconds to chop. While the machine is running, slowly pour in the olive oil in a steady stream until the mixture is smooth, about 10 seconds. Add the Parmesan cheese and lemon juice, processing just until incorporated.

3. PREHEAT GRILL to medium-high and oil the grill grate. Discard marinade and grill chicken 5–6 minutes per side, or until cooked through. Cool and cut into thin slices.

4. PLACE TOMATOES, bocconcini and cooked chicken in a large bowl. Toss with a generous amount of pesto to coat well.

5. TO ASSEMBLE LETTUCE WRAPS, place a lettuce leaf on a plate and top with a large spoonful of the chicken pesto mixture. Garnish with basil if desired.

. . . .

Bocconcini, meaning "a nibble" in Italian, is semisoft, bite-sized fresh mozzarella.

When you close your eyes and blow out your birthday candles, what do you wish for? World peace? Fairy-tale love? Not me. I hunger for a lifetime of endless pizza, slice after slice of cheesy, gooey goodness. Now, thanks to Lisa's pizza prowess, I no longer have to worry about takeout times and delayed deliveries. I know where I'm going to score my next pie—my own kitchen. Using this easy recipe, I can channel my inner Italian and whip up my own perfect pizza—crisp crust topped with sweet caramelized onions, sharp white cheddar, peppery arugula, juicy cherry tomatoes and finished with a sprinkle of tangy Gruyère whenever the mood strikes. See? Dreams really do come true.

MAKES 2 (10-inch) pizzas
PREP 20 minutes
(+30 minutes rising time)
COOK 35 minutes

CARAMELIZED ONION, WHITE CHEDDAR & ARUGULA PIZZA

1. FOR THE PIZZA DOUGH, in a large bowl, combine flour, yeast and salt. Add oil and water and knead lightly to combine ingredients. Turn dough out onto a floured surface and knead by hand for 3–5 minutes, until the dough is smooth and no longer sticky. You may need to add more flour as you are kneading. Coat a large bowl with nonstick cooking spray. Place dough in the bowl, cover with a dish towel and let rise for 30 minutes.

2. PREHEAT OVEN to 450°F and preheat a pizza stone for at least 30 minutes before baking pizzas.

3. TO PREPARE THE CARAMELIZED ONIONS, heat olive oil and butter in a large skillet over medium heat. Stir in onions, sugar and salt. Sauté 20 minutes, until onions are a deep golden color. Stir in balsamic vinegar and cook for 1 minute more. Set aside.

4. TO ASSEMBLE PIZZAS, divide the dough in half and roll each half into a 10-inch round on a lightly floured surface. Spread caramelized onions on the base of both pizzas. Sprinkle with white cheddar cheese. In a medium bowl, toss arugula, tomatoes, olive oil and salt. Place arugula mixture on top of the white cheddar and evenly sprinkle grated Gruyère over both pizzas. Drizzle a few drops of olive oil over the pizzas and sprinkle with salt. Transfer pizza to the preheated stone and bake until crust is golden, about 12–15 minutes.

PIZZA DOUGH
2 cups flour
1 package (¼ oz) active dry yeast (not rapid rise)
1 tsp kosher salt
2 tbsp olive oil
1 cup warm water
Extra flour, for kneading

CARAMELIZED ONIONS
1 tbsp olive oil
1 tbsp butter
2 large yellow onions, halved and thinly sliced
1 tsp sugar
½ tsp kosher salt
1 tbsp balsamic vinegar

1 cup grated sharp white cheddar cheese
3 cups loosely packed arugula
¾ cup cherry tomatoes, halved
2 tsp olive oil
Pinch kosher salt
½ cup grated Gruyère cheese
Olive oil, for drizzling
Kosher salt, to sprinkle

 Buy a prepared crust and top it as above.

MAKES	18 individual servings
PREP	5 minutes
COOK	40 minutes

. . . .

1   lb macaroni pasta

TOPPING

30   Ritz crackers (butter crackers)
5   bacon slices, cooked
½   cup freshly grated Parmesan
     cheese

CHEESE SAUCE

¼   cup butter
¼   cup flour
2½   cups whole milk, warmed
2   cups grated sharp cheddar
     cheese
2   cups grated mild cheddar
     cheese
2   cups grated Swiss cheese
½   tsp kosher salt
¼   tsp freshly ground black
     pepper
Pinch cayenne pepper

Who was your first crush? Mine was Mac (last name Cheese), and it was love at first bite. I simply couldn't resist the creamy, cheesy goodness that each and every bowl delivered. Now, as an adult, I'm reunited with my childhood sweetheart in the form of these heartwarming and drool-worthy individual cups of comfort, brimming with old-fashioned cheddar and Swiss mac 'n' cheese. Topped with crumbly bacon, buttery crackers and Parmesan cheese, each rich and delicious bite has me whispering those three magic words: "Love you, Mac."

MAC & CHEESE CUPS WITH BUTTERY BACON CRUMBLE

1. PREHEAT OVEN to 350°F. Coat 18 (3- × 2-inch-deep) individual ramekins (or one 13- × 9-inch baking dish) with nonstick cooking spray. In a large pot of lightly salted water, cook pasta until just tender. Drain well and set aside.

2. FOR THE TOPPING, in a medium bowl, coarsely crumble crackers and bacon together. Mix in Parmesan cheese and toss to combine. Set aside.

3. IN A LARGE SAUCEPAN, melt butter over medium-low heat. Remove from heat and whisk in flour until smooth. Return to heat and whisk constantly for 2 minutes. Pour in the milk, whisking constantly for 5 minutes, until mixture has thickened and coats the back of a spoon. Remove from heat and stir in the sharp cheddar, mild cheddar, Swiss cheese, salt, pepper and cayenne. Return to heat and stir just until cheese melts. Remove from heat and add cooked pasta and stir to combine. Transfer to prepared baking dishes and top with bacon and cracker crumble. Bake for 15 minutes (20 minutes for 13- × 9-inch baking dish) until golden on top and heated through.

"Once we hit forty, women have about four taste buds left:
one for vodka, one for wine, one for cheese, and one for chocolate."

Gina Barreca

Ah, the classic cheese plate, where you find yourself playing cheese roulette (surprise, it's rank Roquefort!) and trying to balance your cracker and knife and wine glass, and well, you get the messy picture. What if we told you that you could have all that's right about cheese platters (delicious cheese and fruit and jam, oh my!) in one dreamy bite? Feast your eyes on these golden grilled cheese appetizers, each and every morsel overrun with creamy melted Brie, sweet fig jam, tart apples and peppery arugula, sandwiched between crusty, buttery bread. The only challenge you'll have here is finding the strength not to eat them all yourself.

APPLE, FIG JAM & BRIE GRILLED CHEESE BITES

1. TO ASSEMBLE SANDWICHES, spread softened butter on one side of each slice of bread. Flip the bread over and spread fig jam on the other side of each slice. On 6 of the bread slices, layer Brie cheese over the fig jam, followed by the arugula and apples, and finish with more Brie cheese. Top with the remaining 6 slices of bread with the jam side down.

2. HEAT A GRIDDLE over medium heat and cook sandwiches 2–3 minutes per side, until both sides are golden. Remove from heat and cool a few minutes before slicing. Cut each sandwich into thirds or quarters and serve.

MAKES	6 full sandwiches, 18–24 small bites
PREP	5 minutes
COOK	5 minutes

6   tbsp butter, softened
12 pieces crusty, thick-sliced bread
¾   cup fig jam
12 oz Brie cheese
1½ cups baby arugula
1   Granny Smith apple, thinly sliced

Bacon + Honey + Blue Cheese
Pear + Arugula + Havarti
Caramelized Onions + Thyme + Gruyère

"Who do you think would win in a fight between a grilled cheese sandwich and a taco?"

Andy Samberg

Crackers are *so* yesterday. I mean, when was the last time you saw anyone drool over crackers? Exactly, and that's why this inspired and elegant appetizer, a modern take on cheese and crackers, is all the more mouthwatering. Creamy homemade feta polenta is cut into rounds, sautéed until golden and topped with a tangy whipped feta spread, juicy tomatoes, garlic and fresh basil. One taste and you too will discover why we all look to Leading Edge Lisa for *au courant*, front-burner bites.

FRESH TOMATO & WHIPPED FETA POLENTA CRISPS

MAKES 38–40 polenta crisps
PREP 10 minutes
COOK 15 minutes
(+30 minutes cooling time)

. . . .

POLENTA

5 cups water
1 tsp kosher salt
1 cup yellow cornmeal
¼ cup crumbled feta cheese
2 tbsp olive oil

FETA SPREAD

1½ cups crumbled feta cheese
3 tbsp olive oil
1 tbsp fresh lemon juice

TOMATO TOPPING

1½ cups cherry tomatoes, halved
2 tsp olive oil
1 tsp red wine vinegar
½ small garlic clove, minced
⅛ tsp kosher salt

2 tbsp thinly sliced fresh basil

1. FOR THE POLENTA, coat a large rimmed baking sheet with nonstick cooking spray. In a large pot, bring 5 cups water and 1 teaspoon salt to a boil over high heat. Reduce heat to low and slowly add the cornmeal, stirring constantly with a wooden spoon, about 10 minutes. Remove from heat and stir in feta. Spoon polenta on to prepared baking sheet and spread evenly. Let cool 30 minutes, until firm. Once firm, cut out polenta rounds using a 2-inch cookie cutter.

2. IN A LARGE SKILLET, heat olive oil over medium-low heat. Add polenta rounds and cook 4 minutes until golden, flip and continue to cook 2 minutes more. Remove from heat and set aside.

3. FOR THE FETA SPREAD, in a mini food processor, combine feta cheese, olive oil and lemon juice. Process until feta is smooth. Cover and refrigerate until ready to use.

4. FOR THE TOMATO TOPPING, in a medium bowl, toss tomatoes, olive oil, red wine vinegar, garlic and salt.

5. TO ASSEMBLE, spread feta mixture over each polenta crisp. Place tomatoes on top and sprinkle with fresh basil.

. . . .

 Cut rounds from prepared polenta tubes if you don't have time to make your own.

Lisa's all about working smarter, not harder, so why was she telling me to make my own hummus and chips when I could easily buy them? Fast, fresh and delicious topped her list, followed by zesty, healthy and simple. I was sold and got to work (really, when it takes less than 15 minutes, can I call it work?) on creating this smoky, surprising twist on traditional hummus. The results were fantastic—a blend of chipotle peppers, chickpeas and spices, piled high on baked, crunchy, spiced pita chips. Once again, Lisa earns her keep around here (and saves us all a few bucks and calories) with this fantastically flavorful finger food.

LIME CHIPOTLE HUMMUS WITH SPICED PITA CHIPS

1. FOR THE HUMMUS, gently rub the drained chickpeas in a clean dish towel to remove most of the chickpea skins—this will result in a smoother hummus. Place in a food processor along with lime juice, garlic, chipotle pepper, adobo sauce and salt. Pulse a few times and add the olive oil. Continue to process until smooth. Remove and store in an airtight container in the refrigerator until ready to serve. When serving, garnish with flat-leaf parsley.

2. FOR THE PITA CHIPS, preheat oven to 400°F. Line a baking sheet with parchment paper. In a small bowl, combine olive oil, cumin, chili powder, paprika, salt and cayenne pepper, mixing well. Brush both sides of each pita with the olive oil mixture. Cut each pita bread into 8 wedges. Place on prepared baking sheet in a single layer. Bake for 8 minutes, flip and bake 5–6 minutes more, until golden and crispy.

 There are approximately 2 tablespoons of juice in a medium-sized lime.

 MAKES 2 cups of hummus and 32 pita chips
PREP 15 minutes
COOK 15 minutes

HUMMUS
1 (15 oz) can chickpeas, rinsed and drained
2 tbsp fresh lime juice
1 small garlic clove, minced
1 canned chipotle pepper in adobo sauce
1 tsp adobo sauce
¼ tsp kosher salt
¼ cup olive oil

1 tbsp coarsely chopped fresh flat-leaf parsley

PITA CHIPS
2 tbsp olive oil
¼ tsp ground cumin
¼ tsp chili powder
¼ tsp paprika
¼ tsp kosher salt
Pinch cayenne pepper
4 (6-inch) pita breads

MAKES 16–20 mini tostadas

PREP 5 minutes (+30 minute marinade and skewer soak)

COOK 5 minutes

. . . .

Kebab skewers (metal, wood or bamboo)

SPICY SHRIMP

1 lb large shrimp, peeled and deveined
2 tbsp fresh lime juice
1 tbsp olive oil
1 tsp chipotle chili powder
½ tsp ground cumin
½ tsp paprika
½ tsp kosher salt
¼ tsp freshly ground black pepper

GUACAMOLE

2 large ripe avocados
2 tbsp chopped fresh flat-leaf parsley
1 tbsp fresh lime juice
1 large tomato, seeded and chopped
½ small jalapeño pepper, seeded and chopped
¼ tsp kosher salt

16–20 small tortilla chips
1 lime, to squeeze over top

Fresh flat-leaf parsley, coarsely chopped, for garnish

A bunch of sayings come to mind when thinking about this amazing appetizer, namely *good things come in small packages* and *don't sweat the small stuff*. Yes, in this case, great, bold and enormously flavorful things come in small packages, like these one-bite mini tostadas of crispy tortilla chips topped with spice-marinated grilled shrimp and vibrant tomato jalapeño guacamole. As for sweating the small stuff, while the spicy kick from the shrimp and guacamole might leave you aglow, you won't have to mop your brow from hard work—these tiny tostadas can be pulled together in next to no time.

GRILLED SHRIMP & GUACAMOLE MINI TOSTADAS

1. IF THE KEBAB SKEWERS are wood or bamboo, soak them in water for 30 minutes before threading shrimp and vegetables.

2. FOR THE SHRIMP, place in a medium bowl and toss with lime juice, olive oil, chipotle chili powder, cumin, paprika, salt and pepper. Marinate shrimp for 20–30 minutes. Preheat barbecue to medium-high. Skewer shrimp and grill 2 minutes per side, until just cooked through.

3. FOR THE GUACAMOLE, in a medium bowl, mash the avocados. Stir in parsley, lime juice, tomatoes, jalapeño peppers and salt.

4. TO ASSEMBLE, place a spoonful of guacamole on each chip. Top with a grilled shrimp, squeeze lime juice over top and sprinkle with chopped parsley.

. . . .

Shrimp is highly perishable. We recommend buying frozen shrimp and thawing by either placing them in a refrigerator overnight or in a colander under cold running water.

Hold on to your sombrero, amigo, because this grande Tex-Mex treat is going to blow your party hat right off. Layers of bold and flavorful enchilada-spiced meat top crunchy tortilla chips, along with melted cheddar cheese and chunks of tomato and avocado. Tasting every bit like an enchilada-nacho collision, this Juan-in-a-million (too much?) appetizer takes 20 minutes to whip together, making it perfect fare for a fast fiesta.

QUICK & EASY
BEEF ENCHILADA NACHOS

1. IN A LARGE SKILLET, cook the ground beef and chopped onion over medium heat for 5 minutes, or until beef is no longer pink and onions are tender. Drain and return to pan, adding chili powder, cumin, paprika, cayenne, salt, enchilada sauce, black beans and salsa. Simmer for 5 minutes over medium-low heat. Remove from heat and set aside.

2. TO ASSEMBLE, preheat oven to 375°F. Line a baking sheet with aluminum foil and coat with nonstick cooking spray. Spread a single layer of tortilla chips on the baking sheet. Top with half the beef mixture followed by 1 cup of grated cheddar cheese. Pile the remainder of the chips over and layer the remainder of the beef mixture. Finish with 1 cup of grated cheese. Bake for 10 minutes, until cheese has melted. Remove from oven and top with diced tomatoes and avocados.

SERVES 6–8
PREP 5 minutes
COOK 20 minutes

. . . .

1   lb lean ground beef
1   small white onion, chopped
1   tsp chili powder
1   tsp ground cumin
½   tsp paprika
¼   tsp cayenne pepper
Pinch kosher salt
1   cup enchilada sauce
1   cup canned black beans,
     rinsed and drained
½   cup salsa

1   (10 oz) bag tortilla chips
2   cups grated cheddar cheese
3   plum tomatoes, diced
2   ripe avocados, diced

"I don't need a thinner phone. You know what I need? I need a tortilla chip that can support the weight of guacamole."

Ellen DeGeneres

Folks, it's a whole new ball game. You can now ditch those preservative-laden bottles of teriyaki sauce and serve up your own super-simple version, a lustrous sauce of Japanese rice wine, soy sauce, brown sugar and honey. You'll quickly discover that you can't get enough of this terrific teriyaki and since it isn't *sugoi* (translation: "cool") to drink it, you can pour it over these tender baked meatballs, easily helping you hit a home run with this all-star appetizer.

EASY TERIYAKI COCKTAIL MEATBALLS

1. FOR THE TERIYAKI SAUCE, in a medium saucepan, bring mirin to a boil over medium heat. Reduce heat to low and simmer for 4 minutes. Add soy sauce, brown sugar, rice vinegar, honey and ginger, whisking to combine. In a small bowl, stir together cornstarch and water. Add to saucepan, turn heat to medium-high and continue to whisk until slightly thickened, about 3–4 minutes. Remove from heat and set aside.

2. FOR THE MEATBALLS, preheat oven to 400°F. Line a baking sheet with aluminum foil and coat with nonstick cooking spray. In a large bowl, combine beef, panko, 3 tablespoons homemade teriyaki sauce, egg yolks, garlic, ginger, Sriracha and salt. Shape the mixture into approximately 35 (1-inch round) meatballs and place on prepared baking sheet. Bake for 10 minutes, flip meatballs and continue to bake for 10 minutes more. Remove from oven and let meatballs sit on paper towel to drain. Add meatballs to remaining teriyaki sauce and toss well to coat. Garnish meatballs with sliced green onions if desired.

 Easily transform this appetizer into a main course by serving it over rice.

MAKES	35 (1-inch round) meatballs
PREP	20 minutes
COOK	25 minutes

TERIYAKI SAUCE

¾ cup mirin
1 cup soy sauce
¼ cup brown sugar
2 tbsp rice vinegar
1 tbsp honey
½ tsp grated fresh ginger
2 tbsp cornstarch
2 tbsp water

MEATBALLS

1½ lb lean ground beef
½ cup panko (Japanese breadcrumbs)
3 tbsp teriyaki sauce (see above)
2 egg yolks
1 small garlic clove, minced
½ tsp grated fresh ginger
½ tsp Sriracha sauce
½ tsp kosher salt

Green onions, for garnish

MAKES 12 sliders
PREP 15 minutes
COOK 10 minutes

. . . .

PEANUT SAUCE

¼ cup smooth peanut butter
1 small garlic clove, minced
2 tbsp soy sauce
1 tbsp brown sugar
1 tbsp rice vinegar
1 tbsp fresh lime juice
2 tsp honey
1 tsp Sriracha sauce
1 tsp sesame oil
½ tsp grated fresh ginger

CRUNCHY SLAW

2 cups shredded cabbage
1 small carrot, peeled and
  shredded
1 tbsp chopped fresh flat-leaf
  parsley

TURKEY BURGER

1 lb lean ground turkey
2 tbsp smooth peanut butter
1 small carrot, peeled and
  shredded
1 green onion, minced
1 tbsp chopped fresh flat-leaf
  parsley
½ tsp grated fresh ginger
½ tsp Sriracha sauce
Vegetable oil
Kosher salt

12 slider buns

Want to see your guests go nuts? Serve up these Thai Turkey Sliders, the appetizer equivalent of potato chips—there's no such thing as eating just one. What makes these sliders-with-slaw so addictive to eat and fun to make? You don't have to work your buns off to whip up these juicy mini turkey burgers bursting with flavor from peanut butter, ginger and parsley, slathered in a lip-smacking peanut sauce and surrounded by crunchy Asian slaw. So delicious, this crowd-pleaser is bound to become the life of your next party.

THAI TURKEY SLIDERS WITH PEANUT SLAW

1. FOR THE PEANUT SAUCE, in a blender combine peanut butter, garlic, soy sauce, brown sugar, rice vinegar, lime juice, honey, Sriracha, sesame oil and ginger. Blend until smooth. Set aside.

2. FOR THE SLAW, in a medium bowl, toss cabbage, shredded carrots and parsley with 3 tablespoons of peanut sauce. Reserve the remaining peanut sauce to spread on slider buns.

3. FOR THE TURKEY BURGER, in a medium bowl, combine ground turkey, peanut butter, shredded carrot, green onion, parsley, ginger and Sriracha. Stir to incorporate all ingredients. Form into 12 small slider patties. Lightly oil one side of the burgers and sprinkle with kosher salt. Heat a grill pan over medium-high heat. Cook, turning once, until crusty and cooked through, about 3½–4½ minutes per side.

4. TO ASSEMBLE, spread both sides of each slider bun with a generous amount of peanut sauce. Place coleslaw on the bottom bun, top with turkey burger and finish with another small scoop of coleslaw. Place top bun on top and serve.

. . . .

Double the size of the patties (making 6 instead of 12), cook as directed and serve with oven-baked sweet potato fries.

SERVES 6–8
PREP 15 minutes
COOK 40 minutes

. . . .

CHICKEN WINGS

1¼ cups flour
1 tsp brown sugar
1 tsp ground ginger
1 tsp paprika
1 tsp kosher salt
½ tsp freshly ground black
 pepper
¼ tsp cayenne pepper
2 eggs
2 tbsp water
3 lb chicken wings, split,
 wing-tip removed
2 tbsp melted butter

MAPLE SRIRACHA SAUCE

¼ cup butter
2 garlic cloves, minced
¾ cup maple syrup
2 tbsp Sriracha sauce

We two not-so-spring-chicken sisters have been called a lot of things over the years. Lisa's sweet, I'm spicy. Lisa's smooth, I'm bold. Lisa's mellow, I'm peppy. In other words, Lisa's sugary maple syrup and I'm zippy Sriracha sauce, which, when combined, makes one of the most luscious, zesty, addictively sweet and spicy glazes. Tossed with crispy baked chicken wings, this appetizer rules the roost, hereby making us the Superb Saucy Sisters, right?

MAPLE SRIRACHA BAKED CHICKEN WINGS

1. PREHEAT OVEN to 400°F. Line a baking sheet with aluminum foil and place a cooling rack on top of the baking sheet for the wings to cook on. Coat the cooling rack with nonstick cooking spray.

2. FOR THE WINGS, in a large bowl, combine flour, brown sugar, ground ginger, paprika, salt, black pepper and cayenne pepper. In a medium bowl, whisk together eggs and water. Dredge chicken wings in flour and shake off excess. Dip in eggs, letting the excess drip off before dropping back into the flour mixture for a final coat, making sure the chicken wings are coated all over. Place on prepared rack and drizzle with 2 tablespoons of melted butter. Bake for 20 minutes, flip wings over and continue to bake 20 minutes more, until wings are golden and cooked through.

3. IN THE FINAL 10 MINUTES of the wings cooking, prepare the maple Sriracha sauce. In a small saucepan, melt butter over medium heat. Add minced garlic, cooking for 1 minute until softened. Stir in maple syrup and Sriracha sauce and bring to a boil. Reduce heat to low and simmer for 5 minutes or until sauce has thickened slightly. Remove sauce from heat. Place cooked wings in a large bowl and toss with enough sauce to coat them well. Serve with extra sauce.

. . . .

Sriracha (pronounced sir-ah-cha) is the uber-popular Thai condiment of chili peppers, garlic, vinegar, sugar and salt.

When I started going on about how difficult dumplings sound to make, Lisa shushed me and said, "Silence is golden." Very sage advice. But that didn't help me in my quest to become a dumpling doyenne. It turns out I was wrong. The second I stopped my bellyaching and started following Lisa's simple instructions, I was easily able to serve up these golden-bottomed pockets stuffed with a savory combination of edamame, miso, basil and lemon. Dipped in a sweet and spicy Asian dipping sauce, these elegant and utterly delicious edamame dumplings once again prove that when the student is ready (and hungry), the master appears.

GOLDEN EDAMAME DUMPLINGS

1. FOR THE EDAMAME FILLING, in a food processor, combine cooked edamame, basil, olive oil, lemon juice, miso paste, sugar, garlic, ginger, salt and cayenne. Pulse until combined but still chunky.

2. TO ASSEMBLE THE DUMPLINGS, spoon 1 heaping teaspoon of the edamame mixture in the center of each wrapper. Brush a little water around all edges of the dumpling. Fold wrapper over to form a triangle and press to tightly secure edges. Place the dumplings on a baking sheet that has been dusted with cornstarch. Loosely cover finished dumplings with plastic wrap.

3. WHEN READY TO START COOKING, in a large nonstick skillet, heat 1 tablespoon olive oil over medium-high heat. Add ⅓ of the dumplings, placing them seam side up and spread apart. Let cook for 1 minute until the bottom of the dumpling is golden. Pour ¼ cup water into the pan and immediately cover with a tight-fitting lid. Let dumplings steam over medium heat for 4 minutes. Remove dumplings, wipe out skillet and repeat with remaining dumplings. Serve with dipping sauce.

4. FOR THE DIPPING SAUCE, whisk together soy sauce, rice vinegar, honey, Sriracha and green onion.

MAKES 36–40 dumplings
PREP 20 minutes
COOK 10 minutes

· ·

EDAMAME FILLING

1½ cups frozen shelled edamame, cooked
¼ cup chopped fresh basil
3 tbsp olive oil
1 tbsp fresh lemon juice
2 tsp yellow miso paste
1 tsp sugar
1 small garlic clove, minced
½ tsp grated fresh ginger
¼ tsp kosher salt
Pinch cayenne pepper

36–40 wonton or dumpling wrappers
Water
3 tbsp olive oil

DIPPING SAUCE
¼ cup soy sauce
2 tbsp rice vinegar
2 tsp honey
½ tsp Sriracha sauce
1 tbsp chopped green onion

"I am the emperor, and I want dumplings."

Emperor Ferdinand I

Photo on next page →

Golden Edamame Dumplings, page 21

MAKES 10 large wraps

PREP 15 minutes
(+30 minute marinade)

COOK 20 minutes

. . . .

WRAPS

1   package (14 oz) extra-firm tofu
2   tbsp soy sauce
1   tbsp yellow miso paste
1   tbsp rice vinegar
1   tbsp mirin
1   tsp sesame oil
½   tsp grated fresh ginger

MISO DIPPING SAUCE

⅓   cup mayonnaise
2   tbsp yellow miso paste
1   tbsp mirin
1   tsp soy sauce
¼   tsp wasabi paste

10 round (8 ½-inch) rice paper sheets
2   medium carrots, peeled and julienned
2   firm, ripe avocados, thinly sliced
¼   cup coarsely chopped fresh mint
2½ cups baby kale

Under Lisa's tutelage, I've learned to become fearless (or at least fake it) in the kitchen. However, I must confess that when she hauled out the rice paper wraps, my knees were a-knockin'. Would my Hulk-like strength rip these delicate wrappers to shreds? Would my Lennie (as in *Of Mice and Men*)-like hands be able to nimbly wrap these rolls? Turns out, there was no reason to worry because these healthy handheld bites of marinated and baked tofu, wrapped up with carrots, mint and miso sauce, are foolproof. With every fresh and fantastic mouthful, I'm once again reminded that when Lisa's at the helm, the only thing I need to worry about is making sure I get seconds and thirds and fourths and . . .

TOFU SALAD ROLLS WITH MISO DIPPING SAUCE

1. PREHEAT OVEN to 400°F and line a baking sheet with parchment paper.

2. FOR THE WRAPS, slice the tofu into 20 strips and dry with paper towels. Place tofu strips in a flat-bottomed dish. In a small bowl, whisk soy sauce, miso, rice vinegar, mirin, sesame oil and ginger. Pour marinade over tofu, toss and cover for 30 minutes. Discard marinade and place tofu on baking sheet. Bake 8 minutes, flip and continue to bake 8 minutes more. Allow to cool before assembling.

3. FOR THE DIPPING SAUCE, whisk mayonnaise, miso paste, mirin, soy sauce and wasabi paste. When well combined, cover and refrigerate until ready to assemble.

4. TO ASSEMBLE THE WRAPS, place 1 rice paper sheet in a shallow bowl of hot water until just softened, about 1 minute. Lay wet rice paper sheet on a dish towel. Place 2 slices of tofu in the middle of the wrap. Layer with julienned carrots, avocado slices, fresh mint and baby kale. Drizzle a small spoonful of miso dipping sauce. Fold in the right side, followed by the left side and then the top and bottom forming a tight cylinder. Repeat with remaining rice paper sheets and filling. Place finished wraps under a damp cloth until ready to serve to prevent them from hardening. Slice rolls in half diagonally and serve with miso dipping sauce.

. . . .

Mirin is a sweet rice wine used in Japanese cooking. You can find it in the Asian food aisle of all large supermarkets.

STEAMED-UP

[SOUPS]

Tomato Quinoa Soup with Chickpea Crunch | 28

Creamy Corn & Butternut Squash Chowder | 30

Sweet Potato Soup with Pecan Crumble | 31

Roasted Root Vegetable Soup with Herb & Cheese Croutons | 32

Spring Vegetable Minestrone with Orzo | 35

Moroccan Chickpea & Lemon Couscous Soup | 36

Spiced Red Lentil Soup | 38

Slow Cooker Beef, Vegetable & Noodle Soup | 39

Vietnamese Beef & Noodle Pho | 40

Shrimp Ramen Noodle Soup | 42

Chunky Chicken & Vegetable Dumpling Soup | 43

Thai Coconut & Ginger Chicken Soup | 45

Chicken Enchilada Soup Topped with Crunchy Tortillas | 46

Soba Noodle Miso Soup Topped with a Poached Egg | 48

SERVES 6
PREP 10 minutes
COOK 1 hour

. . . .

CHICKPEA CRUNCH

1½ cups canned chickpeas, rinsed
and drained
1 tbsp olive oil
¼ tsp kosher salt

SOUP

1 tbsp butter
1 tbsp olive oil
1 medium yellow onion,
chopped
2 celery stalks, chopped
1 large garlic clove, minced
1½ tsp mild curry powder
1 tsp fresh ginger, minced
½ tsp whole fennel seed
¼ tsp ground cumin
½ tsp kosher salt
¼ tsp freshly ground black
pepper
¾ cup dry white wine
4 cups vegetable broth
1 (28 oz) tin whole tomatoes,
crushed with hands

QUINOA

2 cups vegetable broth
1 cup quinoa, well rinsed
1 tsp minced fresh ginger
¼ tsp ground cumin
¼ tsp kosher salt

2 tbsp butter

Do you know how many times I've been told to put on layers? Countless. Now, do you know how many times I've considered layering soup? Never. That's why I have Lisa, the Queen of Comfort, around to create a soup with so many layers that it's bound to keep me warm from the cold. At the base, there's tomato soup, a velvety soup chock-full of toasty spices such as ginger, cumin, curry and fennel seeds. Next, there's the addition of protein-rich quinoa, a nutritional powerhouse that serves up major fuel and fiber. Finally, there are crunchy baked chickpeas, adding protein-packed bites as the top layer. Yes, with this soup in our bowls (and bellies), we'll only be wearing T-shirts to brave the elements. Just don't tell our mom.

TOMATO QUINOA SOUP WITH CHICKPEA CRUNCH

1. FOR THE CHICKPEA CRUNCH, preheat oven to 400°F. Dry chickpeas off well with paper towel. In a medium bowl, toss chickpeas with olive oil and salt and place on a baking sheet lined with parchment paper. Bake for 30–35 minutes, until the chickpeas are golden and crunchy.

2. TO MAKE THE SOUP, in a large soup pot, heat butter and olive oil over medium heat. Add onion and celery, cooking for 4 minutes to soften. Add garlic, curry, ginger, fennel seed, cumin, salt and pepper. Cook, stirring constantly, for 1 minute. Add white wine and simmer until almost completely evaporated, about 5 minutes. Add vegetable broth and tomatoes and bring to a boil. Reduce heat to low and simmer for 20 minutes.

3. WHILE THE SOUP IS SIMMERING, prepare the quinoa. In a medium saucepan, combine vegetable broth, quinoa, ginger, cumin and salt. Bring to a boil over high heat. Reduce heat to low, cover and simmer for 15 minutes until all liquid is absorbed. Remove from heat and let sit for 5 minutes, covered.

4. REMOVE SOUP FROM HEAT and stir in butter and cooked quinoa. Serve each bowl with a handful of crunchy chickpeas.

"Some friends of mine got me a sweater for my birthday. I'd have preferred a moaner or a screamer, but the sweater was OK."

Steven Wright

When I hear "chowder," I instantly think of New England and Manhattan, and then I spend a few minutes saying "chowder" in different accents. However, Lisa skips the East Coast and tomfoolery and heads straight to the Corn Belt, where she draws inspiration for this *Field of Dreams* Corn and Butternut Squash Chowder. Sweet corn and creamy butternut squash replace clams and potatoes in a richly flavored broth (thanks to the simple trick of adding corncobs as it simmers) that has a little cayenne kick and is topped with toasted, crunchy corn. I assure you—if you make it, they will eat.

CREAMY CORN & BUTTERNUT SQUASH CHOWDER

SERVES 4–6
PREP 10 minutes
COOK 35 minutes

. . . .

SOUP
6 ears fresh corn
2 tbsp butter
1 medium yellow onion, chopped
4 cups butternut squash, cut into 1-inch cubes
1 tsp chopped fresh thyme
¾ tsp kosher salt
¼ tsp freshly ground black pepper
¼ tsp cayenne pepper
4 cups chicken broth
¼ cup heavy cream

CORN TOPPING
1 tsp butter
½ cup reserved corn kernels
Pinch kosher salt
Pinch chopped fresh thyme

1. FOR THE SOUP, cut corn off cobs. Reserve 4 of the cobs to use in the broth and ½ cup corn kernels to top each serving of soup.

2. IN A LARGE SOUP POT, melt butter over medium heat. Add onion and cook to soften, approximately 4 minutes. Add corn kernels to onions, along with butternut squash, thyme, salt, pepper and cayenne. Cover and let cook over low heat for 10 minutes. Add chicken broth and 4 reserved corncobs. Bring to a boil over medium heat and cook, partially covered, for 20 minutes. Remove and discard corncobs.

3. REMOVE SOUP from heat and purée using a handheld immersion blender. Stir in cream.

4. FOR THE CORN TOPPING, melt 1 teaspoon of the butter in a small skillet over medium-high heat. Add reserved ½ cup of corn and sauté with salt and thyme until corn is golden. Remove from heat and garnish each serving with a small spoon of sautéed corn.

. . . .

 An average ear of corn has 800 kernels, with one strand of silk for each kernel.

When is soup like a dessert? "Never," you say? Well, pick up your soup spoon and prepare to eat humble pie with this velvety sweet potato soup. Topped with a homemade pecan crumble and laced with cinnamon and nutmeg, this creamy (yet creamless) soup tastes like sweet potato pie in a bowl. And the best part is you won't break a sweat (dare we say it's as easy as pie?) or your diet.

SWEET POTATO SOUP WITH PECAN CRUMBLE

1. PREHEAT OVEN to 400°F. Wash and prick the sweet potatoes with a fork. Bake 45–55 minutes, until soft and tender.

2. WHILE POTATOES ARE BAKING, in a large soup pot, melt butter over medium heat. Add the onions and cook until softened, 5–6 minutes. Add the garlic, ginger, cinnamon, salt, nutmeg and cayenne. Cook, stirring, for 1 minute. Stir in maple syrup until combined. Stir in vegetable broth and bring to a boil. Reduce heat to low and simmer 15 minutes. Once potatoes are tender, remove from the oven, cooling just enough to be able to handle. Scoop out the flesh of the potatoes and add to the soup. Remove from heat and using a handheld immersion blender, purée the soup. Stir in lemon juice. To serve, garnish the top of each bowl with pecan crumble.

3. TO MAKE THE CRUMBLE, preheat oven to 350°F. In a medium bowl, combine flour, pecans, brown sugar, cinnamon, salt and butter. Mix with your fingers until mixture is crumbly. Place on a baking sheet lined with parchment paper. Bake 10 minutes.

> "I guess I'm just a lucky guy and I'm prepared to tell you why. It's strictly on account of my sweet potato pie."
>
> James Taylor, *Sweet Potato Pie*

SERVES 6

PREP 10 minutes

COOK 1 hour, 20 minutes

. . . .

SOUP

3 lb (about 5) sweet potatoes
2 tbsp butter
1 medium yellow onion, chopped
1 small garlic clove, minced
1 tsp minced fresh ginger
¼ tsp ground cinnamon
¼ tsp kosher salt
Pinch ground nutmeg
Pinch cayenne pepper
2 tsp maple syrup
6½ cups vegetable broth
1 tbsp fresh lemon juice

PECAN CRUMBLE

½ cup flour
½ cup chopped raw pecans
2 tbsp brown sugar
¼ tsp ground cinnamon
¼ tsp kosher salt
3 tbsp butter, softened

SERVES 6
PREP 20 minutes
COOK 1 hour

. . . .

SOUP

1½ cups Yukon gold potatoes,
     peeled, cut into 1-inch cubes
1½ cups sweet potatoes, peeled
     and cut into 1-inch cubes
1   cup parsnips, peeled and cut
     into 1-inch cubes
1   cup carrots, peeled and cut
     into 1-inch cubes
2   tbsp olive oil
4   sprigs of thyme, leaves only
½   tsp kosher salt
½   tsp freshly ground black
     pepper
2   tbsp butter
1   medium red onion, chopped
½   cup dry white wine
6   cups vegetable broth
1   tbsp butter
1   tbsp fresh lemon juice
¼   tsp kosher salt, or more to taste

HERB & CHEESE CROUTONS

2   cups 1-inch cubes baguette
     bread
2   tsp olive oil
¼   tsp dried thyme
¼   tsp kosher salt
2   tbsp grated Gruyère cheese

When Lisa told me to start roasting, I immediately announced to everyone that she's a crybaby who can't ride a bike. When the room went silent, I realized she was talking about *veggies*. Yes, while Lisa can be a bit of a trike-riding blubberer, she sure knows her stuff—roasting root vegetables such as potatoes, parsnips and carrots does magically enhance their natural sweetness and help bring a depth of flavor to this scrumptious soup of vegetables, thyme and white wine. And if that isn't enough, Lisa has topped this smooth soup with homemade crunchy herb and cheese croutons. Guess I'm not going to be invited to emcee her roast anytime soon.

ROASTED ROOT VEGETABLE SOUP WITH HERB & CHEESE CROUTONS

1. FOR THE SOUP, preheat the oven to 425°F. Place cut vegetables in a large bowl and toss with olive oil, thyme, salt and pepper. Place on a baking sheet lined with parchment paper and cook 25–30 minutes, until vegetables are tender. Stir halfway through cooking.

2. IN A LARGE SOUP POT, melt 2 tablespoons butter over medium heat. Add onion and cook until softened, 5 minutes. Add white wine and let evaporate, scraping any browned bits from the bottom of the pot. Add vegetable broth and bring to a boil. Reduce heat to low and stir in roasted vegetables, continuing to simmer for 10 minutes.

3. REMOVE POT FROM STOVE and using a handheld immersion blender, purée the soup until smooth. Return soup to stove and over low heat, stir in 1 tablespoon butter, lemon juice and salt. Sprinkle each serving of soup with croutons.

4. FOR THE CROUTONS, preheat oven to 375°F. In a medium bowl, toss cubed bread with olive oil, thyme and salt. Place on a baking sheet lined with parchment paper and bake 10 minutes. Remove from oven and sprinkle Gruyère cheese over top. Bake 3 minutes more, until golden.

Minestrone soup recipes vary by region and by *nonna*. While we always enjoy the hearty tomato-based variety, we're also huge fans of this healthy Spring Vegetable Minestrone, a soup that's created straight from the garden patch—chunks of zucchini, carrots and new potatoes mingle with leafy spinach, sweet peas and fresh herbs. With the addition of tender orzo and protein-packed chickpeas, this scrumptious soup is perfect as a satisfying lunch or dinnertime addition.

SPRING VEGETABLE MINESTRONE WITH ORZO

1. IN A LARGE SOUP POT, heat olive oil over medium heat. Add onion and cook for 3 minutes. Stir in white wine and let evaporate, scraping any browned bits from the bottom of the pot. Add carrots, zucchinis and potatoes. Cook 5 minutes, stirring occasionally. Stir in garlic, thyme, oregano, salt and pepper, cooking for 1 minute. Add chicken broth and bring to a boil. Reduce heat and simmer, partially covered, for 15 minutes.

2. WHILE SOUP SIMMERS, cook orzo in lightly salted boiling water for 10 minutes, or until tender. Drain well and add to soup along with chickpeas and green peas. Cook over low heat for 2 minutes to heat. Remove from heat and stir in baby spinach. Top each bowl with a generous serving of grated Parmesan cheese.

"Despite the forecast, live like it's spring."

Lilly Pulitzer

SERVES   8–10
PREP   15 minutes
COOK   30 minutes

- 1 tbsp olive oil
- 1 medium yellow onion, chopped
- ½ cup dry white wine
- 2 medium carrots, peeled and chopped
- 2 medium zucchinis, chopped
- 15 new potatoes, halved
- 2 large garlic cloves, minced
- 1 tsp chopped fresh thyme
- 1 tsp chopped fresh oregano
- ½ tsp kosher salt
- ½ tsp freshly ground black pepper
- 10 cups chicken broth
- 1 cup orzo pasta, uncooked
- 1¼ cups canned chickpeas, rinsed and drained
- 1 cup frozen green peas, thawed
- 4 well-packed cups baby spinach, stems removed if preferred

Freshly grated Parmesan cheese, for serving

SERVES 4–6
PREP 10 minutes
COOK 20 minutes

- -

2   tbsp olive oil
1   medium yellow onion, chopped
2   large garlic cloves, minced
1   tbsp tomato paste
1   tsp ground cumin
½   tsp paprika
½   tsp ground cinnamon
¼   tsp ground turmeric
⅛   tsp cayenne pepper
½   cup dry white wine
2   medium carrots, peeled and chopped
2   cups canned chickpeas, rinsed and drained
4   cups vegetable broth
1   (14.5 oz) can diced tomatoes
1   tbsp butter
1   tbsp fresh lemon juice
1   tsp lemon zest

LEMON COUSCOUS

2   cups water
1   tbsp fresh lemon juice
¼   tsp kosher salt
1   cup uncooked couscous
½   tsp lemon zest

Fresh mint, thinly sliced, for garnish

Does the whole Meatless Monday trend make your taste buds want to take a nap? Fear not, because Lisa is hopping on her magic carpet and transforming blah into breathtaking with this Moroccan Chickpea & Lemon Couscous Soup. Grab your spoon and take a trip to the spice market with this vegetarian soup, a perfect blend of cumin, paprika, cinnamon, turmeric and cayenne, along with refreshing mint, creamy chickpeas and zesty lemon couscous. Whip up this simple, healthy and hearty soup and prepare yourself for an unforgettable, any-thing-but-mundane, aromatic adventure.

MOROCCAN CHICKPEA & LEMON COUSCOUS SOUP

1. IN A LARGE SOUP POT, heat olive oil over medium heat. Add onion and cook until softened, 4 minutes. Stir in garlic, tomato paste, cumin, paprika, cinnamon, turmeric and cayenne pepper, cooking for 1–2 minutes. Add white wine and reduce until almost completely evaporated. Add carrots and chickpeas, stirring to combine with spices. Add vegetable broth and diced tomatoes and bring to a boil. Lower heat and simmer for 15 minutes.

2. WHILE THE SOUP SIMMERS, prepare the couscous. In a small saucepan, bring water and lemon juice to a boil over medium-high heat. Remove saucepan from heat and stir in couscous and lemon zest. Cover and let stand for 5 minutes. Uncover the couscous and fluff using a fork.

3. ONCE SOUP FINISHES SIMMERING, remove from heat. Using a hand-held immersion blender, lightly purée soup, leaving it slightly chunky. Stir in butter, lemon juice and lemon zest. Top each bowl of soup with a mound of lemon couscous and sprinkle with fresh mint.

"We were the Spice Boys."

George Harrison

You know when you're super excited because you think you've discovered something only to learn that someone has beaten you to the punch? This has happened to me twice. Once with LED slippers (genius, right?) and again with a little legume called the lentil. It appears that I'm 10,000 years too late to jump on the lentil bandwagon, but better late than never, right? Lentils are filling, delicious, nutritious and inexpensive, lending this steamy soup a buttery (no, there's no butter) flavor. We have a feeling that this soup, the perfect combination of vegetables, spices and lentils, has some serious staying power . . . at least another 10,000 years.

"If you see a bandwagon, it's too late."

James Goldsmith

SPICED RED LENTIL SOUP

SERVES   4–6
PREP   10 minutes
COOK   35 minutes

. . . .

2   tbsp olive oil
1   medium yellow onion, chopped
2   celery stalks, chopped
2   carrots, peeled and chopped
2   small garlic cloves, minced
1   tsp ground cumin
¼   tsp kosher salt
¼   tsp freshly ground black pepper
Pinch ground cayenne pepper
7½   cups chicken broth
1½   cups red lentils, well rinsed
1   tbsp fresh lemon juice

¼   cup chopped fresh flat-leaf parsley, for garnish

1. IN A LARGE SOUP POT, heat olive oil over medium heat. Add onion, celery and carrots, cooking for 6 minutes until softened. Add garlic, cumin, salt, pepper and cayenne. Cook 1 minute, stirring continuously. Add chicken broth and lentils and bring to a gentle boil. Simmer, covered, over low heat for 25 minutes.

2. REMOVE FROM HEAT and using a handheld immersion blender, lightly purée the soup, leaving it slightly chunky. Stir in lemon juice and garnish each serving with chopped parsley.

When I generously offered my services as sous-chef, Lisa declined and said she already had a dependable one. "What a crock!" I replied. "Exactly," she countered. Turns out she was talking about her crock-pot (aka slow cooker), an invaluable appliance that toils tirelessly without throwing her attitude. Within minutes, she has her slow cooker loaded up with seared beef and sautéed vegetables and sits back while it works away using low heat to build intensely rich flavor. The result? A hearty, nourishing and delicious stew-like soup chock-full of fork-tender beef, vegetables and noodles. Sigh. Looks like I'm going to be Chief Bottle Washer for a bit longer.

SLOW COOKER BEEF, VEGETABLE & NOODLE SOUP

1. HEAT 1 TABLESPOON of vegetable oil in a large skillet over medium-high heat. Sprinkle beef cubes with salt and pepper. Add half the beef in a single layer to the skillet. Sear beef for 2–3 minutes per side or until browned. Remove from skillet, add remaining 1 tablespoon of vegetable oil and add remaining beef to skillet. Place all seared beef in slow cooker. Using the same skillet, heat olive oil over medium-high heat. Add onion, carrots and celery and cook, stirring, for 3–4 minutes. Add garlic, tomato paste, thyme, salt and pepper. Cook 1 minute more. Stir in red wine and cook for 1 minute, loosening any browned bits from the bottom of the skillet. Transfer to slow cooker and add beef broth. Cover and cook on low for 8–10 hours, until beef is very tender.

2. TOWARDS THE END OF COOKING, in a large pot of salted water, cook noodles until tender. Drain and add to slow cooker when it finishes cooking. Season to taste with salt and pepper. Garnish each serving with fresh thyme sprig.

 When it comes to the crock-pot, follow the Beatles' advice and "Let It Be." If you constantly open the lid to check what's going on, the heat will escape and extend the cooking time.

SERVES   6–8
PREP   10 minutes
COOK   8–10 hours

2   tbsp vegetable oil
2   lb beef chuck, fat trimmed, cut into bite-sized cubes
½   tsp kosher salt
½   tsp freshly ground black pepper
1   tbsp olive oil
1   medium white onion, chopped
2   carrots, peeled and chopped
2   celery stalks, chopped
1   large garlic clove, minced
2   tbsp tomato paste
½   tsp dried thyme
½   tsp kosher salt
¼   tsp freshly ground black pepper
½   cup dry red wine
8   cups beef broth
½   lb egg noodles
Kosher salt and freshly ground black pepper, to taste

Fresh thyme, for garnish

. . . .

9   cups beef broth
2   large shallots, peeled and
    chopped
2   celery stalks, chopped
2   carrots, peeled and chopped
2   large garlic cloves, chopped
1   (2-inch) piece of fresh ginger,
    peeled and chopped
1   cinnamon stick
2   tsp coriander seeds
2   tsp cumin seeds
1   tsp whole fennel seeds
½   lb dried rice noodles
2   tbsp fresh lime juice
1   lb beef filet or flank steak
2   cups bean sprouts
2   cups shredded napa cabbage

GARNISHES

½   cup sliced fresh mint
1   chili pepper, thinly sliced into
    rounds
1   lime, cut into 6 wedges

I must admit to a slight phobia of pho bo—while this classic rice noodle soup is a staple and sold from food carts all over Vietnam, I can't shake the fear of the two-day commitment (not to mention beef bones) required to make the traditional broth. Well, as luck would have it, we have Ho Chi Lisa stationed at the stove, ready to bring us the quick version of this comforting soup. In less than an hour, you can cook up this fast pho, a bowl of richly seasoned beef broth, tender rice noodles and beef, and fragrant herbs and spices. So, what are you going to do with those 47 hours Lisa just saved you?

VIETNAMESE BEEF & NOODLE PHO

1. IN A LARGE SOUP POT, bring beef broth to a boil. Add shallots, celery, carrots, garlic, ginger, cinnamon stick, coriander seeds, cumin seeds and fennel seeds. Turn heat to low and simmer, covered, for 45 minutes. While the broth is cooking, bring a large pot of water to a boil. Following package directions, cook rice noodles until tender. Drain and divide among 6 bowls.

2. WHEN THE BROTH IS READY, strain through a fine mesh sieve. Discard solids, return broth to pot and stir in lime juice. Keep broth hot over low heat until ready to serve.

3. FOR THE BEEF, slice your filet or flank as thin as possible across the grain. To make it easier to slice, freeze for 15 minutes. Heat a grill pan over high heat and cook in batches, 30 seconds per side. Transfer to a plate and cook remaining beef.

4. TO ASSEMBLE EACH BOWL, arrange bean sprouts and napa cabbage over noodles. Ladle hot broth into the bowl and top with beef slices, sliced mint, chili peppers and a lime wedge.

"All of us are born with a set of instinctive fears—of falling, of the dark, of lobsters, of falling on lobsters in the dark, of speaking before a Rotary Club, and of the words 'Some Assembly Required.'"

Dave Barry

In my early years, I majored in Ramen 101. Now, much like then, I rely on Lisa to keep me acting my age, and that's why I'm so grateful for this Asian noodle soup, a dressed-up-for-adulthood version of the quintessential college staple. This Shrimp Ramen Noodle Soup covers our three favorite Fs: fast, flavorful and foolproof. Carrots, bok choy and tender noodles float about in a chicken broth infused with garlic, ginger, soy and sake. The addition of shrimp elevates each satisfying slurp, making me momentarily believe I can act my age, not my shoe size.

SERVES 8
PREP 5 minutes
COOK 25 minutes

. . . .

2 tbsp olive oil
2 medium carrots, peeled and chopped
1 lb baby bok choy, washed and chopped
2 small garlic cloves, minced
2 tsp minced fresh ginger
¼ tsp red pepper flakes
¼ cup sake
¼ cup soy sauce
10 cups chicken broth
1½ lb small raw shrimp, peeled
1 tbsp fresh lime juice
8 oz ramen noodles

Sliced green onions, for garnish

SHRIMP RAMEN NOODLE SOUP

1. IN A LARGE SOUP POT, heat olive oil over medium heat. Add carrots and cook until slightly softened, 4 minutes. Stir in bok choy, garlic, ginger and red pepper flakes. Cook, stirring constantly, for 2 minutes. Add sake and stir to deglaze the pan. Add soy sauce and chicken broth and bring to a boil. Reduce heat to low and simmer for 15 minutes. Add shrimp and continue to cook over low heat for 2–3 minutes. Remove from heat and stir in lime juice.

2. SOAK THE RAMEN NOODLES in boiling water just until tender. Drain and divide between 8 bowls. Ladle soup with shrimp into each bowl and garnish with sliced green onions.

. . . .

The "correct" way to eat ramen noodles is to noisily slurp them. This will (a) cool the noodles down, (b) allow you to eat them faster and keep the other noodles from getting mushy, and (c) bring oxygen (and thus added flavor) to the noodles and broth.

I believe in the power of suggestion. Why else, I ask, would I call Lisa "Dumpling" for the last few months? No other reason than to be able to sink my spoon into this supremely comforting Chicken & Vegetable Dumpling Soup. Filled with chunks of fresh vegetables and shredded roast chicken, this soup is elevated to new heights with the addition of easy, pillowy, drop-in dumplings. Can you just imagine what Lisa will create when I start calling her "Honey Bun"?

CHUNKY CHICKEN & VEGETABLE DUMPLING SOUP

1. FOR THE CHICKEN, rub the chicken breasts with 1 tablespoon olive oil, salt and pepper. In a large skillet, heat remaining 1 tablespoon olive oil over medium heat. Sauté chicken until just cooked through, about 8 minutes per side. When cool enough to handle, shred the chicken and set aside.

2. FOR THE SOUP, heat olive oil in a large soup pot over medium heat. Add leeks, carrots and celery, cover and cook 6–8 minutes, until slightly tender. Add garlic, thyme, salt and pepper and cook, stirring constantly, for 1 minute. Add chicken broth and bring to a boil. Lower heat and simmer, covered, for 20 minutes.

3. WHILE THE SOUP IS SIMMERING, prepare the dumpling dough. In a medium bowl, combine flour, baking powder, salt and thyme. Mix well to combine. Stir in olive oil and warm water just until a soft dough is formed. A teaspoon at a time, drop dough into simmering soup. Cover and continue to simmer soup for 15 minutes. Stir in peas, zucchini and shredded chicken. Simmer 5 minutes more. Serve and garnish with thyme sprig.

 Keep fresh peas in the fridge—it takes only 6 hours at room temperature for half their sugar to turn to starch.

SERVES 8–10
PREP 20 minutes
COOK 1 hour

CHICKEN

3 boneless skinless chicken breasts
2 tbsp olive oil
½ tsp kosher salt
¼ tsp freshly ground black pepper

VEGETABLE SOUP

2 tbsp olive oil
2 leeks, white part only, washed and thinly sliced
4 carrots, peeled and chopped
4 celery stalks, chopped
2 garlic cloves, minced
½ tsp dried thyme
½ tsp kosher salt
½ tsp freshly ground black pepper
12 cups chicken broth
1½ cups fresh peas (or frozen, thawed)
1½ cups chopped zucchini

DUMPLINGS

1½ cups flour
2 tsp baking powder
1 tsp kosher salt
¼ tsp dried thyme
2 tbsp olive oil
¾ cup warm water

Thyme sprigs, for garnish

Pack your bags because we're taking you on a trip down the Mekong River. And by bags, we mean of the grocery variety. With this quick and easy recipe, you're going to get all the exotic tastes of Thailand—lemongrass, ginger and coconut—combined in one steamy, superb soup. From the aromatic lemongrass and ginger to the creamy coconut milk and hint of spice from red curry paste, this classic Thai chicken soup is your taste buds' passport to jetlag-free international travel.

THAI COCONUT & GINGER CHICKEN SOUP

1. IN A LARGE SOUP POT, heat olive oil over medium heat. Add garlic, ginger, lemongrass paste, red curry paste and salt. Cook, stirring, for 2 minutes. Add chicken broth, coconut milk and fish sauce. Over medium heat, bring to a gentle simmer. Add peppers and snow peas and continue to simmer for 10 minutes.

2. WHILE THE SOUP IS SIMMERING, cook rice vermicelli noodles according to package directions. Drain and rinse with cold water to prevent sticking. Add noodles to soup, along with shredded chicken. Remove soup from heat and stir in lime juice. Garnish each serving with fresh mint and a lime wedge.

 To quickly poach chicken breasts, place in saucepan with enough water or broth to cover, bring to a boil over high heat, reduce heat to low, cover and simmer for 12 minutes, or until cooked through.

SERVES 6–8
PREP 10 minutes
COOK 15 minutes

1	tbsp olive oil
2	large garlic cloves, minced
1	tbsp grated fresh ginger
1	tbsp lemongrass paste
2	tsp red curry paste
½	tsp kosher salt
8	cups chicken broth
1½	cups coconut milk
1	tbsp fish sauce
1	red bell pepper, sliced in strips
1	cup snow peas
8	oz rice vermicelli noodles
2	cups shredded cooked chicken
1	tbsp fresh lime juice

Fresh mint, chopped, for garnish
Lime wedges, for garnish

SERVES 8
PREP 15 minutes
COOK 1 hour, 30 minutes

· ·

SPICE MIXTURE

1	tsp ground cumin
½	tsp chili powder
½	tsp ancho chili powder
½	tsp paprika
½	tsp kosher salt

2	boneless skinless chicken breasts
2	tsp + 1 tbsp olive oil
1	large yellow onion, chopped
1	green bell pepper, chopped
1	red bell pepper, chopped
2	large garlic cloves, minced
2	tbsp tomato paste
1	(15.5 oz) can diced tomatoes
1	(4 oz) can diced green chilies
8	cups chicken broth
½	cup masa harina
1	cup water
1¼	cups canned black beans, rinsed and drained
¼	cup chopped flat-leaf parsley

CRUNCHY TORTILLA STRIPS

2	tbsp olive oil
1	tsp fresh lime juice
2	(10-inch) corn tortilla wraps
½	tsp kosher salt

GARNISHES

Avocado, chopped
Monterey Jack cheese, shredded
Lime wedges

Despite the fact that "La Cucaracha" is one of my favorite tunes, my limited Spanish has left me intimidated by Mexican ingredients … until now. Gracias to El Loco Lisa, I'm no longer scared of masa harina (how was I to know it's simply Mexican corn flour available in the international aisle of every grocery store?) and excitedly add it to this flavorful Chicken Enchilada Soup. Chock-full of southwestern spices, zesty chicken, tomatoes, peppers and beans, this meal in a bowl is topped with crunchy tortilla strips, making every bite of this superb *sopa* (soup) a fiesta in my *boca* (mouth).

CHICKEN ENCHILADA SOUP TOPPED WITH CRUNCHY TORTILLAS

1. PREHEAT OVEN to 375°F.

2. FOR THE SPICE MIXTURE, in a small bowl, combine cumin, chili powder, ancho chili powder, paprika and salt. Set aside.

3. PLACE CHICKEN on baking sheet lined with parchment paper. Drizzle 2 teaspoons of olive oil over chicken and sprinkle with 1 teaspoon of the spice mixture. Bake chicken for 18 minutes or until cooked through. Remove from oven and let cool. Once chicken is cool enough to handle, cut into 1-inch cubes and set aside.

4. FOR THE SOUP, heat 1 tablespoon of the olive oil in a large soup pot over medium heat. Add onion and cook until softened, about 4 minutes. Add green and red peppers, garlic, tomato paste and remaining spice mixture. Stir well to combine, cooking for 2 minutes. Add canned tomatoes, green chilies and chicken broth. Bring to a boil, reduce heat and stir in cooked chicken. Simmer, uncovered, for 30 minutes.

5. IN A SMALL BOWL, whisk the masa harina and water until well blended. Pour into soup along with the black beans and simmer 30 minutes more. Remove from heat and stir in chopped parsley. Garnish each serving with crispy tortilla strips, avocado, cheese and lime wedges.

6. FOR THE CRUNCHY TORTILLA STRIPS, preheat oven to 350°F. In a small bowl, combine olive oil and lime juice. Brush on both sides of each tortilla wrap and sprinkle with salt. Cut into thin strips and place on a baking sheet lined with parchment paper. Bake for 10 minutes, stir and bake 4 minutes more. They will crisp more as they cool.

While there are already many geniuses in Japanese cuisine—Morimoto and Matsuhisa, to name a few—there's still space for our Sensei Lisa and her savory soup, the tastiest this side of the Pacific. Not only has Lisa sumo-sized traditional miso soup, but she has also kept it super healthy. Along with a quick-to-create, rich-tasting miso broth, the nutritional benefits are multiplied with the addition of tofu, edamame, leafy bok choy, buckwheat soba noodles and a perfectly poached egg, guaranteed to have you saying "domo arigato" with each scrumptious spoonful.

SOBA NOODLE MISO SOUP TOPPED WITH POACHED EGG

SERVES 6
PREP 10 minutes
COOK 20 minutes

- 2 tsp vegetable oil
- 1 medium yellow onion, chopped
- 2 small garlic cloves, minced
- 1 tsp minced fresh ginger
- 5 cups vegetable broth
- 3 cups water
- 1 tbsp soy sauce
- 1 large carrot, peeled and cut into matchsticks
- 1 cup shelled edamame, defrosted
- 6 oz buckwheat soba noodles
- 6 tbsp white miso paste
- 1 lb baby bok choy, washed well and cut in half
- 8 oz firm tofu, drained and cut into ½-inch cubes

POACHED EGGS

- 6 eggs
- 2 tsp white vinegar

1. IN A LARGE SOUP POT, heat vegetable oil over medium heat. Add onion, garlic and ginger, cooking 4 minutes until softened. Add vegetable broth, water and soy sauce. Bring to a boil. Reduce heat to low and add carrots and edamame. Simmer.

2. MEANWHILE, in a large pot of boiling water, cook soba noodles until soft and tender. Drain and rinse the noodles so they are no longer sticky. Divide noodles among 6 bowls.

3. PLACE 1 CUP OF HOT BROTH in a small bowl. Whisk in miso paste until smooth with no lumps. Add miso mixture back into the pot. Add bok choy and tofu, simmering 5–10 minutes, until the bok choy is slightly softened. Divide the soup among the bowls of noodles and top each bowl with a poached egg. Serve immediately.

4. FOR THE POACHED EGGS, bring a medium saucepan of water to a boil over high heat. Reduce heat to medium and add vinegar. Working with eggs one at a time, crack each egg into its own small bowl. Give the water a quick whirl with a whisk right before adding the egg. Slide each egg into the water and poach for 3½ minutes. Remove with a slotted spoon, drain on paper towel and place on soup.

Don't boil the broth after adding the miso paste or your soup will get cloudy.

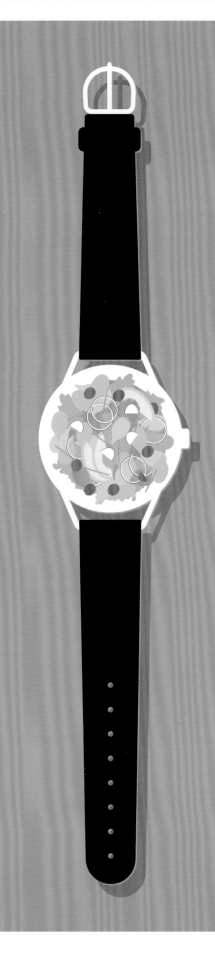

CRUNCH TIME

Cornbread Panzanella Salad | 52

Mediterranean Orzo Salad with Feta & Tomatoes | 54

Pesto & Roasted Red Pepper Pasta Salad | 55

Italian Chopped Salad with Creamy Parmesan Dressing | 56

Falafel Salad with Lemon Tahini Dressing | 58

Harvest Salad with Honey Roasted Walnuts | 60

Quinoa, Spinach & Berry Salad | 61

Roasted Beet, Goat Cheese & Farro Salad | 62

Winter Couscous Salad with Roasted Vegetables, Pomegranates & Cranberries | 64

Wheat Berry, Kale & Apple Salad with Maple Sherry Vinaigrette | 67

Sugar Snap, Green Bean & Mint Couscous Salad | 68

Crispy Tofu, Quinoa & Edamame Salad | 69

Asian Chicken Salad with Ramen Croutons | 70

Cajun Chicken Cobb Salad | 72

Moroccan Chicken Salad with Crispy Pita Chips | 74

Baja Fish Taco Salad with Creamy Chipotle Dressing | 75

Chunky Potato, Tuna & Bean Salad | 78

Grilled Thai Steak Salad | 80

SERVES 6–8
PREP 20 minutes
COOK 45 minutes

. . . .

CORNBREAD CROUTONS

1 cup flour
1 cup yellow cornmeal
¼ cup sugar
1 tbsp baking powder
½ tsp kosher salt
¼ tsp cayenne pepper
1 cup buttermilk
¼ cup melted butter
¼ cup honey
2 eggs

LIME DRESSING

¼ cup fresh lime juice
¼ cup olive oil
2 tbsp vegetable oil
2 tbsp chopped fresh flat-leaf parsley
1 tbsp honey
¼ tsp kosher salt
¼ tsp freshly ground black pepper

SALAD

1 tbsp butter
3 ears fresh corn, kernels removed
¼ tsp paprika
¼ tsp chili powder
¼ tsp kosher salt
¼ tsp freshly ground black pepper
8 cups chopped romaine lettuce
1 red bell pepper, chopped
1 yellow pepper, chopped
1 large ripe avocado, chopped
¼ cup chopped fresh basil

1 large jalapeño pepper, seeds removed, chopped, for garnish (optional)

Lisa hates when I speak in accents ("Like nails on a chalkboard," she claims), but I simply can't resist getting all Scarlett O'Hara breathy about this Cornbread Panzanella Salad, a Southern spin on the classic Italian salad. I do declare that this citrus-dressed salad, crammed with homemade cornbread croutons, crunchy sweet peppers, sautéed fresh corn and creamy avocado, is a marvelous meal in a bowl. As God is my witness, you'll never be hungry again . . .

CORNBREAD PANZANELLA SALAD

1. PREHEAT OVEN to 400°F. Line an 8-inch-square baking pan with parchment paper and coat lightly with nonstick cooking spray.

2. FOR THE CORNBREAD, in a large bowl, combine flour, cornmeal, sugar, baking powder, salt and cayenne pepper. In a medium bowl, whisk buttermilk, melted butter, honey and eggs until combined. Pour the wet ingredients into the flour mixture and gently mix ingredients together. Do not overmix. Pour batter into prepared pan and bake for 18–20 minutes, until the edges are golden and a toothpick inserted into the center comes out clean. Remove from oven and let cool before slicing into croutons.

3. ONCE CORNBREAD HAS COOLED, lower oven temperature to 350°F and line a baking sheet with parchment paper. Cut the cornbread into 1-inch cubes and place on parchment paper. Bake for 10 minutes, flip the cubes and continue baking for 10 minutes more. Remove from oven and let croutons cool completely before using them.

4. FOR THE DRESSING, place lime juice, olive oil, vegetable oil, parsley, honey, salt and pepper in a container with a lid. Shake well to combine.

5. FOR THE SALAD, in a medium skillet, melt the butter over high heat. Add corn, paprika, chili powder, salt and pepper. Cook 2–3 minutes, until corn is golden. Remove from heat and cool. Place the lettuce in a large serving bowl. Add red and yellow peppers, avocado, basil, sautéed corn and cornbread croutons. Gently toss with dressing to combine. Garnish with chopped jalapeños. Serve immediately.

. . . .

 Buy premade cornbread and toast as above.

Lisa of Troy has created a pasta salad that easily will launch a thousand meals. A Greek-inspired orzo salad full of fresh tomatoes, cucumbers, Kalamata olives and feta cheese, each bowlful also benefits from the addition of creamy chickpeas, savory sun-dried tomatoes and fresh basil. Whipped up in less than 15 minutes, this stunningly simple salad is the tastiest quick fix for fighting the war on mealtime madness.

MEDITERRANEAN ORZO SALAD WITH FETA & TOMATOES

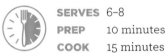

SERVES 6–8
PREP 10 minutes
COOK 15 minutes

- ¾ lb orzo pasta
- 1½ cups cherry tomatoes, halved
- 1½ cups chopped English cucumber
- 1¼ cups canned chickpeas, rinsed and drained
- 1 cup crumbled feta cheese
- ¼ cup chopped oil-packed sun-dried tomatoes
- ¼ cup Kalamata olives, halved
- 3 tbsp chopped fresh basil

VINAIGRETTE

- ¼ cup olive oil
- 2 tbsp fresh lemon juice
- 1 tbsp white wine vinegar
- 1 tsp honey
- ½ tsp dried oregano
- ½ tsp kosher salt
- ¼ tsp freshly ground black pepper

1. BRING A LARGE POT of salted water to a boil. Cook orzo until tender, 8–10 minutes. Drain and rinse under cold water. Drain well and set aside.

2. IN A LARGE BOWL, combine cherry tomatoes, cucumber, chickpeas, feta cheese and sun-dried tomatoes. Stir in the cooked orzo.

3. FOR THE DRESSING, in a medium bowl, whisk olive oil, lemon juice, white wine vinegar, honey, oregano, salt and pepper. Drizzle over the orzo salad and toss well to coat. Stir in Kalamata olives and chopped basil.

Add grilled chicken or shrimp for a complete meal.

You're standing with the refrigerator door wide open. Are you (a) checking to see if the light bulb is still working, (b) cooling down from a hot flash or (c) wishing something delicious would magically appear? Fear not because the bulb will last, the sweats won't, and in less than 20 minutes you can have a show-stopping salad. Made using basic ingredients (nothing complicated here!), this homemade pesto—a beautiful blend of almonds, basil and Parmesan—coats tender pasta, creamy mozzarella cheese, sweet roasted red peppers and leafy arugula. What are you waiting for? Quit your daydreaming (no, we don't know how old that jar of pickles is), close the refrigerator door and use your noodle.

PESTO & ROASTED RED PEPPER PASTA SALAD

1. USING A BLENDER or food processor, combine basil, ground almonds, garlic and salt. Process until finely chopped. Add olive oil and process until smooth. Add Parmesan cheese and pulse on and off until well incorporated.

2. FOR THE PASTA, bring a large pot of lightly salted water to a boil. Cook pasta until tender, drain well and transfer to a large serving bowl. Let cool slightly before continuing.

3. ADD THE ROASTED RED PEPPERS, mozzarella and arugula. Toss with pesto until well coated. Serve with extra Parmesan cheese, if desired.

> "Everybody likes pesto. You walk into a restaurant, that's all you hear— pesto, pesto, pesto."
>
> George Costanza, *Seinfeld*

SERVES 8
PREP 10 minutes
COOK 15 minutes

PESTO
2   cups lightly packed fresh basil
½   cup ground almonds
1   small garlic clove, minced
¾   tsp kosher salt
½   cup olive oil
1   cup freshly grated Parmesan cheese

1   lb penne pasta
1   cup jarred roasted red peppers, drained and chopped
1   cup diced fresh mozzarella
3   cups lightly packed arugula

Freshly grated Parmesan cheese, for serving

SERVES 6–8
PREP 25 minutes
COOK 5 minutes

CREAMY PARMESAN HERB DRESSING

1   cup mayonnaise
½   cup sour cream
⅓   cup freshly grated Parmesan cheese
1   small garlic clove, minced
2   tbsp chopped fresh flat-leaf parsley
2   tbsp chopped fresh basil
1   tbsp fresh lemon juice
¼   tsp dried oregano
¼   tsp kosher salt
¼   tsp freshly ground black pepper
Pinch cayenne pepper

CANDIED PECANS

2   tbsp butter
2   tbsp sugar
1   cup pecans
¼   tsp kosher salt

SALAD

6   cups chopped iceberg lettuce
3   cups chopped romaine lettuce
1½ cups chopped broccoli florets
1½ cups chopped cauliflower florets
1   cup cherry tomatoes
1   cup canned chickpeas, rinsed and drained
2   celery stalks, chopped
1   large carrot, peeled and chopped
1   large red bell pepper, chopped
½   cup freshly grated Parmesan cheese
½   cup coarsely chopped dates
¼   cup roasted sunflower seeds
¼   cup chopped fresh flat-leaf parsley

What did I do (other than drool?) when my sis dreamt up this Italian Chopped Salad? Blared some Bryan Adams (it *does* cut like a knife), grabbed my Ginsu (Lisa bans me from the "good" knives) and got to work. Yes, while this salad might take a bit of effort in the slicing and dicing department, it's most certainly worth the time—chunks of vegetables (broccoli, cauliflower and carrots, to name a few), crisp lettuce, candied pecans and sweet dates, all tossed in a creamy Parmesan herb dressing, make this Italian Chopped Salad a cut above all others. What are you waiting for? Chop-chop!

ITALIAN CHOPPED SALAD WITH CREAMY PARMESAN DRESSING

1. FOR THE DRESSING, in a food processor, combine mayonnaise, sour cream, Parmesan cheese, garlic, parsley, basil, lemon juice, oregano, salt, pepper and cayenne. Pulse until puréed and smooth. Cover and refrigerate until ready to dress salad.

2. FOR THE CANDIED PECANS, in a medium skillet, melt butter over medium heat. Add sugar and stir until it dissolves. Add pecans and salt and continuously stir for 1–2 minutes, until coated and toasted. Remove from heat and transfer to a piece of parchment paper to cool—nuts will harden as they cool. Once cool, chop coarsely and set aside.

3. FOR THE SALAD, in a large bowl, combine iceberg lettuce, romaine lettuce, broccoli, cauliflower, tomatoes, chickpeas, celery, carrots, red peppers, Parmesan cheese, dates, sunflower seeds and parsley. Toss with dressing, top with candied pecans and serve immediately.

> "The best thing I have is the knife from *Fatal Attraction.* I hung it in my kitchen. It's my way of saying, 'Don't mess with me.'"
>
> Glenn Close

. . . .

LEMON TAHINI DRESSING

½	cup tahini
⅔	cup water
2	tbsp fresh lemon juice
1	tbsp soy sauce
1	small garlic clove, minced
2	tsp maple syrup
1	tsp lemon zest
½	tsp Sriracha sauce
½	tsp kosher salt

FALAFEL

2	cups canned chickpeas, rinsed and drained
½	cup panko (Japanese breadcrumbs)
¼	cup chopped red onion
¼	cup chopped fresh flat-leaf parsley
1	small garlic clove, minced
1	egg
1	tbsp + 2 tsp olive oil
1	tbsp fresh lemon juice
1	tsp lemon zest
1	tsp ground cumin
½	tsp ground coriander seed
½	tsp kosher salt
¼	tsp cayenne pepper

SALAD

8	cups shredded romaine lettuce
2½	cups seeded, diced tomatoes
2½	cups diced English cucumber
½	cup chopped fresh flat-leaf parsley

Lisa knows I'm a falafel fanatic. I'm instantly roped in by the charm of chickpeas, spellbound by spices and tantalized by tahini—and she has captured the magic of this Middle Eastern classic with this incredible salad. Not only has my little Baba Ghanoush Gnat made this traditionally grease-laden delight healthy (baked and not deep-fried), but she's also brought all the zippy flavors to this deconstructed falafel, including a zesty lemon tahini dressing, tomatoes, cucumbers, parsley and of course, cumin-spiced crispy falafel. Now, whenever I hear the siren song of this street food, I can bring it on home with this superbly satisfying salad.

FALAFEL SALAD WITH LEMON TAHINI DRESSING

1. FOR THE DRESSING, combine tahini, water, lemon juice, soy sauce, garlic, maple syrup, lemon zest, Sriracha and salt in a blender. Blend until smooth and refrigerate until ready to use. The dressing will thicken slightly and flavors will develop while you prepare the rest of the salad.

2. PREHEAT OVEN to 400°F. Line a baking sheet with parchment paper and set aside.

3. FOR THE FALAFEL, using a food processor, combine the chickpeas, panko, red onion, parsley and garlic. Pulse several times to chop. Add egg, 1 tbsp olive oil, lemon juice, lemon zest, cumin, coriander seed, salt and cayenne pepper. Pulse a few times until a coarse paste forms, scraping down the sides of the bowl once or twice. Shape into 20–22 small patties and place on prepared baking sheet. Brush tops with remaining 2 teaspoons olive oil and bake 15 minutes, flip and continue to bake 10 minutes more. Remove from oven and let cool slightly.

4. FOR THE SALAD, in a large serving bowl, combine lettuce, tomatoes, cucumbers and parsley. Toss with half the tahini dressing until well coated. Slice each falafel in half and place on top of salad. Drizzle remaining dressing over falafel and serve.

. . . .

Stuff the falafel in a pita along with salad and dressing for a portable meal.

We already feel lucky to reap what Lisa sows, but now we've hit the mother lode with this superb, quick and easy Harvest Salad. It's a cornucopia of crunch as refreshing red and green apples and juicy pears are tossed with tart cranberries and creamy goat cheese. As if that wasn't enough of a bountiful bowlful, honey roasted walnuts add a sweet and salty bite to every balsamic-dressed forkful. With such a delicious combination of textures and flavors, we'd bet the farm you'll love it.

SERVES 4–6
PREP 10 minutes
COOK 15 minutes

. . . .

HONEY ROASTED WALNUTS

1 cup walnut halves
2 tbsp honey
1 tbsp brown sugar
½ tsp kosher salt
Pinch cayenne pepper

HONEY BALSAMIC DRESSING

¼ cup olive oil
2 tbsp balsamic vinegar
1 tbsp honey
1 tsp Dijon mustard
¼ tsp kosher salt
¼ tsp freshly ground black pepper

SALAD

5 cups baby spinach
5 cups baby arugula
1 Honeycrisp (or any red) apple, cut into chunks
1 Granny Smith apple, cut into chunks
1 Bartlett or bosc pear, cut into chunks
⅓ cup dried cranberries
½ cup crumbled goat cheese

HARVEST SALAD
WITH HONEY ROASTED WALNUTS

1. PREHEAT OVEN to 325°F and line a baking sheet with parchment paper. In a medium bowl, toss walnut halves with honey, brown sugar, salt and cayenne pepper. Place on baking sheet and bake for 6 minutes, stir and continue to bake for 5–6 minutes. Remove from oven; walnuts will harden as they cool. Set aside.

2. FOR THE BALSAMIC DRESSING, in a small bowl, whisk olive oil, balsamic vinegar, honey, Dijon mustard, salt and pepper.

3. TO ASSEMBLE THE SALAD, in a large serving bowl, combine baby spinach, arugula, apples, pear and cranberries. Toss with balsamic dressing just before serving. Top with crumbled goat cheese and honey roasted walnuts.

"I'd consider being a farmer.
As long as I could live on the Pepperidge Farm.
And raise Milanos."

Author Unknown

Are you expecting me to praise the numerous nutritional benefits (whole grains, leafy greens, antioxidants) of this power-packed salad? Well, surprise, because while all that's fantastically true, this Quinoa, Spinach & Berry Salad also has a hidden super power: much like myself (and Hangin' Loose Lisa), it's extremely easygoing. Prefer arugula to spinach? Go for it. Like blackberries more than blueberries? Not a problem. Have a perfectly ripe avocado? Toss it in. Complete with zesty lemon and fresh basil, this simple, healthy and delicious salad is perfect by the book or freestyled your own way.

> "I have the reputation of being easygoing. But inside, I'm like nails. I will kill."
>
> Calvin Klein

QUINOA, SPINACH & BERRY SALAD

1. TO COOK QUINOA, in a medium saucepan, combine quinoa, water and salt. Bring to a boil over high heat. Reduce heat to a simmer, cover and cook for 15 minutes. Remove from heat and let sit, covered, for 5 minutes. Place in a large bowl and let cool.

2. FOR THE DRESSING, in a small bowl, whisk together olive oil, lemon juice, basil, honey, lemon zest and salt. Set aside.

3. PLACE SPINACH in a large serving bowl and toss with a few table-spoons of dressing. Toss remaining dressing with cooled quinoa, along with strawberries, blueberries, raspberries, mango and basil. Place in the center of the spinach leaves and serve.

SERVES 6–8
PREP 10 minutes
COOK 20 minutes

QUINOA
1 cup quinoa, rinsed well and drained
2 cups water
½ tsp kosher salt

LEMON BASIL DRESSING
⅓ cup olive oil
¼ cup fresh lemon juice
1 tbsp chopped fresh basil
2 tsp honey
½ tsp lemon zest
½ tsp kosher salt

SALAD
8 cups coarsely chopped baby spinach
2 cups sliced strawberries
1 cup blueberries
1 cup raspberries
1 large ripe mango, peeled and chopped
¼ cup chopped fresh basil

Farro (pronounced FAHR-oh) may be as old as the hills (20,000 years and counting) but definitely not past its prime. In fact, this protein- and fiber-rich ancient cereal grain is hitting its stride in mainstream cuisine, gracing everything from soups to salads with its nutty flavor and chewy texture. In this superb salad, along with this go-to grain, we've added equally earthy beets that have been roasted until sweet and tender, along with crunchy celery, mixed greens and creamy goat cheese to create a flavorful, healthy and comforting dish that'll instantly make you a farro fan.

ROASTED BEET, GOAT CHEESE & FARRO SALAD

SERVES 6
PREP 10 minutes
COOK 40 minutes

. . . .

DIJON VINAIGRETTE
⅓ cup olive oil
¼ cup Champagne vinegar
1 tsp Dijon mustard
1 tsp honey
½ tsp kosher salt
¼ tsp freshly ground black pepper

ROASTED BEETS
6 medium-sized beets, trimmed and rinsed

FARRO
1½ cups uncooked farro, rinsed
6 cups water
½ tsp kosher salt

SALAD
6 cups mixed greens
3 celery stalks, chopped
¾ cup crumbled goat cheese

1. FOR THE DRESSING, in a small bowl, whisk olive oil, Champagne vinegar, Dijon mustard, honey, salt and pepper. Set aside.

2. FOR THE ROASTED BEETS, preheat oven to 400°F. Pat beets dry after washing and wrap each individually in aluminum foil. Place all on a baking sheet and roast 30–40 minutes, until fork tender. Remove from oven, discard aluminum foil and place beets in a bowl of cold water. When cool enough to handle, rub off the peel, cut into wedges and set aside.

3. WHILE THE BEETS ARE ROASTING, prepare the farro. In a large saucepan, combine farro, water and salt. Bring to a boil over high heat, reduce heat to low and simmerfor 20–25 minutes until tender. Drain and set aside to cool.

4. TO ASSEMBLE SALAD, in a large serving bowl, combine mixed greens, chopped celery, roasted beets and farro. Add dressing and toss well to combine. Sprinkle goat cheese over top and serve.

. . . .

 To store beets, cut the majority of the greens away (leave about 2 inches intact), place in a plastic bag, remove air and keep in the refrigerator for up to 3 weeks.

SERVES 6–8
PREP 15 minutes
COOK 30 minutes

. . . .

2   cups trimmed and halved
    Brussels sprouts
1½ cups peeled and cubed
    butternut squash
1½ cups peeled and cubed sweet
    potato
1   tbsp olive oil
1   tbsp maple syrup
¾   tsp kosher salt
⅛   tsp ground cinnamon

COUSCOUS
1¾ cups Israeli (also known as
    pearl) couscous
3   cups vegetable or chicken
    broth

MAPLE VINAIGRETTE
¼   cup olive oil
2   tbsp white balsamic vinegar
2   tsp maple syrup
1   tsp Dijon mustard
¼   tsp kosher salt
¼   tsp freshly ground black
    pepper

¼   cup pomegranate seeds
¼   cup dried cranberries
½   cup roasted and salted
    almonds, coarsely chopped

Do flurries and frostbite leave you feeling bitter? Do thoughts of hibernating bears make you green with envy? Us too, and that's why we've come up with a bright and delicious way to warm up to winter: a couscous salad that's overrun with cinnamon-roasted vegetables, studded with pomegranate seeds and cranberries, tossed in a maple vinaigrette and finished with crunchy almonds. This comforting and filling salad will fuel your inner furnace and brighten your blustery day, even if you did spend 20 minutes scraping your windshield.

WINTER COUSCOUS SALAD WITH ROASTED VEGETABLES, POMEGRANATES & CRANBERRIES

1. PREHEAT OVEN to 400°F and line a large baking sheet with parchment paper. In a large bowl, combine Brussels sprouts, butternut squash and sweet potatoes. Toss with olive oil, maple syrup, salt and cinnamon. Spread vegetable mixture on prepared baking sheet. Cook for 15 minutes, stir and cook for 10 minutes more, or until vegetables are just tender. Remove from oven and let cool slightly.

2. FOR THE COUSCOUS, in a large saucepan, combine couscous and broth. Bring to a boil over high heat. Reduce heat to medium-low, cooking uncovered until couscous is tender. Strain excess liquid if necessary and set aside to cool.

3. FOR THE DRESSING, in a small container, combine olive oil, white balsamic vinegar, maple syrup, Dijon mustard, salt and pepper. Shake well to combine.

4. TO ASSEMBLE SALAD, in a large bowl, combine roasted vegetables, couscous, pomegranate seeds and dried cranberries. Toss with dressing to coat well and top with roasted almonds.

"Winter is nature's way of saying, 'Up yours.'"

Robert Byrne

We've gone and done it. We've separated the wheat from the chaff and elevated it to new heights in this Wheat Berry, Kale & Apple Salad. Wheat berries add a chewiness and nut-like flavor that perfectly complements crunchy Granny Smith apples, sweet and spicy roasted pecans, sharp cheddar and nutritious kale. One bite of this marvelous maple sherry–dressed salad and we know you'll agree—the wheat should never be stuck with the chaff again.

WHEAT BERRY, KALE & APPLE SALAD WITH MAPLE SHERRY VINAIGRETTE

1. TO COOK WHEAT BERRIES, in a medium saucepan, combine wheat berries, water and salt. Bring to a boil over high heat. Turn heat to low, cover and cook 1 hour or until berries are bursting and chewy. Drain excess water and transfer to a large bowl to cool.

2. FOR THE SHERRY MAPLE DRESSING, in a small container, combine olive oil, sherry vinegar, maple syrup, shallots, thyme, salt and pepper. Shake well to combine and set aside.

3. FOR THE SPICED PECANS, preheat oven to 325°F and line a baking sheet with parchment paper. Place pecans in a medium bowl and toss with corn syrup, sugar, salt and cayenne pepper. Spread in a single layer on baking sheet and bake 5 minutes, stir and continue to bake 10 minutes more. Remove from oven and let cool completely.

4. TO ASSEMBLE SALAD, combine kale, apples, white cheddar and parsley with the cooked wheat berries. Toss with dressing and top each portion with spiced pecans.

Talk about superfoods—wheat berries are satisfying grains that are super high in fiber, potassium and B vitamins, and a cup of kale has 684% of your daily vitamin K needs, 206% of your vitamin A and 134% of your vitamin C.

SERVES 6
PREP 10 minutes
COOK 1 hour, 15 minutes

WHEAT BERRIES
1 cup red spring wheat berries, rinsed well and drained
3½ cups water
1 tsp kosher salt

MAPLE SHERRY VINAIGRETTE
3 tbsp olive oil
2 tbsp sherry vinegar
2 tsp maple syrup
½ tsp minced shallots
½ tsp chopped fresh thyme
½ tsp kosher salt
¼ tsp freshly ground black pepper

SPICED PECANS
1½ cups pecan halves
2 tbsp corn syrup
2 tbsp sugar
½ tsp kosher salt
⅛ tsp cayenne pepper

6 cups coarsely chopped baby kale leaves
2 Granny Smith apples, cored and diced
¾ cup sharp white cheddar cheese, cut into ½-inch cubes
2 tbsp chopped fresh flat-leaf parsley

You know about not sweating the small stuff, right? We never do, especially when it comes to couscous. These teeny tiny grains require absolutely no sweat (read: only 5 minutes) to cook, are the perfect sub for pasta and rice and are superb at soaking up flavors all around them. The fluffy granules do their part in contributing to this super simple and tasty salad, a creative combo of healthy chickpeas, green beans, snap peas and tomatoes with a lemony shallot dressing, tangy feta and refreshing mint. Don't sweat it—this quick and delicious couscous salad is easy peasy, lemon squeezy.

SERVES 4–6
PREP 15 minutes
COOK 10 minutes

· ·

COUSCOUS
1 cup couscous
1 cup boiling water

LEMON SHALLOT DRESSING
⅓ cup olive oil
¼ cup fresh lemon juice
1 tsp sugar
½ small shallot, minced
½ tsp kosher salt
¼ tsp freshly ground black pepper

1½ cups sugar snap peas, trimmed
1½ cups green beans, ends trimmed
1 cup canned chickpeas, rinsed and drained
1 cup cherry tomatoes
1 cup crumbled feta cheese
¼ cup chopped fresh mint

SUGAR SNAP, GREEN BEAN & MINT COUSCOUS SALAD

1. FOR THE COUSCOUS, in a large bowl, combine couscous with boiling water. Cover and let stand for 5 minutes. Fluff with a fork and set aside to cool.

2. FOR THE DRESSING, in a small container combine olive oil, lemon juice, sugar, shallot, salt and pepper. Shake well to combine and set aside.

3. BRING WATER TO A BOIL in a large saucepan. Turn heat to low and add sugar snap peas and green beans. Cook 1 minute, drain and plunge sugar snap peas and green beans into a bowl of cold water. Drain well and add to the bowl of couscous, along with the chickpeas, tomatoes, feta cheese and mint. Pour dressing over the couscous salad and toss to combine.

"Don't sweat the petty things and don't pet the sweaty things."

George Carlin

Lisa challenged me to an arm wrestling competition. I quickly discovered that those pipe-cleaner-sized arms of hers are surprisingly strong and pack a mighty punch. How was I going to compete? Instead of hitting the gym, I hit the stove. Thanks to Lightweight Lisa, I was able to create this knockout salad, a protein-packed meal in a bowl with crispy tofu, quinoa and edamame. Topped with baked wonton crisps and tossed in a creamy Asian vinaigrette, this healthy salad definitely gave me the upper hand. In case you're wondering, I'm now known in some circles as Janitor Julie (read: I cleaned the floor with her).

CRISPY TOFU, QUINOA & EDAMAME SALAD

1. FOR THE TOFU, preheat oven to 400°F. Line a baking sheet with parchment paper. Cut the tofu into cubes and place in a medium bowl. In a small bowl, whisk sesame oil, soy sauce, mirin and rice vinegar. Toss marinade with tofu and let sit for 30 minutes. When ready to bake the tofu, arrange on baking sheet in a single layer. Bake for 10 minutes, flip tofu pieces and bake 8 minutes more, until golden. Set aside.

2. FOR THE DRESSING, using a blender, combine rice vinegar, mayonnaise, lime juice, soy sauce, vegetable oil, honey and wasabi. Blend until well combined.

3. FOR THE QUINOA, in a medium saucepan, bring water to a boil over high heat and stir in quinoa. Turn heat to low, cover and let simmer 15 minutes, or until the water is absorbed. Remove from heat and cool.

4. IN A LARGE MIXING BOWL, combine edamame, cucumber, carrots, avocados and chopped parsley. Add quinoa and baked tofu. Pour enough dressing over top to coat salad well. Garnish with wonton crisps.

5. FOR THE WONTON CRISPS, preheat oven to 375°F. Line a baking sheet with parchment paper. Brush both sides of each wonton wrapper with oil. Sprinkle with salt and cut each wrapper diagonally in half. Place wonton wrappers on the baking sheet in a single layer. Bake for 7 minutes, or until golden. Remove from oven—wrappers will crisp more as they cool.

"The first rule about fight club is you don't talk about fight club."

Tyler Durden, *Fight Club*

SERVES 6
PREP 15 minutes
(+30 minute marinade)
COOK 45 minutes

. . . .

CRISPY TOFU
1   package (12 oz) firm tofu, pressed dry between layers of paper towel
1   tbsp sesame oil
1   tbsp soy sauce
1   tbsp mirin
1   tbsp rice vinegar

ASIAN VINAIGRETTE
¼   cup rice vinegar
¼   cup mayonnaise
1   tbsp fresh lime juice
1   tbsp soy sauce
1   tbsp vegetable oil
1   tsp honey
1   tsp wasabi paste

QUINOA SALAD
1¼ cups quinoa, rinsed and drained
2   cups water
1   cup shelled and cooked edamame
1   small English cucumber, chopped
1   large carrot, peeled and sliced diagonally
2   small ripe avocados, chopped
2   tbsp chopped fresh flat-leaf parsley

WONTON CRISPS
12 wonton wrappers
1   tbsp vegetable oil
½   tsp kosher salt

SERVES 6–8

PREP 15 minutes
(+30 minute marinade)

COOK 40 minutes

. . . .

HOISIN SOY MARINADE

5   boneless skinless chicken
    breasts
3   tbsp soy sauce
3   tbsp hoisin sauce
2   tbsp vegetable oil
2   tsp honey
½   tsp grated fresh ginger
½   tsp Sriracha sauce

HOISIN GINGER DRESSING

⅓   cup vegetable oil
1   tbsp soy sauce
1   tbsp hoisin sauce
1   tbsp rice vinegar
1   tbsp honey
¼   tsp grated fresh ginger

RAMEN CROUTONS

2   packages (3 oz each) ramen
    noodles
2   tbsp melted butter
¼   tsp kosher salt

SALAD

8   cups chopped romaine lettuce
4   cups thinly sliced napa
    cabbage
2   cups snow peas, trimmed and
    cut diagonally
2   large carrots, peeled and
    julienned
½   cup coarsely chopped roasted
    almonds

To the meat-and-potatoes posse who scoff at the notion of salad for supper: prepare to eat your words. This Asian Chicken Salad with Ramen Croutons is supremely satisfying, a tasty combo of hoisin-marinated grilled chicken, roasted almonds, crunchy ramen croutons and vibrant veggies, all tossed in a sweet and tangy Asian dressing. Really, if this is rabbit food, we're some blissful bunnies.

ASIAN CHICKEN SALAD WITH RAMEN CROUTONS

1. PLACE CHICKEN BREASTS in a large resealable plastic bag. In a small bowl, whisk soy sauce, hoisin sauce, vegetable oil, honey, ginger and Sriracha sauce until well combined. Pour half the marinade in with the chicken and toss to coat. Reserve the remaining marinade to toss with the cooked chicken. Let marinate for 30 minutes.

2. FOR THE SALAD DRESSING, combine vegetable oil, soy sauce, hoisin sauce, rice vinegar, honey and ginger in a jar with a tight-fitting lid. Shake well until ingredients are combined. Set aside.

3. FOR THE RAMEN CROUTONS, preheat oven to 350°F. Line a baking sheet with parchment paper. Discard spice packets from the ramen noodles. Break the dry ramen noodles into large chunks and place in a medium bowl. Toss with melted butter and salt. Place on baking sheet and bake for 8 minutes, stir and continue to bake 8 minutes more. Remove from oven, set aside and let cool.

4. PREHEAT BARBECUE to medium-high heat and lightly oil the grill grate. Remove chicken from marinade, and discard the marinade. Grill chicken 8–10 minutes per side, until cooked through. Remove from heat and let rest 5 minutes. Chop chicken into bite-sized pieces and toss with the marinade reserved earlier. Set aside.

5. TO ASSEMBLE THE SALAD, in a large bowl, combine romaine lettuce, napa cabbage, snow peas and carrots. Toss with salad dressing until well coated. Pile cooked chicken in the center and scatter ramen croutons and chopped almonds over top.

. . . .

 If you don't have time to fire up the barbecue, replace the grilled chicken with chopped rotisserie chicken.

SERVES 6–8
PREP 15 minutes
COOK 30 minutes

. . . .

BUTTERMILK RANCH DRESSING

1   cup buttermilk
½   cup sour cream
¼   cup mayonnaise
2   tbsp cider vinegar
2   tbsp chopped fresh flat-leaf
     parsley
1   tbsp snipped fresh chives
1½   tsp kosher salt
1   tsp sugar
1   tsp paprika
1   tsp Dijon mustard
¼   tsp garlic powder

CAJUN CHICKEN

¼   cup flour
¼   tsp kosher salt
1   egg
2   tbsp water
½   cup cornmeal
½   cup breadcrumbs
½   tsp kosher salt
¼   tsp freshly ground black
     pepper
¼   tsp paprika
¼   tsp dried oregano
¼   tsp garlic powder
⅛   tsp cayenne pepper
4   boneless skinless chicken
     breasts

SALAD

10   cups chopped romaine lettuce
4   ears fresh corn, shucked
8   slices of bacon, cooked crisp
     and crumbled
2   ripe avocados, cut into 1-inch
     pieces
2   cups grated cheddar cheese
4   hard-boiled eggs, sliced
1½   cups cherry tomatoes, halved

I love it when my sister travels. It always results in terrifically tasty rewards for me, such as this Cajun Chicken Cobb courtesy of my very own Louisiana Lisa. Full of gumbo and grits, my little ragin' Cajun came up with this super tasty twist on the classic Cobb Salad: chopped spicy baked chicken alongside crunchy lettuce, cheddar cheese, fresh corn, avocado, bacon and eggs, all topped with a homemade ranch dressing (that's also great with a veggie platter). You too will be thrilled that when Lisa hits the road, she brings home more than just a snow globe.

CAJUN CHICKEN COBB SALAD

1. FOR THE DRESSING, using a blender, combine buttermilk, sour cream, mayonnaise, cider vinegar, parsley, chives, salt, sugar, paprika, Dijon mustard and garlic powder. Blend until well combined and refrigerate, covered, until needed.

2. TO PREPARE THE CAJUN CHICKEN, preheat oven to 375°F. Line a baking sheet with aluminum foil and place a cooling rack on top of the baking sheet for the chicken to cook on. Coat the cooling rack with non-stick cooking spray.

3. PLACE THE FLOUR and ¼ teaspoon salt in a large plastic bag. In a medium bowl, whisk together the egg and water. In a large bowl, combine cornmeal, breadcrumbs, salt, pepper, paprika, oregano, garlic powder and cayenne pepper. Place the chicken breasts in the flour bag and shake well. Shake off excess flour and then dip in eggs, letting excess drip off before coating in cornmeal and breadcrumb mixture. Press well to adhere coating and place on prepared rack. Bake 20–22 minutes, until chicken is cooked through. Remove from oven, let cool and cut into strips.

4. TO ASSEMBLE THE COBB SALAD, lay the romaine lettuce on a large serving platter. To prepare the corn, in a large pot of boiling water, cook the corn for 2 minutes. Drain, cool and cut the kernels off the cob. Arrange the corn, bacon, avocado, cheddar cheese, hard-boiled eggs, tomatoes and chicken individually sectioned over the romaine lettuce. Drizzle with buttermilk ranch dressing or toss each salad serving with dressing.

. . . .

To make the perfect hard-boiled egg, place eggs in single layer in saucepan and cover with 1 inch of cold water. Bring to a boil over high heat, turn heat off, cover pan and let sit 12 minutes. Run eggs under icy water, gently crack and peel.

SERVES 6

PREP 20 minutes
(+2–8 hour marinade)

COOK 40 minutes

. . . .

4   boneless skinless chicken
    breasts
2   tbsp olive oil
1   tbsp brown sugar
2   tsp smoked paprika
2   tsp ground cumin
1   tsp *za'atar* spice blend
½   tsp ground ginger
½   tsp kosher salt
¼   tsp ground cinnamon
2   tbsp fresh lemon juice

PITA CHIPS

2   large pita breads
1   tbsp olive oil
1   tsp *za'atar* spice blend
¼   tsp kosher salt

CREAMY LEMON DRESSING

2   tbsp fresh lemon juice
2   tbsp olive oil
2   tbsp mayonnaise
2   tbsp sour cream
2   tsp honey
½   tsp kosher salt
¼   tsp ground cumin

SALAD

3   celery stalks, chopped
2   large tomatoes, seeded and
    chopped
1   large green bell pepper,
    chopped
1   cup canned chickpeas, rinsed
    and drained
⅓   cup roughly chopped fresh
    mint

Looking to add some Moroccan mystery to your cooking repertoire? You don't need to watch *Ishtar* or head to the dusty desert—all you need to do is raid your spice rack. So simple to pull together, this aromatic, full-flavored, fantastic salad is the result of crunchy greens, chickpeas, tomatoes and fresh mint being combined with Middle Eastern–spiced grilled chicken and tossed in a creamy and refreshing lemon dressing. Topped with *za'atar*-spiced pita chips, this striking salad will have you rocking the casbah (and your kitchen) in no time.

MOROCCAN CHICKEN SALAD WITH CRISPY PITA CHIPS

1. PLACE CHICKEN in a large resealable plastic bag. In a small bowl, combine olive oil, brown sugar, smoked paprika, cumin, *za'atar*, ginger, salt and cinnamon. Rub spice mixture into chicken breasts and refrigerate for 2–8 hours to marinate. Remove from refrigerator 30 minutes before grilling and add lemon juice to chicken. Preheat barbecue to medium-high and lightly oil the grill grate. Remove chicken from marinade and grill 8–10 minutes per side, until cooked through. Let rest for 5 minutes before cutting into large cubes. Set aside.

2. FOR THE PITA CHIPS, preheat oven to 350°F. Cut each pita into 8 wedges. In a large bowl, toss pita wedges with olive oil, *za'atar* and salt until combined. Place on a baking sheet lined with parchment paper and bake for 10 minutes, flip and continue to bake for 5 minutes more. Remove from oven and let cool.

3. FOR THE LEMON DRESSING, in a small bowl, whisk lemon juice, olive oil, mayonnaise, sour cream, honey, salt and cumin until well combined.

4. TO ASSEMBLE THE SALAD, in a large bowl, combine celery, tomatoes, green peppers, chickpeas, fresh mint and cubed chicken. Drizzle dressing over and toss well to coat. Serve with pita chips.

. . . .

Za'atar **is a Middle Eastern spice mixture of thyme, sumac, sesame seeds and salt.**

When I go fishing for compliments, I'm looking for words such as "brilliant," "stunning" and "hi-*larious*" to be tossed around. When Lisa pursues praise, it's "healthy," "flavorful" and "inventive" that put a spring in her step. Well, she can stop angling for adoration because this salad garners her a rousing round of applause, and rightfully so. Lisa's take on these scrumptious but typically greasy SoCal tacos is so very exciting. Instead of getting battered and deep-fried, mild white fish is marinated in a spicy lime sauce, grilled to flaky perfection and perched atop a fresh mango, avocado and smoky grilled corn salad. Served with crunchy corn tortilla chips and tossed in a spicy chipotle dressing, this deconstructed taco serves up all the fixings without all the fat.

PS: Do you like how I did my hair today? Stunning?

SERVES 4–6
PREP 15 minutes
(+30 minute marinade)
COOK 10 minutes

. . . .

FISH MARINADE

1 lb firm white fish (halibut, cod or tilapia), cut into 4–6 pieces
2 tbsp olive oil
2 tbsp fresh lime juice
1 tsp adobo sauce
½ tsp kosher salt
¼ tsp freshly ground black pepper

CREAMY CHIPOTLE DRESSING

1 cup plain yogurt
½ cup mayonnaise
1 tbsp fresh lime juice
1 tbsp honey
2 tsp apple cider vinegar
1 canned chipotle pepper in adobo sauce, seeds removed
1 tsp adobo sauce
½ tsp ground cumin
½ tsp kosher salt

SALAD

6 cups chopped romaine lettuce
4 cups thinly sliced napa cabbage
2 ears fresh corn, grilled, kernels removed
1 large ripe mango, peeled and chopped
1 large ripe avocado, chopped

Lime, thinly sliced, for garnish
Corn tortilla chips

BAJA FISH TACO SALAD WITH CREAMY CHIPOTLE DRESSING

1. PLACE FISH in a glass baking dish with olive oil, lime juice, adobo sauce, salt and pepper. Turn the fish in the marinade until evenly coated. Cover and set aside for 30 minutes to marinate.

2. FOR THE DRESSING, in a food processor, combine yogurt, mayonnaise, lime juice, honey, apple cider vinegar, chipotle pepper, adobo sauce, cumin and salt. Purée mixture until combined.

3. PREHEAT BARBECUE to medium-high heat and lightly oil grill grate. Remove fish from marinade and place on the grill. Grill 3 minutes, flip and grill 2–3 minutes more, until fish flakes easily with a fork. Remove from heat and set aside.

4. FOR THE SALAD, in a large bowl, combine romaine lettuce and napa cabbage. Toss with a few tablespoons of dressing to coat. Add corn, mango and avocado and toss with a little more dressing. Top each serving of salad with a piece of grilled fish. Drizzle dressing over fish and garnish with a slice of lime. Add a handful of corn tortilla chips on the side of the salad.

. . . .

To grill corn, shuck corn and place on a medium-high barbecue for 4–6 minutes, turning occasionally.

Baja Fish Taco Salad, page 75

Oui, oui, I remember. We were pedaling in Bordeaux, châteaus and vineyards a blur as our scarves flew behind and our baguettes bounced in our baskets. Fine, we weren't (Lisa doesn't know how to ride a bike), but we do dream of a glass of crisp, fruity sauvignon blanc alongside this *fantastique* Potato, Tuna & Bean Salad. Rustic and healthy, this chunky potato salad is loaded with arugula, tuna and creamy white beans, and dressed in a fresh thyme and Dijon vinaigrette. A meal on its own (an impressive lunch served with crusty bread) or as part of a bigger spread, this *magnifique* salad delivers all the deliciousness and elegance of the French countryside without having to humiliate Lisa on a tricycle.

SERVES 4
PREP 10 minutes
COOK 15 minutes

DIJON VINAIGRETTE

¼ cup olive oil
2 tbsp red wine vinegar
1 tsp Dijon mustard
1 tsp minced fresh thyme
1 tsp sugar
1 tsp kosher salt
½ tsp freshly ground black pepper
¼ tsp minced fresh garlic

SALAD

1½ lb small Yukon Gold potatoes, halved
Kosher salt
2 cups baby arugula
1 cup canned cannellini (white kidney) beans, rinsed and drained
1 can (6 oz) of tuna in water, drained and broken into chunks
1 small red bell pepper, chopped
1 small green bell pepper, chopped
¼ cup chopped fresh flat-leaf parsley

CHUNKY POTATO, TUNA & BEAN SALAD

1. FOR THE VINAIGRETTE, in a small container, combine olive oil, red wine vinegar, Dijon mustard, thyme, sugar, salt, pepper and garlic. Shake well to combine and set aside.

2. TO MAKE THE SALAD, place potatoes in a medium pot with water to cover and a generous pinch of salt. Bring to a boil over medium-high heat and cook 10–12 minutes, until potatoes are just tender. Drain potatoes, place in a large mixing bowl and toss with 2 tablespoons of vinaigrette. Set potatoes aside to cool.

3. ONCE POTATOES HAVE COOLED, add arugula, cannellini beans, tuna, red and green peppers and parsley. Toss gently with remaining dressing to combine.

"I thought of that while riding my bike."

Albert Einstein, on the Theory of Relativity

I believe that Homer (as in Simpson), once said something about not winning friends with salad. While this may be the case for those who throw together limp lettuce doused in bottled dressing, we've won many a friend with this healthy and hearty Grilled Thai Steak Salad. Flank steak, a naturally lean and tasty cut, is made all the more delicious when marinated in an Asian-inspired mixture and then grilled to melt-in-your-mouth, crusted perfection. Much like other Thai dishes, all the parts—fresh herbs, juicy mango, aromatic peanut dressing, tender beef—work together to create a most harmonious mix of bold, exotic and addictive flavors. Serve this up and get ready to fill your friend list.

GRILLED THAI STEAK SALAD

1. FOR THE FLANK STEAK, place in a large resealable plastic bag. In a small bowl, whisk lime juice, soy sauce, fish sauce, honey, garlic and ginger. Pour over flank steak, seal bag and marinate 30 minutes on the counter. Remove steak from marinade and pat dry with paper towels. Heat grill to high and cook for 6 minutes. Flip steak and cook another 5–6 minutes, or until desired doneness. Allow steak to rest for 10 minutes before thinly slicing flank steak against the grain.

2. FOR THE DRESSING, in a blender, combine peanut butter, water, vegetable oil, lime juice, rice vinegar, soy sauce, honey, brown sugar and Sriracha sauce. Pulse until combined.

3. TO ASSEMBLE SALAD, toss mixed greens, parsley, basil, carrots, mango and red pepper with half the dressing and toss to coat well. Finish the salad with steak slices and roasted cashews on top. Serve immediately with remaining dressing to drizzle over each serving.

 Use beef tenderloin for a special occasion in place of flank steak.

SERVES 6
PREP 15 minutes
(+30 minute marinade)
COOK 15 minutes
(+10 minutes resting)

FLANK STEAK
1½ lb flank steak
2 tbsp fresh lime juice
2 tbsp soy sauce
1 tbsp fish sauce
1 tbsp honey
1 large garlic clove, minced
1 tsp grated fresh ginger

PEANUT LIME DRESSING
¾ cup peanut butter
¼ cup warm water
2 tbsp vegetable oil
2 tbsp fresh lime juice
2 tbsp rice vinegar
2 tbsp soy sauce
1 tbsp honey
1 tbsp brown sugar
½ tsp Sriracha sauce

SALAD
12 cups mixed greens, baby kale, spinach or romaine lettuce
½ cup chopped fresh flat-leaf parsley
½ cup chopped fresh basil
2 small carrots, peeled and julienned
1 large mango, peeled and chopped into chunks
1 red bell pepper, julienned
½ cup roasted cashews

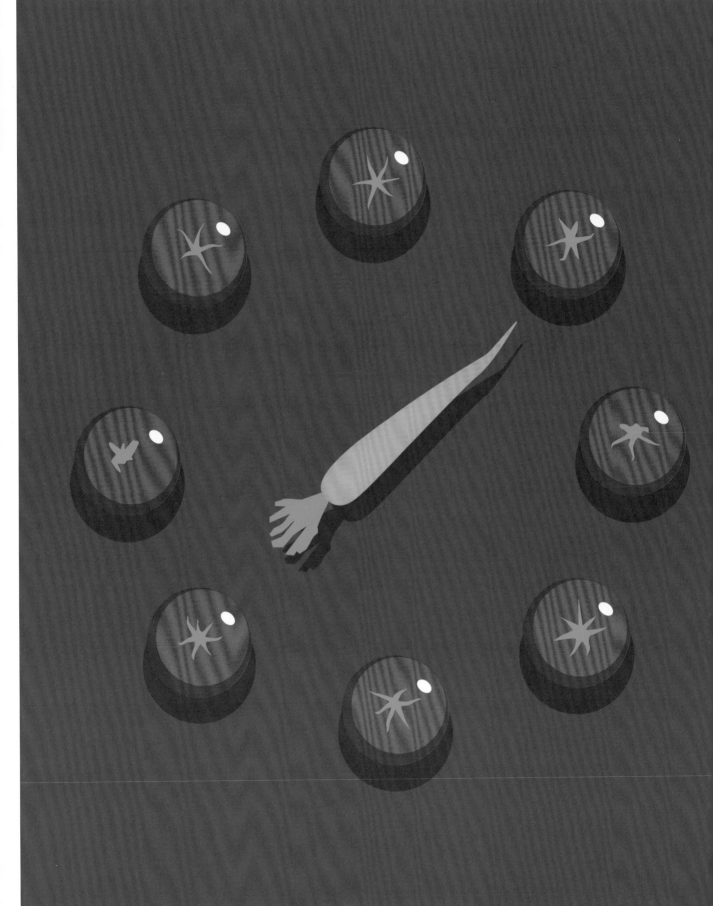

PICK OF THE CROP

[**VEGETABLES**]

Mashed potatoes are the Goldilocks of side dishes—you're going to want to get them "just right." This simple recipe is the key to elevating a classic side dish (it first appeared in 1747) from bland and boring to must-have mashed. How so? Our homemade ranch dressing, with buttermilk and herbs galore, adds a richness and terrific tang to these creamy and luscious mashed potatoes, making them all-star spuds.

BUTTERMILK RANCH MASHED POTATOES

SERVES 6-8
PREP 10 minutes
COOK 15 minutes

· ·

4   lb russet potatoes, peeled and quartered
½   cup butter, room temperature

1   cup buttermilk
½   cup sour cream
¼   cup mayonnaise
2   tbsp cider vinegar
2   tbsp chopped fresh flat-leaf parsley
1   tbsp snipped fresh chives
1½   tsp kosher salt
1   tsp sugar
1   tsp Dijon mustard
½   tsp paprika
¼   tsp freshly ground black pepper
¼   tsp garlic powder

Fresh chives, for garnish

1. ADD POTATOES to a large pot of salted water and bring to a boil over high heat. Lower to medium heat and cook until potatoes are fork tender, about 10–13 minutes. Drain potatoes well. Put the potatoes through a ricer or mash with a potato masher in a large bowl. Mix in butter until melted.

2. IN A MEDIUM BOWL, whisk buttermilk, sour cream, mayonnaise, cider vinegar, parsley, chives, salt, sugar, Dijon mustard, paprika, pepper and garlic powder. Whisk until well combined and stir into potato mixture until creamy. Garnish with fresh chives.

· ·

No buttermilk? Make your own by putting a tablespoon of fresh lemon juice or white vinegar in a glass measuring cup. Add milk until you reach 1 cup total. Stir to combine and let sit 5–10 minutes to become buttermilk.

"Think twice." If I had a nickel for every time someone said that to me . . . well, you get the picture. Now, if only someone had told me to "bake twice," I would have beat my sis to the punch and come up with this spudalicious side dish on my own. Not only are russet potatoes baked, scooped, mashed, mixed and then piled high with a flavorsome filling of spinach, feta and Parmesan, but they're also perfect prepared in advance, refrigerated and then slid into the oven for the second baking just before dinner. With my mouth full of these crisp-on-the-outside, creamy-on-the-inside, delectable double-baked potatoes, eating my words never tasted so good.

SPINACH & FETA TWICE-BAKED POTATOES

1. PREHEAT OVEN to 400°F. Rub the outside of each potato with olive oil, sprinkle with salt and pierce each with a fork several times. Bake 60–65 minutes, until tender. Remove potatoes from oven and let cool slightly. Cut potatoes in half lengthwise and scoop out flesh into a large mixing bowl, leaving ¼ inch of potato all around the inside as a shell. Place shells on a baking sheet and set aside.

2. MASH POTATOES WITH BUTTER, sour cream and milk. Fold in spinach, 1 cup of the feta, Parmesan, salt, pepper, oregano and cayenne pepper. After discarding 4 of the potato skins (so that the remaining potato skins can be filled high), pile the mixture in the remaining shells, top with ½ cup feta cheese and lightly sprinkle with paprika. Bake at 400°F for 10–15 minutes, until heated through and golden on top.

SERVES	6–8
PREP	10 minutes
COOK	1 hour, 20 minutes

6   large russet potatoes, scrubbed
1   tbsp olive oil
¼   tsp kosher salt
¼   cup butter, softened
¾   cup sour cream
½   cup whole milk
1   package (18 oz) frozen chopped spinach, thawed, squeezed very dry
1   cup crumbled feta cheese
½   cup freshly grated Parmesan cheese
1   tsp kosher salt
½   tsp freshly ground black pepper
½   tsp dried oregano
Pinch cayenne pepper
½   cup crumbled feta cheese, for topping
Paprika, for topping

"I have made a lot of mistakes falling in love, and regretted most of them, but never the potatoes that went with them."

Nora Ephron

We all know that when sweet potatoes are baked, they get sweeter. So, can you just imagine what happens when they're baked twice? That's right, you end up with this out-of-this-world, sweet Southern-inspired side dish. Tasting much like scrumptious sweet potato pie, sweet potatoes are baked, mashed with brown sugar, cinnamon and ginger, piled back in their skins, topped with a buttery and crunchy streusel topping and baked a second time. With this clever take on a classic, you won't have to convince anyone to dig into these easy-as-pie, creamy and candy-like sweet potatoes.

SERVES 6–10
PREP 10 minutes
COOK 1 hour, 30 minutes

. . . .

7 sweet potatoes, washed and dried
2 tsp vegetable oil
¼ tsp kosher salt
3 tbsp butter, softened
3 tbsp brown sugar
4 oz whipped cream cheese, room temperature
½ tsp vanilla extract
½ tsp ground cinnamon
½ tsp kosher salt
⅛ tsp ground ginger

PECAN STREUSEL
¾ cup pecans, toasted and chopped
¼ cup flour
¼ cup brown sugar
¼ tsp ground cinnamon
⅛ tsp kosher salt
3 tbsp cold butter, cubed

Maple syrup, for drizzle

TWICE-BAKED SWEET POTATOES WITH PECAN STREUSEL

1. PREHEAT OVEN TO 375°F. Rub the sweet potatoes with vegetable oil and sprinkle with salt. Prick the potatoes a few times to let steam escape while cooking. Place sweet potatoes on a baking sheet and bake 60–75 minutes, until tender. Let cool slightly.

2. WHILE THE POTATOES BAKE, prepare pecan streusel. In a small bowl, combine pecans, flour, brown sugar, cinnamon and salt. Add butter with your fingertips, combining until mixture is crumbly. Set aside.

3. ONCE THE POTATOES are cool enough to handle, cut a thin slice off the top of each potato and scoop out potato flesh into a large bowl, leaving a border all around the inside as a shell. Discard 1 potato once flesh has been removed so that the remaining potato shells can be filled high. Mash scooped-out potato with butter, brown sugar, cream cheese, vanilla extract, cinnamon, salt and ginger. Evenly scoop filling into 6 remaining potato shells and top with pecan streusel. Bake 10–15 minutes, until topping is golden and heated through. Drizzle with maple syrup before serving.

"I'm a hot little potato right now."

Mugatu, *Zoolander*

I'm a gold digger. When I see anything made with buttery Yukon Gold potatoes, I dig right in. This classic stick-to-your-ribs (but not your thighs, as we've done away with the traditional two cups of heavy cream) side dish is some serious comfort food currency—tender potatoes are layered with an onion herb mixture, a creamy combination of white cheddar and Parmesan cheese, and finished with a crunchy crumb topping. Easy and impressive, these creamy scalloped potatoes will most definitely be treasured at your table.

SERVES   8
PREP   20 minutes
COOK   1 hour, 30 minutes

3   lb (about 6 large) Yukon Gold potatoes, peeled and thinly sliced crosswise
1   tbsp olive oil
½   cup grated white cheddar or Gruyère cheese
½   cup freshly grated Parmesan cheese
¾   tsp kosher salt
1   medium yellow onion, chopped
1   tsp chopped fresh thyme
1   tsp chopped fresh rosemary

BÉCHAMEL
¼   cup butter
¼   cup flour
1   tsp dried mustard powder
½   tsp kosher salt
Pinch cayenne pepper
3   cups whole milk, warmed

TOPPING
½   cup panko (Japanese breadcrumbs)
½   cup grated white cheddar or Gruyère cheese
¼   cup freshly grated Parmesan cheese
2   tbsp melted butter

THE PERFECT SCALLOPED POTATOES

1. PREHEAT OVEN to 400°F. Coat a 9-inch square baking dish with non-stick cooking spray.

2. IN A LARGE BOWL, toss sliced potatoes with olive oil, white cheddar, Parmesan cheese and salt. Set aside. In a small bowl, toss chopped onion, thyme and rosemary. Set aside.

3. TO MAKE THE BÉCHAMEL, in a medium saucepan, melt butter over medium heat. Add flour, mustard powder, salt and cayenne. Stir continuously for 30 seconds. Gradually whisk in milk and continue to whisk until sauce thickens, 4–5 minutes. Remove from heat.

4. FOR THE TOPPING, in a small bowl, toss together panko, white cheddar, Parmesan cheese and melted butter.

5. TO ASSEMBLE, pour 1 cup béchamel over the bottom of the baking dish. Arrange ⅓ of the sliced potato mixture in a pattern on top. Sprinkle with half the onion mixture and top evenly with 1 cup béchamel. Layer ⅓ of the potato slices, the remaining half of the onions, followed by remaining potato slices. Pour last cup of béchamel and evenly scatter topping over potatoes. Cover with aluminum foil and bake 50 minutes. Lower heat to 350°F, uncover and continue to bake for 30 minutes, or until the potatoes are fork tender and top is beginning to turn golden.

You can assemble the scalloped potatoes up to 6 hours in advance. Refrigerate covered with foil and allow to come to room temperature before baking.

What's hot in Spain? A close second to Rafa Nadal is romesco, the go-to sauce (aka Spanish ketchup) for everything from grilled chicken and veggies to pasta and pizza. Here, we've recreated this sought-after sauce, a bold blend of roasted red peppers, almonds, garlic and tomatoes, and paired it with creamy roasted fingerling potatoes and caramelized Brussels sprouts. Satisfying and savory, this ace dish is a real crowd-pleaser, even more so than "The King of Clay" in his tennis whites.

SERVES 4–6
PREP 20 minutes
COOK 1 hour, 15 minutes

ROMESCO SAUCE

4   medium plum tomatoes, cored and halved
2   tbsp olive oil
1   small garlic head
1   cup chopped roasted red peppers
½   cup roasted almonds
2   tbsp sherry vinegar
1   tsp kosher salt
¼   cup olive oil

POTATOES AND BRUSSELS SPROUTS

2   lb fingerling potatoes, cut lengthwise in thirds
1   lb Brussels sprouts, stems removed and sprouts halved
1   tbsp olive oil
1   tsp kosher salt
1   tsp dried rosemary
¼   tsp freshly ground black pepper

ROASTED FINGERLING POTATOES & BRUSSELS SPROUTS WITH ROMESCO SAUCE

1. FOR ROMESCO SAUCE, preheat oven to 375°F. Place tomato halves on a baking sheet lined with parchment paper. Drizzle 1 tablespoon olive oil over tomatoes. Slice about ¼ inch off the top of the head of garlic. Drizzle with remaining 1 tablespoon olive oil, wrap in aluminum foil and place on baking sheet with tomatoes. Roast for 45 minutes, until tomatoes are starting to caramelize around the edges and the center clove of the garlic is soft. Remove from oven, let cool slightly. Place tomatoes in a blender and squeeze garlic out of its skin into the blender. Add roasted red peppers, almonds, sherry vinegar and salt. Pulse to purée, slowly adding olive oil until emulsified and smooth. Remove from blender. Can be refrigerated covered for 1 week.

2. TO PREPARE POTATOES and Brussels sprouts, preheat oven to 400°F. Line a large baking sheet with parchment paper. In a large bowl, toss potatoes, Brussels sprouts, olive oil, salt, rosemary and pepper. Place on baking sheet and roast for 15 minutes. Stir and continue roasting 15 minutes more, or until potatoes are golden and Brussels sprouts are tender. Serve romesco sauce with roasted potatoes and Brussels sprouts.

If you have trouble finding fingerling potatoes, you can use baby red potatoes, cutting the larger ones in half.

Live-It-Up Lisa believes that variety is the spice of life and thus, doesn't believe in serving up predictable potatoes. Can't say we're sorry, especially after trying her kicked-up Cajun Oven Fries. Creamy russet potatoes are hand cut, roasted until crisp on the outside and fluffy on the inside, and then tossed in aromatic toasted cumin and chili powder. Smoky, spicy and superb, these healthy baked french fries add zip, zing and, along with a delectable dipping sauce, excitement to the everyday meal.

CAJUN OVEN FRIES WITH SWEET & SPICY KETCHUP

SERVES 4–6
PREP 15 minutes
COOK 25 minutes

. . . .

KETCHUP

1   tsp ground cumin
1   tsp chili powder
½   cup ketchup
1   tbsp apricot jam
2   tsp fresh lime juice

BAKED FRIES

2½ lb (about 6 medium) russet
      potatoes, unpeeled, scrubbed,
      cut into ¼-inch strips
2   tbsp olive oil
1   tsp kosher salt
2   tsp ground cumin
1   tsp chili powder
¼   tsp ground ginger
¼   tsp garlic powder
Pinch cayenne pepper

1. FOR THE KETCHUP, in a small dry skillet, toast the cumin and chili powder for 30 seconds over medium-low heat. Transfer to a small bowl and let cool slightly. Add ketchup, apricot jam and lime juices to the toasted spices and whisk to combine. Cover and refrigerate until ready to serve.

2. FOR THE BAKED FRIES, preheat oven to 450°F. Line 2 baking sheets with aluminum foil and coat very well with nonstick cooking spray. After cutting potatoes, dry between 2 kitchen towels. In a large bowl, toss potatoes with olive oil and salt. Arrange potatoes in a single layer on prepared baking sheets. Bake for 15 minutes, stir and bake 10 minutes more, until golden and crispy.

3. WHILE POTATOES ARE BAKING, in a small skillet, toast cumin and chili powder, stirring constantly, over medium-low heat for 30 seconds, until spices are fragrant. Remove from heat and empty spices into a small bowl. Add ground ginger, garlic powder and cayenne. Set aside. Once potatoes are cooked, remove from oven and transfer to a large bowl. Toss with spice mixture. Serve immediately with ketchup.

Frank Sinatra once said, "Orange is the happiest color." We couldn't agree more with Ol' Blue Eyes—this orange-hued Butternut Squash & Carrot Bake makes us extremely happy. Cooked and puréed together, squash and carrots are sweetened with honey and brown sugar and spiced with cinnamon and nutmeg. Topped with a crispy crunchy cornflake topping, this superb side dish is fly-me-to-the-moon marvelous.

"I wish Frank Sinatra would just shut up and sing."

Lauren Bacall

SWEET BUTTERNUT SQUASH & CARROT BAKE

1. PREHEAT OVEN to 350°F. Coat a 12- × 8-inch (or 11- × 7-inch) baking dish with nonstick cooking spray.

2. PLACE BUTTERNUT SQUASH and carrots in a large saucepan and fill with enough water to cover vegetables. Bring to a boil, reduce heat to medium and cook for 15–20 minutes until tender. Drain well. Using a food processor or blender, add ¼ cup butter and half the butternut squash-carrot mixture. Purée until smooth and transfer to a large mixing bowl. Repeat with remaining ¼ cup butter and butternut squash–carrot mixture. Stir in honey, brown sugar, eggs, vanilla extract, salt, cinnamon and nutmeg. Spoon mixture into prepared dish.

3. FOR THE CORNFLAKE CRUMBLE, in a medium bowl, combine cornflakes, brown sugar, cinnamon and butter. Mix until crumbly. Sprinkle over butternut squash–carrot mixture. Cover with aluminum foil and bake 30 minutes. Remove foil and bake 20 minutes more.

SERVES 6–8
PREP 15 minutes
COOK 1 hour, 15 minutes

. . . .

4   cups peeled and cubed butternut squash
4   cups peeled and cubed carrots
½   cup butter, softened
¼   cup honey
¼   cup brown sugar
2   eggs, lightly whisked
1   tsp vanilla extract
¾   tsp kosher salt
¼   tsp ground cinnamon
¼   tsp ground nutmeg

CORNFLAKE CRUMBLE
2   cups crushed cornflakes
½   cup brown sugar
¼   tsp ground cinnamon
¼   cup butter, softened

> "Nobody likes beets, Dwight. You should grow something everybody does like. You should grow candy."
>
> Michael Scott, *The Office*

It's time to get back to your roots. No, not the color your hair used to be, but the root vegetables that, when roasted, become nature's candy. Here, the trio of carotene-rich carrots, fiber-packed parsnips and vitamin-filled beets are coated with tart balsamic vinegar, sweet honey and a kick of spice from cayenne pepper, and roasted until caramelized. Tasty and healthy, this marvelous medley can also be made using other root vegetables and can be served atop salads for an extra delicious bite. How's that for a rooting-tooting side dish?

BALSAMIC ROASTED CARROTS, PARSNIPS & BEETS

SERVES 4–6
PREP 15 minutes
COOK 40–45 minutes

. . . .

2 tbsp olive oil
2 tbsp balsamic vinegar
1 tbsp honey
2 tsp chopped fresh thyme
¾ tsp kosher salt
⅛ tsp cayenne pepper
5 large yellow beets, peeled and cut into wedges
5 large carrots, peeled and cut lengthwise
5 large parsnips, peeled and cut lengthwise

Fresh thyme sprigs, for garnish

1. PREHEAT OVEN to 400°F. Line a large baking sheet with parchment paper.

2. IN A LARGE BOWL, whisk olive oil, balsamic vinegar, honey, thyme, salt and cayenne pepper together. Add chopped beets, carrots and parsnips and toss to coat. Spread vegetables on baking sheet. Roast 20–22 minutes, stir and continue to cook 20–22 minutes more, until vegetables are tender. Garnish roasted vegetables with fresh thyme sprigs and serve.

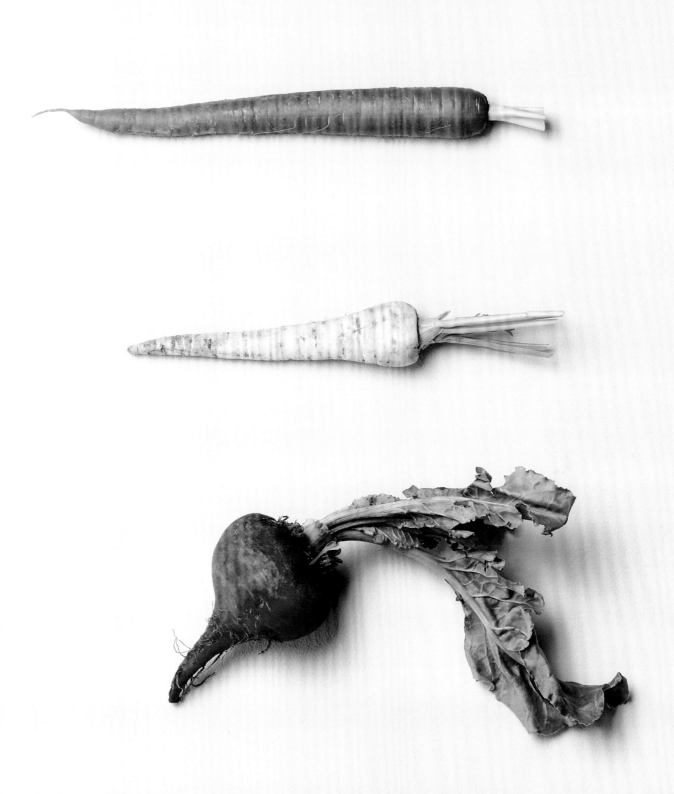

"Eat your broccoli," is one of the many phrases I vowed I'd never say as a mom. Wrong. So when I caught myself repeating it on a loop, I turned to Lisa for help. Her answer was simple: a five-ingredient recipe for Cheesy Lemon Roasted Broccoli. Tossed with lemon juice, olive oil and salt, broccoli is roasted until tender and crisp, and finished with a sprinkle of sharp white cheddar that gets melted under the broiler. Thankfully, I no longer need to bellyache about broccoli, but sorry kiddos, you still have to pick up your socks, do your homework and brush your teeth.

CHEESY LEMON ROASTED BROCCOLI

SERVES 6
PREP 10 minutes
COOK 20 minutes

· · · · · · · · · · · · · · · · · · · ·

2   heads broccoli, cut into florets with some stem
2   tbsp olive oil
1   tbsp fresh lemon juice
½   tsp kosher salt
2   tsp fresh lemon juice
¾   cup grated sharp white cheddar

1. PREHEAT OVEN to 425°F. Line a baking sheet with parchment paper.

2. IN A LARGE BOWL, toss broccoli with olive oil, 1 tablespoon of the lemon juice and salt. Arrange broccoli in a single layer on prepared baking sheet. Roast the broccoli for 15 minutes, tossing once halfway through cooking. Remove broccoli from oven and turn oven to broil. Drizzle broccoli with 2 teaspoons of lemon juice and sprinkle with white cheddar. Place under broiler for 1 minute, or until cheese melts. Watch carefully to prevent burning.

"I do not like broccoli. And I haven't liked it since I was a little kid and my mother made me eat it. And I'm President of the United States and I'm not going to eat any more broccoli."

George Bush

Cauliflower gets a bad rap. It's been berated as boring, knocked as nasty and even dissed by Larry David. Well, you cauliflower condemners, your days of disapproval are over because no one, we repeat, no one can resist this melt-in-your-mouth Parmesan Roasted Cauliflower. A vegetable low in carbs and high in fiber and vitamins, cauliflower is caramelized in the oven, tossed with a zesty Dijon dressing, sprinkled with Parmesan cheese and broiled until golden. It takes only one bite of this flavorful, tender veggie to know why this recipe will kick-start a cauliflower craze among kids and adults alike.

PARMESAN ROASTED CAULIFLOWER

1. PREHEAT OVEN to 400°F. Line a baking sheet with parchment paper and set aside.

2. IN A LARGE BOWL, toss the cauliflower florets with olive oil, salt and pepper. Spread on baking sheet and bake for 10 minutes. Flip cauliflower and continue roasting 10 minutes more.

3. WHILE THE CAULIFLOWER IS ROASTING, prepare the lemon Dijon dressing. In a mini food processor or blender, combine olive oil, lemon juice, parsley, Dijon mustard, sugar and salt. Process until well combined.

4. WHEN THE CAULIFLOWER IS FINISHED ROASTING, remove from oven and turn broiler to high heat. Toss the cauliflower in a large bowl with the lemon Dijon dressing. Return cauliflower to the baking sheet and sprinkle Parmesan cheese evenly over top. Broil 1–2 minutes, watching carefully until the cauliflower is golden and the Parmesan cheese is melted. Remove from oven, garnish with parsley and serve.

SERVES 4
PREP 5 minutes
COOK 25 minutes

1   large head cauliflower, cut into florets, about 6–7 cups
2   tbsp olive oil
½   tsp kosher salt
¼   tsp freshly ground black pepper
¼   cup freshly grated Parmesan cheese

LEMON DIJON DRESSING
2   tbsp olive oil
1   tbsp fresh lemon juice
1   tbsp chopped fresh flat-leaf parsley
½   tsp Dijon mustard
½   tsp sugar
⅛   tsp kosher salt

Fresh flat-leaf parsley, for garnish

"There's no deceit in the cauliflower. This is a totally honest meal. You don't know what a pleasure it is in this day and age to eat food that you can believe in."

Lenny Cantrow, *The Heartbreak Kid*

We know that your time is precious, so we aren't going to encourage you to fritter it away. Or are we? These fantastic fritters are a mere 20-minute investment and the results are worth every second. Cooked until golden-crusted yet soft and creamy inside, these crispy cakes are the combination of grated sweet zucchini mixed with fresh creamy ricotta and flavorful Parmesan cheese. A delicious, fast and easy side dish, these crowd-pleasing Zucchini Ricotta Fritters will definitely free up some time for you to dilly-dally.

GOLDEN ZUCCHINI RICOTTA FRITTERS

MAKES	10 fritters
PREP	10 minutes
COOK	10 minutes

- 2 medium zucchinis
- ¾ cup ricotta cheese
- ¾ cup breadcrumbs
- ½ cup freshly grated Parmesan cheese
- 1 small garlic clove, minced
- 1 egg, lightly whisked
- 1 tsp lemon zest
- ½ tsp kosher salt
- ¼ tsp freshly ground black pepper
- 2 tbsp olive oil

Lemon wedges, to squeeze over cooked zucchini fritters

1. GRATE ZUCCHINIS and remove excess liquid by squeezing the zucchini in small sections with your hands. Place grated zucchini on paper towels to remove remaining liquid. Place in a large bowl and combine with ricotta cheese, breadcrumbs, Parmesan cheese, garlic, whisked egg, lemon zest, salt and pepper. Mix thoroughly until well combined.

2. USING A ¼-CUP SCOOP, form zucchini mixture into 10 round, flat patties. Heat olive oil in a large skillet over medium-low heat. Add zucchini patties and cook until golden, 2–3 minutes per side. Remove from heat and serve with squeezed lemon juice.

Choose small to medium-sized, darker-skinned zucchinis, as they have more flavor and nutrients than large ones.

Kermit was right. It's not easy being green, especially when trying to get kids and carnivores to eat their veggies. Well, thanks to this creative recipe, we can all sit back and let these quick and delicious Caesar Asparagus with Mini Croutons speak volumes. Vibrant, crisp and tender asparagus are topped with tangy Caesar dressing and mini crunchy croutons, making the selling of these superb spears child's play.

CAESAR ASPARAGUS WITH MINI CROUTONS

1. FOR THE CROUTONS, in a small bowl, toss diced bread with olive oil, Parmesan cheese and salt. Heat a medium skillet over medium-high heat. Add bread and cook 4–5 minutes, until golden all over. Remove from skillet and set aside.

2. FOR THE CAESAR DRESSING, in a mini food processor or blender, combine Parmesan cheese, lemon juice, garlic, Dijon mustard, sugar, salt and pepper. Process until combined. With the machine running, add olive oil and process until smooth. Transfer to a bowl and set aside.

3. BRING A LARGE pot of water to a boil. Add asparagus, turn heat to low and cook until just tender, about 2 minutes. Drain and immediately plunge into a bowl of cold water. Drain well. Transfer asparagus to a serving platter. Drizzle with Caesar dressing and top with mini croutons and shaved Parmesan cheese.

Did you know that asparagus are either male or female? Of course, it's the female stalks that are plumper.

SERVES 6
PREP 10 minutes
COOK 20 minutes

MINI CROUTONS

1   cup diced French bread
1   tbsp olive oil
1   tbsp freshly grated Parmesan cheese
¼   tsp kosher salt

CAESAR DRESSING

6   tbsp freshly grated Parmesan cheese
2   tbsp fresh lemon juice
1   small garlic clove, minced
1   tsp Dijon mustard
¼   tsp sugar
¼   tsp kosher salt
¼   tsp freshly ground black pepper
3   tbsp olive oil

30–36 asparagus stalks, woody ends trimmed

Shaved Parmesan cheese, for garnish

These aren't your garden-variety green beans—we've given them a makeover, elevating them from dull to drool-worthy. Steamed yet crispy, the warm and vibrant green beans are tossed in a lemon shallot vinaigrette and topped with creamy goat cheese and crunchy toasted walnuts. Such a simple, scrumptious and speedy (20 minutes, tops) side dish has us all full of beans.

GREEN BEANS WITH GOAT CHEESE & WALNUTS

1. FOR THE BEANS, bring a large pot of water to a boil over high heat. Reduce heat to low, add green beans, cover and cook until tender-crisp, about 3 minutes. Drain and rinse with cold water immediately to stop further cooking. Spread beans on paper towel and pat dry.

2. FOR THE VINAIGRETTE, in a small bowl, whisk olive oil, white balsamic vinegar, lemon juice, shallot, Dijon mustard, honey, salt and pepper. Toss beans with half the vinaigrette, place on serving plate and sprinkle with goat cheese and chopped walnuts. Drizzle with more dressing if desired.

SERVES 6–8
PREP 10 minutes
COOK 10 minutes

· ·

1½ lb green beans, ends trimmed

LEMON SHALLOT VINAIGRETTE
3 tbsp olive oil
1 tbsp white balsamic vinegar
2 tsp fresh lemon juice
1 tsp minced shallot
1 tsp Dijon mustard
¼ tsp honey
¼ tsp kosher salt
¼ tsp freshly ground black
   pepper

¼ cup crumbled goat cheese
½ cup toasted chopped walnuts

"Green Beans, or string beans as they are usually called, must be done [boiled] till very tender— it takes nearly an hour and a half."

Sarah Josepha Hale, *The Good Housekeeper*, 1839

Walk around the block. Count the shoes in your closet. Make a stir-fry. What do these three things have in common? They can all be done in five minutes or less. Yes, as in you're 300 seconds away from serving up this sizzling Asian Vegetable Stir-Fry, a cruciferous combo of cauliflower, broccoli, carrots, peppers and bok choy. Lightning fast and super healthy, this stir-fry can be easily altered (want different veggies? why not?) or bulked up (add tofu, chicken or beef) into a complete meal, making it the tastiest way to make the most of your time.

ASIAN VEGETABLE STIR-FRY

1. FOR THE STIR-FRY SAUCE, in a small bowl, whisk chicken broth, soy sauce and sherry cooking wine. In another bowl, dissolve cornstarch in water. Whisk cornstarch mixture into stir-fry sauce and set aside.

2. IN A LARGE WOK, heat vegetable oil over high heat. When the oil is very hot, add onion, garlic, ginger and salt. Stir constantly for 1 minute. Add broccoli, cauliflower and carrots. Cook for 1 minute, lower heat to medium, add 2 tablespoons water, cover and cook for 2 minutes. Remove cover and add red bell peppers, bok choy and stir-fry sauce. Cook until sauce thickens and vegetables are tender and coated. Garnish with roasted cashews.

Stir-Fry Secrets

1. Have all your ingredients prepped before you start cooking.

2. Heat your wok until very hot before beginning.

3. Don't overcrowd your wok or you'll steam, not stir-fry.

SERVES 4–6
PREP 20 minutes
COOK 5 minutes

STIR-FRY SAUCE

¼ cup chicken broth (vegetable broth for a vegetarian stir-fry)

2 tbsp soy sauce

1 tbsp cooking sherry

1 tbsp cornstarch

1 tbsp water

1 tbsp vegetable oil

1 medium red onion, halved and then sliced

1 small garlic clove, minced

½ tsp grated fresh ginger

¼ tsp kosher salt

2 cups broccoli florets

2 cups cauliflower florets

1 large carrot, peeled and sliced diagonally

2 tbsp water

1 red bell pepper, julienned

4 cups sliced bok choy

½ cup chopped roasted cashews, for garnish

SERVES 4–6
PREP 15 minutes (+30–60 minute marinade and skewer soak)
COOK 10 minutes

· ·

Kebab skewers (metal, wood or bamboo)

MISO DRESSING
½ cup yellow miso paste
¼ cup warm water
2 tbsp vegetable oil
2 tbsp mirin
2 tbsp brown sugar
1 tbsp rice vinegar
½ tsp grated fresh ginger

TOFU
1 package (12 oz) extra-firm tofu, patted dry with paper towels

2 medium green zucchinis, cut into 24 thick round slices
2 medium yellow zucchinis, cut into 24 thick round slices
1 red bell pepper, cut into large chunks
1 yellow pepper, cut into large chunks

When I think of food-on-a-stick, my mind instantly jumps to corn dogs, caramel apples and cotton candy. Unsurprisingly, Lisa skips over skewered fried butter and heads straight to fresh produce, fantastic flavors and a fired-up barbecue for these Grilled Miso Tofu & Veggie Kebabs. Marinated in a sweet and salty miso dressing and grilled until smoky and tender, these tofu, zucchini and pepper kebabs prove once again that despite sometimes being a stick-in-the-mud, Lisa's always on the right end of the stick.

GRILLED MISO TOFU & VEGGIE KEBABS

1. IF THE KEBAB SKEWERS are wood or bamboo, soak them in water for 30 minutes before threading tofu and vegetables.

2. FOR THE MISO DRESSING, in a blender, combine miso paste, water, vegetable oil, mirin, brown sugar, rice vinegar and ginger. Blend until smooth. Set aside.

3. FOR THE TOFU, cut into 24 (1-inch) cubes and place in a medium bowl. Toss with ¼ cup miso dressing, cover and set aside to marinate for 30–60 minutes. Place cut-up vegetables in another bowl and toss with ¼ cup miso dressing, setting aside to marinate. Reserve remaining dressing to brush on while grilling.

4. LIGHTLY OIL GRILL and preheat to medium. Thread the tofu and vegetables, alternating tofu, green zucchini, yellow zucchini, red peppers and yellow peppers. Grill skewers, brushing with more dressing as needed. Turn skewers occasionally, until lightly charred, about 8–10 minutes. Remove from grill and drizzle with any remaining miso dressing if desired.

"Speak softly and carry a big stick; you will go far."

Theodore Roosevelt

SERVES 4–6
PREP 20 minutes
COOK 1 hour

. . . .

THYME PECANS

1   cup coarsely chopped pecans
1   tbsp melted butter
1   tsp chopped fresh thyme
¼   tsp kosher salt
Pinch cayenne pepper

SWEET POTATOES

2   medium sweet potatoes,
    peeled and cut into ½-inch
    cubes
1   tbsp olive oil
¼   tsp kosher salt
¼   tsp freshly ground black
    pepper

RISOTTO

4   cups vegetable broth
2   tbsp butter
1   tbsp olive oil
1   small yellow onion, finely
    chopped
1   large garlic clove, minced
½   tsp kosher salt
1½ cups Arborio rice
¾   cup dry white wine
½   cup freshly grated Parmesan
    cheese
1   tsp chopped fresh thyme
½   tsp kosher salt, to taste

"'Excellent!' I cried.
'Elementary,' said he."

Arthur Conan Doyle,
The Complete Sherlock Holmes

Until recently, I ranked risotto right up there with Gordon Ramsay as most-temperamental-in-the-kitchen. I worried about the rumored hours of stirring and watching and waiting I would have to endure, a cooking experience that would end in me channeling the bad-boy Brit and uttering a string of @#$% words. Well, I worried for nothing because Lisa has let me in on a little chef's secret: Risotto is easy. Good rice, a hot stock and 20 minutes of frequent stirring are all it takes to make this creamy, dreamy dish of caramelized roasted sweet potatoes folded into Parmesan, thyme and white wine risotto. Topped with roasted pecans, this no-sweat, restaurant-worthy risotto is easygoing and most-comforting-in-the-kitchen.

SWEET POTATO RISOTTO WITH THYME ROASTED PECANS

1. PREHEAT OVEN to 350°F.

2. FOR THE PECANS, in a medium bowl, toss together chopped pecans, butter, thyme, salt and cayenne. Place on a baking sheet lined with parchment paper and bake for 10 minutes, until lightly toasted. Set aside.

3. FOR THE SWEET POTATOES, increase oven temperature to 425°F. In a large bowl, combine sweet potatoes, olive oil, salt and pepper. Spread on a baking sheet lined with parchment paper and roast for 10 minutes. Stir and roast 8–10 minutes more, just until tender but not mushy. Remove from oven and set aside.

4. IN A MEDIUM SAUCEPAN, bring vegetable broth to a simmer over low heat. In a large saucepan, heat butter and olive oil over medium heat. Add onion and cook 3 minutes to soften. Add garlic, salt and Arborio rice and cook, stirring, for 2 minutes. Add wine, stirring continually until evaporated. Reduce heat to medium-low and add ½ cup of vegetable broth, stirring frequently until the liquid is absorbed. Add another ½ cup and repeat, making sure each addition of liquid is absorbed before adding the next. Continue for 18–20 minutes, until rice is creamy and tender. Remove from heat and stir in Parmesan cheese, thyme and salt (to taste). Gently fold in roasted sweet potatoes. Top with roasted pecans and serve immediately.

SERVES 6
PREP 15 minutes
COOK 15 minutes

· ·

BASIL & WALNUT PESTO

1   cup firmly packed fresh basil
     leaves
½   cup coarsely chopped toasted
     walnuts
1   small garlic clove, minced
½   tsp kosher salt
¼   tsp freshly ground black
     pepper
½   cup olive oil
¾   cup freshly grated Parmesan
     cheese
1   tbsp fresh lemon juice

1   lb bowtie pasta
1   tbsp olive oil
2   green onions, chopped
1   cup fresh green peas
15   asparagus spears, trimmed
     and cut on the diagonal into
     bite-sized pieces
¼   tsp kosher salt
¼   tsp freshly ground black
     pepper

Freshly grated Parmesan cheese,
     for garnish
Fresh basil leaves, for garnish

Watergate, Vietnam and the oil crisis marked the 1970s, but there were also some great things to come out of the "'Me' Decade," including the Hustle, *Annie Hall*, Led Zeppelin and pasta primavera. Yes, the combo of pasta and spring vegetables was made famous in the '70s at New York landmark restaurant Le Cirque. Count on Lisa to boogie on down and bring this classic dish to the 21st century. A creamy, aromatic basil and walnut pesto is tossed with a bright mix of peas, asparagus and tender pasta to create this quick, easy, delicious and ultra-fresh dish. Totally rad, right?

PASTA PRIMAVERA
WITH BASIL & WALNUT PESTO

1. FOR THE WALNUT PESTO, combine basil, walnuts, garlic, salt and pepper in a food processor. Process until finely chopped. With the motor running, slowly pour in olive oil and process until mixture is well combined. Add Parmesan cheese and lemon juice, pulsing once or twice to combine. Cover and set aside.

2. IN A LARGE POT of boiling salted water, cook pasta until tender. Reserve ½ cup cooking water and drain pasta well. Place pasta in a large mixing bowl and set aside.

3. IN A LARGE SKILLET, heat olive oil over medium-high heat. Add chopped green onions, peas, asparagus, salt and pepper. Stir 3–4 minutes, until vegetables are just tender. Add to pasta and toss with walnut pesto. If pasta needs to be loosened, add reserved pasta water a small amount at a time. Sprinkle each serving with Parmesan cheese and garnish with fresh basil.

· ·

You can store nuts in the refrigerator for 9 months and for up to 2 years in the freezer.

Are you staring into the abyss of your fridge, wondering how dinner will appear? This superb Spaghetti with Chunky Marinara Sauce (note: "marinara" comes from the Italian word for sailor) is going to be your port in the eating and feeding storm. A pantry pasta that requires little to no planning, this chunky southern Italian sauce is perfect for everyone from those trying to get sea legs in the kitchen to the seasoned home cook, and, thanks to the combination of sweet Italian tomatoes, garlic, olive oil, onions and basil, you'll never have a futiny™ (food + mutiny) on your hands.

SERVES 4–6
MAKES 2½ cups sauce
PREP 5 minutes
COOK 50 minutes

⅓ cup olive oil
3 garlic cloves, thinly sliced
¼ cup thinly sliced fresh basil
½ cup chopped yellow onions
1 can (28 oz) San Marzano tomatoes
½ tsp kosher salt
¼ tsp freshly ground black pepper
Pinch crushed red pepper flakes
1 lb dry spaghetti, linguine or fettuccini
1 tbsp butter
¼ cup freshly grated Parmesan cheese
2 tbsp thinly sliced fresh basil

Freshly grated Parmesan cheese, for serving

SPAGHETTI WITH CHUNKY MARINARA SAUCE

1. IN A SMALL SAUCEPAN, heat olive oil over medium-low heat. Add sliced garlic and cook for 2 minutes. Remove from heat and stir in basil. Let cool for 15 minutes. Strain oil and discard solids.

2. IN A LARGE SAUCEPAN, heat 2 tablespoons of reserved oil over medium heat. Add onions and cook 2–3 minutes, until tender. Stir in tomatoes, salt, pepper and red pepper flakes. Using a potato masher, mash tomatoes just until chunky. Reduce heat to low and simmer sauce, stirring occasionally, for 30 minutes.

3. WHILE SAUCE IS COOKING, bring a large pot of salted water to a boil and cook spaghetti until tender. Drain well and divide between serving bowls.

4. REMOVE SAUCE FROM HEAT and stir in butter, Parmesan cheese and basil. Spoon a generous serving of sauce over each bowl of spaghetti, drizzle with remaining oil and sprinkle with freshly grated Parmesan cheese, if desired.

Stir in a spoonful of pesto, add cream for a tomato cream sauce or kick up the sauce with some extra red pepper flakes, capers and olives.

SERVES   4
PREP   15 minutes
COOK   35 minutes (+1 hour, 30
         minute refrigeration)

. . . .

**HOMEMADE RICOTTA CHEESE
(MAKES 1 CUP)**

3½   cups whole milk
½   cup heavy cream
½   tsp kosher salt
3   tbsp fresh lemon juice

ANGEL HAIR PASTA

½   lb angel hair pasta or
     spaghetti
1   tbsp olive oil
1   medium yellow onion, cut in
     half and thinly sliced
2   medium zucchinis, cut into
     ½-inch cubes
1   large garlic clove, minced
1   tsp chopped fresh thyme
1   tsp kosher salt
¼   tsp freshly ground black
     pepper
¼   tsp crushed red pepper flakes
2   tbsp tomato paste
1½   cups cherry tomatoes, halved
½   cup dry white wine
⅓   cup freshly grated Parmesan
     cheese
1   tsp lemon zest
Kosher salt and freshly ground
     black pepper, to taste

Freshly grated Parmesan cheese,
     to serve

Little Lisa Muffet sat on her tuffet eating her curds and ricotta cheese whey. That is, until I came along and almost scared her away by screeching that no one but she has the skill required to make homemade ricotta. She laughed and told me that whipping up a batch of this creamy, fluffy white Italian cheese is as easy as ABC. True enough, this rich and flavorful ricotta is simple yet impressive, and made even more so when tossed with angel hair pasta, sautéed zucchini and onions, Parmesan cheese and lemon zest. Once again, Mother Goose Gnat has it all goin' on.

ANGEL HAIR PASTA WITH ZUCCHINI, TOMATOES & HOMEMADE RICOTTA

1. FOR THE RICOTTA CHEESE, in a large saucepan, heat milk, cream and salt over medium heat. Stir frequently until it comes to a simmer. Simmer gently for 2 minutes. Remove from heat and stir in lemon juice. Set aside for 10 minutes. Place a strainer over a mixing bowl and line the strainer with cheesecloth. Ladle the curds and whey into the cheesecloth. Cover and refrigerate for 1½ hours. Remove ricotta from cheesecloth and place in a covered container until ready to use.

2. FOR THE PASTA, bring a large pot of salted water to a boil. Cook pasta until tender. Drain pasta, reserve ½ cup of the water, and set aside.

3. IN A LARGE SKILLET, heat olive oil over medium heat. Add onion and cook, stirring, for 3–4 minutes to soften. Add zucchini, garlic, thyme, salt, pepper and red pepper flakes. Cook, stirring, for 4 minutes until zucchini is tender. Stir in tomato paste until well combined. Reduce heat to low and stir in cherry tomatoes and white wine, cooking for 2 minutes. Add cooked pasta, reserved ½ cup pasta water, Parmesan cheese and lemon zest and heat through. Remove from heat and season to taste with salt and pepper. Top each serving of pasta with a large spoonful of homemade ricotta cheese. Sprinkle with extra Parmesan cheese if desired.

Looking for the food pyramid in a bowl? You've found it. At the base of the pyramid is pasta (tender fusilli), followed by vegetables (onions, kale and spinach), fruit (yes, tomatoes fall into this category), protein (chickpeas), dairy (Parmesan, milk and butter), and topped off with a little bit of flavorful fat (hello, cream). The Egyptians couldn't have built a better pyramid (and in 18 minutes, at that) than this creamy, comforting, kid- and family-friendly dinnertime dish.

FUSILLI WITH SUN-DRIED TOMATOES, SPINACH & KALE

SERVES 4–6
PREP 10 minutes
COOK 20 minutes

1. IN A LARGE POT of salted boiling water, cook pasta according to package directions. Drain and set aside.

2. IN A LARGE SKILLET, melt butter over medium heat. Add onion and cook until softened, 2–3 minutes. Stir in garlic, tomato paste, salt and red pepper flakes, stirring constantly for 1 minute. Add flour and stir until well combined. Slowly whisk in milk and cream, stirring continuously to incorporate. Add sun-dried tomatoes and whisk until sauce has thickened slightly, 2–3 minutes. Stir in diced tomatoes, kale, spinach and chickpeas. Cook for 1–2 minutes over low heat. Add cooked pasta and fresh Parmesan cheese, stirring well. Serve garnished with fresh basil.

¾	lb fusilli pasta
2	tbsp butter
1	small yellow onion, chopped
1	large garlic clove, minced
2	tbsp tomato paste
½	tsp kosher salt
Pinch crushed red pepper flakes	
2	tbsp flour
2	cups 2% milk
½	cup heavy cream
⅓	cup oil-packed sun-dried tomatoes, drained and finely minced
1	can (14 oz) diced tomatoes, drained, liquid discarded
2	cups coarsely chopped baby kale
2	cups coarsely chopped spinach
1	cup canned chickpeas, rinsed and drained
½	cup freshly grated Parmesan cheese
¼	cup chopped fresh basil, for garnish

Turn leftover kale into healthy kale chips by pulling the leaves off stems, tossing with a little olive oil and salt, spreading in a single layer on a parchment-lined baking sheet and baking at 300°F for 5–8 minutes, until crisp but not browned.

SERVES   4–6
PREP   15 minutes
         (+30 minutes
         of eggplant draining)
COOK   1 hour, 5 minutes

· ·

8   cups 1-inch cubes of peeled
    eggplant
1   tbsp kosher salt
2   tbsp olive oil
¾   lb orzo pasta
2   tbsp butter
1   small yellow onion, chopped
1   large garlic clove, minced
1   tsp kosher salt
Pinch crushed red pepper flakes
¼   cup flour
1¼ cups whole milk, warmed
1   cup freshly grated Parmesan
    cheese
1   tbsp fresh lemon juice
1   tsp lemon zest
1   cup ricotta cheese
2   tbsp freshly grated Parmesan
    cheese
1   cup panko (Japanese bread-
    crumbs)
2   tbsp melted butter

"I'm not normally a
praying man, but if
you're up there,
please save me,
Superman!"

Homer Simpson

Orzo is the superhero of pasta. How so? Resembling a pumped-up, Hulk-like rice, this pasta has a transformative quality as flexible as Plastic Man, and is often used as a hearty addition to soup or served as a simple side dish. Well, look out because Legendary Lisa has struck again and taken orzo to new heights with this grown-up noodle and cheese bake, an elegant mealtime marvel of roasted eggplant, creamy ricotta cheese and tender pasta, all topped with a golden, crispy panko crumble. Cooked up faster than a speeding bullet, this warm, comforting and delicious dish will definitely morph you into the Amazing Eating Machine.

EGGPLANT & RICOTTA BAKED ORZO

1. PREHEAT OVEN to 425°F. To prepare eggplant, place eggplant cubes in a large colander and toss with salt. Let them drain for 30 minutes. Without rinsing the eggplant, pat dry with paper towels. In a large bowl, toss eggplant with olive oil and spread out on a baking sheet lined with parchment paper. Bake 25–30 minutes, until golden brown, stirring halfway through. Remove from oven and place eggplant in a large mixing bowl.

2. LOWER OVEN temperature to 350°F.

3. COOK ORZO PASTA in a large pot of salted, boiling water until al dente (it will cook more in the oven). Drain pasta and place in mixing bowl with roasted eggplant. In a medium saucepan, melt 2 tablespoons of butter over medium heat. Add onion and cook 3 minutes. Add garlic, salt and crushed red pepper flakes, cooking 1 minute more. Add flour, stirring until incorporated. Gradually stir in the milk and continue to stir until there are no lumps. Remove from heat and stir in Parmesan cheese, lemon juice and lemon zest. Pour sauce over orzo and eggplant and add ½ cup ricotta cheese. Toss gently to coat orzo.

4. COAT an 11- × 7-inch baking dish with nonstick cooking spray. Transfer orzo mixture to baking dish and top with dollops of remaining ½ cup ricotta cheese followed by 2 tablespoons of Parmesan cheese. In a small bowl, combine panko crumbs and 2 tablespoons of melted butter. Sprinkle panko mixture over orzo and bake, uncovered, for 20 minutes.

I love when Lisa listens to music in the kitchen because some solid gold recipes have been born as a result—"Cheeseburger in Paradise" (page 200), "Blueberry Hill" (page 276) and "Breakfast in America" (page 223), to name a few. So it shouldn't come as a surprise that "Scenes from an Italian Restaurant" was playing when she came up with this Creamy Chicken Marsala Penne, a dish inspired by the old-school Italian menu item. To bring it on home, Lisa has taken the classic combo of juicy chicken, earthy mushrooms and sweet Marsala wine and made it a meal by tossing it with tender pasta. Can you imagine what she's going to serve up when she hears the song, "I Eat Heavy Metal"?

CREAMY CHICKEN MARSALA PENNE

1. IN A LARGE POT of boiling salted water, cook pasta according to package directions. Drain and set aside.

2. FOR THE CHICKEN, season with salt and pepper. Dredge chicken pieces in flour, shaking off excess. In a large skillet, heat olive oil and butter over medium-high heat. Brown chicken in 2 batches, until golden brown, about 4 minutes. Transfer to a plate.

3. FOR THE MARSALA SAUCE, melt butter in a skillet over medium-high heat. Add onion, shallots, garlic and mushrooms. Cook for 6–8 minutes, until mushroom liquid evaporates. Stir in flour and salt; cook for 1 minute. Add Marsala wine and cook, stirring, until most of the liquid is evaporated. Add chicken broth and bring to a boil. Reduce heat to low and stir in heavy cream and cooked chicken. Simmer, covered, for 5 minutes. Remove from heat and stir in pasta and Parmesan cheese. Season to taste with salt and pepper. Garnish with Parmesan cheese and chopped parsley. Serve immediately.

 If you don't have Marsala wine, simmer 2 parts white wine with 1 part brandy plus a little brown sugar and a pinch of salt.

¾ lb penne pasta

CHICKEN

4 boneless skinless chicken breasts, cut into bite-sized pieces
¼ tsp kosher salt
¼ tsp freshly ground black pepper
¼ cup flour
2 tbsp olive oil
1 tbsp butter

MARSALA SAUCE

2 tbsp butter
1 small white onion, chopped
2 tbsp minced shallots
1 large garlic clove, minced
3 cups sliced white mushrooms
1 tbsp flour
½ tsp kosher salt
½ cup dry Marsala wine
1 cup chicken broth
¼ cup heavy cream
½ cup freshly grated Parmesan cheese
Kosher salt and freshly ground black pepper, to taste

Freshly grated Parmesan cheese, for garnish
Chopped fresh flat-leaf parsley, for garnish

SERVES 4–6
PREP 10 minutes
COOK 1 hour, 30 minutes

. . . .

PARMESAN GNOCCHI

2 lb (about 3 large) russet
   potatoes
½ cup freshly grated Parmesan
   cheese
2 egg yolks
½ tsp kosher salt
1¼–1½ cups flour
Cornmeal, for dusting baking
   sheet

MUSHROOM WHITE WINE SAUCE

2 tbsp olive oil
1 tbsp butter
½ cup chopped shallots
2 large garlic cloves, minced
1 tsp chopped fresh thyme
6 cups stemmed and sliced
   cremini mushrooms
½ tsp kosher salt
½ cup dry white wine
½ cup chicken broth
½ cup freshly grated Parmesan
   cheese
¼ cup heavy cream

Freshly grated Parmesan cheese,
   for garnish
Fresh thyme sprigs, for garnish

"How come the dove
gets to be the peace
symbol? How about the
pillow? It has more
feathers than the dove,
and it doesn't have that
dangerous beak."

Jack Handy

Ready for some pillow talk? While I'm neither going to divulge Lisa's crush (name starts with Wolfgang, ends with Puck), nor tell you what she fears (peanut butter sticking to the roof of her mouth), I am going to reveal that she makes perfectly pillowy potato gnocchi. What's her secret? Listen closely and you won't lose a wink of sleep making these soft dumplings—to keep gnocchi light in texture, don't add too much flour or over-knead the dough. Simple, right? Pair these fluffy one-biters with this quick, rich and tasty white wine and mushroom cream sauce, and you've got a satisfying dish that dreams are made of.

PARMESAN GNOCCHI WITH WHITE WINE & MUSHROOM CREAM SAUCE

1. FOR THE GNOCCHI, preheat oven to 425°F. Scrub potatoes, pat dry and poke holes with a fork to allow steam to escape during baking. Bake potatoes until tender, 50–60 minutes. Remove potatoes from oven and allow to cool 10 minutes for easier handling. The gnocchi needs to be made while the potatoes are still warm. Cut potatoes in half, scoop out the flesh and put through a potato ricer into a large bowl. Add Parmesan cheese, egg yolks and salt, mixing well to combine. Incorporate 1 cup of flour and mix until the dough is formed. Turn out onto floured surface and lightly knead remaining ¼–½ cup flour until soft dough is formed. You don't need to overwork the dough. Cut the dough into 4 pieces. Roll each piece on a lightly floured surface into long strips. Cut the strips into ½-inch gnocchi and place on a cornmeal-dusted baking sheet. Once sauce is ready, cook gnocchi.

2. FOR THE MUSHROOM SAUCE, in a large skillet, heat olive oil and butter over medium heat. Add shallots and cook, stirring, until softened, 2 minutes. Add garlic and thyme, cooking 1 minute more. Increase heat to high and add mushrooms and salt, cooking 5–6 minutes, until lightly browned and most of the moisture is removed from the mushrooms. Add wine and cook until almost evaporated, 3 minutes. Add chicken broth and bring to a boil. Remove from heat and stir in Parmesan cheese and cream. Keep warm while cooking gnocchi.

3. TO COOK THE GNOCCHI, bring a large pot of salted water to a boil. Add half of the gnocchi and when they float to the surface, cook 1 minute longer. Remove gnocchi with a flat slotted spoon and add to mushroom sauce. Repeat with remaining gnocchi. Sprinkle with Parmesan cheese and garnish with a sprig of fresh thyme. Serve immediately.

When Lisa asked me if I wanted to warm up, I immediately took it as my chance to showcase my toe touching and one-arm pushups. After shooting me the Gnat Grimace, she took the top off her slow cooker and got me seriously fired up. The aroma, an enveloping scent of slow-cooked beef simmering all day along with sautéed vegetables, garlic and red wine, was intoxicating. With this meltingly tender and hearty beef ragu spooned atop creamy, cheesy polenta, the only exercise I'm going to be doing is the fork-to-mouth mambo.

CREAMY POLENTA WITH SLOW-COOKED BEEF RAGU

1. FOR THE BEEF RAGU, heat olive oil in a large skillet over high heat. Season the roast with ½ teaspoon salt and pepper and place in skillet. Cook 4 minutes per side until a golden brown crust forms and then transfer to slow cooker. Do not wipe out skillet. Add onion, celery and carrots over medium heat. Cook 4 minutes, stirring frequently. Add tomato paste, garlic, oregano, 1 teaspoon salt and pepper and cook 1 minute. Add red wine and cook for 1 minute. Along with San Marzano tomatoes, add mixture to the beef in the slow cooker. Cover and cook on low setting for 8–10 hours, until the beef easily falls apart. Using 2 forks, shred beef and stir to combine with sauce. Serve over polenta and garnish with chopped parsley.

2. FOR THE POLENTA, in a large saucepan, bring water and 1 teaspoon salt to a boil. Gradually whisk in cornmeal over low heat. Cook for 40 minutes, stirring every 10 minutes. Remove from heat and stir in butter, cream, Parmesan cheese and ½ teaspoon salt. Serve immediately.

The traditional way to cook polenta involves a fireplace, a large copper pot and a wooden stick. While we use the stovetop, we like to use a heavy-bottomed pot and a wooden spoon to keep the polenta from sticking or scorching.

SERVES 8–10
PREP 10 minutes
COOK 8–10 hours

BEEF RAGU
1 tbsp olive oil
1 (3 lb) beef rump roast
½ tsp kosher salt
½ tsp freshly ground black pepper
1 yellow onion, chopped
2 celery stalks, chopped
2 carrots, peeled and chopped
3 tbsp tomato paste
2 large garlic cloves, minced
1 tsp dried oregano
1 tsp kosher salt
½ tsp freshly ground black pepper
½ cup dry red wine
1 can (28 oz) San Marzano whole tomatoes

CREAMY POLENTA
9 cups water
1 tsp kosher salt
2 cups yellow cornmeal
¼ cup butter
⅓ cup heavy cream
⅓ cup freshly grated Parmesan cheese
½ tsp kosher salt

Chopped fresh flat-leaf parsley, for garnish

SERVES   6
PREP   10 minutes
COOK   1 hour, 30 minutes

. . . .

TURKEY BOLOGNESE

1   lb ground turkey
1   small red onion, chopped
1   large garlic clove, minced
1   celery stalk, chopped
1   large carrot, peeled and
    chopped
2   tbsp chopped fresh flat-leaf
    parsley
1   tsp dried oregano
1   tsp kosher salt
½   tsp freshly ground black
    pepper
¼   tsp crushed red pepper flakes
½   cup whole milk
1   can (28 oz) diced tomatoes
2   tbsp tomato paste

MANICOTTI

12 manicotti shells
2½ cups ricotta cheese
2   cups shredded mozzarella
    cheese
½   cup freshly grated Parmesan
    cheese
1   egg
2   tbsp chopped fresh flat-leaf
    parsley
½   tsp dried oregano
½   tsp kosher salt
¼   tsp garlic powder
⅓   cup freshly grated Parmesan
    cheese

It takes a lot for Lisa to lose her cool (me playing pirate with a manicotti tube as my spyglass does the trick) so it's no shock that even on the busiest, most harried of days, she's cool as a cucumber. How does she do it? She knows she has this incredibly easy and comforting baked pasta in her back pocket (and sometimes in her freezer), one that she can make ahead of time and bake off just before serving. In this hearty and filling Italian favorite, manicotti noodles are stuffed with the perfect blend of ricotta, mozzarella and Parmesan cheese, and then blanketed in a chunky Turkey Bolognese sauce. One bite and you too will instantly discover that Landlubber Lisa (yes, this annoys her too) cooks up some seriously blow-me-down delicious fare.

CHEESY MANICOTTI WITH TURKEY BOLOGNESE

1. FOR THE TURKEY BOLOGNESE, place ground turkey, red onion, garlic, celery, carrot, parsley, oregano, salt, pepper and red pepper flakes in a large skillet over medium heat. Using a wooden spoon, break up turkey as it cooks, and when it's no longer pink, reduce heat to low, cover and simmer for 10 minutes. Uncover, increase heat to high and add milk, stirring constantly, until most of the milk is absorbed. Stir in diced tomatoes and tomato paste and bring to a boil. Reduce heat and gently simmer for 30 minutes, stirring occasionally.

2. FOR THE MANICOTTI, cook the manicotti shells in a large pot of salted boiling water until slightly softened, 6 minutes. Drain, rinse under cold water and set aside.

3. PREHEAT OVEN to 350°F and coat a 13- × 9-inch baking dish with nonstick cooking spray. Spread 2 cups of prepared Bolognese over the base of the baking dish. In a mixing bowl, stir together ricotta cheese, shredded mozzarella, ½ cup Parmesan cheese, egg, parsley, oregano, salt and garlic powder. Using a small spoon, stuff this cheese mixture into the manicotti shells. Line stuffed manicotti in prepared baking dish. Cover with remaining 2 cups of Bolognese. Sprinkle ⅓ cup Parmesan cheese over top and bake, covered, for 20 minutes. Uncover and continue to bake 10 minutes more.

. . . .

Instead of using a small spoon, place filling in a resealable plastic bag, cut off the corner and use to squeeze filling into manicotti shells.

I'm elated that Lisa aced Latin in high school. Not only did she teach me "Semper ubi sub ubi," (translation: "Always wear underwear"), but she has also capitalized on the fact that the name "lasagna" comes from the Latin word *lasanum*, meaning "cooking pot." Taking this literally, she has created a simple and superb skillet lasagna that is a deliciously hearty combination of rich meat sauce, tender noodles, ricotta, Parmesan cheese and mozzarella cheese. Easy prep, quick cooking, A+ reviews and only one skillet to wash at the end of the night make this *optimus* (translation: "the best") dinner fare for every night "of the week.

> "Can I borrow your underpants for 10 minutes?"
>
> The Geek, *Sixteen Candles*

SERVES 4–6
PREP 10 minutes
COOK 35 minutes

HEARTY MEAT & 3-CHEESE SKILLET LASAGNA

1. PREHEAT OVEN to 425°F.

2. IN A LARGE OVEN-SAFE SKILLET, heat olive oil over medium heat. Add onion and cook until softened, 3 minutes. Add garlic and cook 30 seconds more. Stir in ground beef and cook until no longer pink, occasionally stirring and breaking up the beef into small pieces. Drain off any excess liquid. Stir in tomato paste, Italian seasoning, salt, brown sugar, fennel seed, red pepper flakes and pepper until well combined. Add red wine and cook for about 2 minutes, until the wine is reduced. Stir in tomato sauce, beef broth and diced tomatoes. Bring to a boil, reduce heat to low and stir in broken lasagna noodles. Cover and cook for 20 minutes, stirring occasionally, until the pasta is tender.

3. ONCE PASTA IS TENDER, remove skillet from heat and stir in ½ cup ricotta cheese and Parmesan cheese. Top with sliced mozzarella cheese and ½ cup ricotta cheese scattered on top. Bake, uncovered, for 10 minutes. Top with fresh basil and serve.

Try this with Caesar Asparagus, page 101.

1	tbsp olive oil
1	small yellow onion, diced
2	garlic cloves, minced
1	lb lean ground beef
2	tbsp tomato paste
1	tsp dried Italian seasoning
1	tsp kosher salt
½	tsp brown sugar
½	tsp fennel seed
½	tsp crushed red pepper flakes
½	tsp freshly ground black pepper
½	cup dry red wine
2	cups tomato sauce
1	cup beef broth
1	can (28 oz) diced tomatoes
12	curly-edged lasagna noodles, broken into large pieces
½	cup ricotta cheese
½	cup freshly grated Parmesan cheese
4	oz fresh mozzarella cheese, thinly sliced
½	cup ricotta cheese

Fresh basil leaves, for garnish

SERVES 8
PREP 15 minutes
COOK 1 hour, 30 minutes
(+30 minutes cooling
time)

. . . .

MEAT SAUCE

3 tbsp olive oil
1 large yellow onion, chopped
1½ lb lean ground beef
2 large garlic cloves, minced
1 tsp dried oregano
½ cup dry white wine
1 (28 oz) can crushed tomatoes
1 tsp kosher salt
½ tsp freshly ground black
pepper
2 dried bay leaves

¾ lb ziti or any tubular pasta
1 tbsp olive oil
1½ cups crumbled feta cheese

BÉCHAMEL

⅓ cup butter
⅓ cup flour
3 cups whole milk, warmed
2 quick grates of fresh nutmeg
½ tsp kosher salt
2 egg yolks
¾ cup grated kefalotyri (or
another hard yellow cheese
from Greece, or freshly grated
Parmesan cheese)

When Lisa announced that she was making pastitsio, I was at a loss. I responded with, "That's Greek to me." She congratulated me on my culinary comprehension. I wasn't sure why until I discovered that pastitsio (pronounced pa-STEE-tsee-oh) is in fact Greek comfort food, a Hellenic lasagna composed of hearty meat sauce, ziti pasta and creamy béchamel sauce, layered and baked until golden. Dotted with tangy feta and full of fantastic flavor, this lasagna freezes well and reheats easily, proving once again that the goddess known as Glykeria Gnat (that's the Greek name I've given Lisa) has created the Mount Olympus of feasts.

GREEK PASTITSIO

1. PREHEAT OVEN to 350°F. Coat a 9- × 9-inch baking dish (note: dish should be 3 inches deep) with nonstick cooking spray. If you don't have this dish, you can use a 13- × 9-inch baking dish; however, you won't get the same look with the height of the final dish.

2. FOR THE MEAT SAUCE, in a large skillet, heat olive oil over medium heat. Add onion and cook until softened, 5 minutes. Add ground beef and break it up with a wooden spoon, cooking for 5 minutes until browned. Add garlic and oregano, cooking for 1 minute. Pour in wine and let it evaporate for 2–3 minutes. Stir in tomatoes, salt and pepper. Bring to a boil and then turn heat down to a simmer, add bay leaves and partially cover skillet. Cook for 30 minutes, stirring occasionally. Remove the bay leaves and set sauce aside.

3. COOK THE PASTA in a large pot of boiling water until al dente, 2 minutes less than the package directions. Drain and toss with olive oil. Add just over half the cooked pasta to the base of the baking dish. Sprinkle feta cheese over top.

4. TO MAKE THE BÉCHAMEL, melt the butter in a large saucepan over medium-low heat. Add the flour and stir until it turns golden but doesn't burn. Slowly whisk in milk, whisking continually to prevent lumps. Cook until smooth and slightly thickened. Remove pan from heat and whisk in nutmeg, salt, egg yolks and kefalotyri or Parmesan cheese, stirring continuously to prevent the eggs from cooking. When smooth, set aside.

5. TO FINISH ASSEMBLING, spread meat sauce evenly over the pasta and feta cheese layer. Pour remaining pasta over meat sauce and finish with the béchamel sauce evenly over the top. Bake, uncovered, for 30–35 minutes. Let cool at least 30 minutes before serving.

While we don't cook ours the way a paella purist in Valencia might (over an open fire and including rabbit and snails), we do bring all that's great about this classic Spanish dish to our hearty and vibrant Paella with Chicken & Peppers. With saffron infusing our broth and Spanish paprika lending a subtle smokiness and deep, woodsy flavor, our juicy chicken and sweet pepper paella is truly a one-pan weeknight wonder—simple to make and quick to disappear.

SERVES   6–8
PREP   15 minutes
COOK   1 hour

8   cups chicken broth
2   large pinches of saffron threads
2   tbsp olive oil
4   boneless skinless chicken breasts, cut into bite-sized pieces
½   tsp kosher salt
¼   tsp freshly ground black pepper
1   tbsp olive oil
2   small yellow onions, chopped
2   large garlic cloves, minced
½   tsp kosher salt
¼   tsp freshly ground black pepper
1   red bell pepper, chopped
1   green bell pepper, chopped
½   cup dry white wine
1   can (14 oz) diced tomatoes
1   tsp smoked paprika (Spanish paprika)
3   cups Arborio rice

Lemon wedges, for garnish

EASY PAELLA WITH CHICKEN & PEPPERS

1. PLACE CHICKEN BROTH in a medium saucepan and bring to a boil. Simmer over low heat and add saffron threads to infuse broth. Keep warm while preparing paella.

2. IN A 16- TO 18-INCH PAELLA PAN, heat 2 tablespoons of olive oil over medium-high heat. Season chicken with salt and pepper, add to pan and stir occasionally, cooking for 6 minutes until golden. Remove chicken from pan and set aside.

3. USING THE SAME PAELLA PAN, add 1 tablespoon olive oil over medium heat. Add onions, garlic, salt and pepper and cook, stirring, for 3–4 minutes, until softened. Add red and green peppers, stirring for 1 minute. Add white wine, diced tomatoes and smoked paprika. Cook 5–6 minutes, stirring occasionally, until most liquid has evaporated. Return chicken to pan and add warm saffron-infused chicken broth. Bring to a boil, lower heat to medium-low and simmer for 10 minutes. Add rice and stir until well combined. Cook over medium heat for 20 minutes without stirring, allowing a crust to form. When rice is tender and liquid is absorbed, remove from heat and cover with a cloth towel for 5–10 minutes to rest. Serve with lemon wedges.

Saffron, made from the dried stamens of crocus flowers, is the world's most expensive spice. Harvested by hand, it can take between 70,000 and 250,000 flowers to make 1 pound of saffron.

Do you need a quick and easy, tasty and healthy dinner? Lisa's on it like white on rice. Literally. You can get this stellar dish from fridge to feast in less than 25 minutes. Yes, nutritious Chinese food is within reach with this vegetarian meal in a bowl, a tasty combination of stir-fried golden tofu, protein-rich scrambled eggs, crunchy vegetables and, of course, rice. Whip up this perfect weeknight meal and breathe easy, because even if you're racing against the clock (you'll always win with this dish) or don't have certain vegetables (feel free to use what you have), you'll always come out ahead with this fantastic Crispy Tofu Fried Rice.

CRISPY TOFU FRIED RICE

SERVES 4–6
PREP 10 minutes
COOK 15 minutes

- 2 tsp vegetable oil
- 1 package (14 oz) firm tofu, drained, patted dry with paper towels and cut into ½-inch cubes
- 1 tbsp soy sauce
- 1 tbsp fresh lime juice
- ¼ tsp Sriracha sauce
- 1 tsp vegetable oil
- 2 eggs, lightly whisked
- 1 tbsp vegetable oil
- 2 small carrots, peeled and chopped
- 1 small yellow onion, chopped
- 1 garlic clove, minced
- 5 cups cold, cooked long-grain rice
- 1 cup frozen peas, thawed
- 2 tbsp soy sauce
- 1 tbsp oyster sauce

1. IN A LARGE SKILLET OR WOK, heat 2 teaspoons vegetable oil over medium-high heat. Add tofu and cook until lightly browned, 4–5 minutes, stirring occasionally. Stir in 1 tablespoon soy sauce, lime juice and Sriracha sauce, stirring well to coat for 30 seconds. Remove tofu from pan and set aside.

2. USING THE SAME PAN, add 1 teaspoon vegetable oil over medium heat. Add eggs and scramble until almost cooked. Remove from pan and set aside with tofu.

3. USING THE SAME PAN, heat 1 tablespoon vegetable oil over medium-high heat. Add carrots and onions and cook, stirring, for 4 minutes. Stir in garlic, cooking 1 minute more. Add cold, cooked rice and cook for 2 minutes. Reduce heat to low and add peas, tofu and eggs, stirring well to combine. Stir in 2 tablespoons soy sauce and the oyster sauce. Cook, stirring, until heated through.

Day-old rice makes the best fried rice because it's drier and will keep your fried rice from becoming wet and mushy.

Ready for a side dish you can make faster than you can say olé? Here it is: a flavorful, quick, easy and healthy Mexican twist on a Middle Eastern staple. Within 10 minutes (yes, you read that right), you can serve up tender couscous, along with zesty Mexican spices, creamy black beans and fresh corn. Whether served on its own, wrapped in a burrito or piled over top of nachos with melted cheese, this fresh and zesty Mexican Couscous is a south-of-the-border bonanza.

10-MINUTE MEXICAN COUSCOUS

1. IN A LARGE SAUCEPAN, heat olive oil over medium heat. Add onion and continually stir for 2 minutes to soften. Stir in garlic, chili powder, cumin and salt and cook for 1 minute. Add chicken broth, salsa, black beans and corn kernels. Bring to a boil, stir in couscous, remove from heat, cover and let stand for 5 minutes. Stir in lime juice and garnish with chopped parsley.

"If everything seems under control, you're not going fast enough."

Mario Andretti

SERVES 6–8
PREP 2 minutes
COOK 8 minutes

. . . .

1   tbsp olive oil
1   small yellow onion, chopped
1   garlic clove, minced
1   tsp chili powder
½   tsp ground cumin
½   tsp kosher salt
1½ cups chicken broth
1   cup salsa (mild or medium spice)
1   cup canned black beans, rinsed and drained
1   cup (2 ears) fresh corn kernels
1½ cups couscous
1   tbsp fresh lime juice

2   tbsp chopped fresh flat-leaf parsley, for garnish

If you've ever witnessed her on the beam, you too would know that Lisa's no Nadia Comăneci; however, that hasn't stopped her from finding the perfect balance in this Shrimp & Tofu Pad Thai. A tricky mix to master, using readily available ingredients from the Asian aisle at your local supermarket, Lisa has expertly blended the salty, sweet, spicy and sour flavors that best characterize this classic Thai stir-fry. A quick meal to pull together, tender rice noodles are combined with sautéed tofu, scrambled eggs, crunchy bean sprouts and sweet shrimp, all tossed in a super-flavorful Pad Thai sauce and topped with roasted peanuts. Make this crowd-pleasing dish and you'll get a guaranteed perfect 10, every time.

THE ULTIMATE SHRIMP & TOFU PAD THAI

1. PLACE RICE NOODLES in a large bowl and cover noodles with boiling water. Let soak until softened, about 10–15 minutes or according to package directions. Drain noodles and rinse under cold water, then drain again and set aside.

2. WHILE THE NOODLES are soaking prepare the pad Thai sauce. In a medium bowl, whisk chicken broth, brown sugar, lime juice, tamarind paste, soy sauce, fish sauce and Sriracha sauce. Set aside.

3. IN A LARGE SKILLET, heat 1 tablespoon of oil over medium-high heat. Add tofu and cook 5 minutes, until golden. Add shallots and garlic, stirring continuously for 2 minutes. Push tofu and shallot mixture to the side of the skillet and add remaining 1 tablespoon of oil. Stir in the eggs and scramble until nearly cooked, 1–2 minutes. Add shrimp, sprinkle with salt and cook for 1 minute, tossing with all ingredients in the skillet. Add rice noodles and sauce and cook, stirring gently, for 2 minutes. Add bean sprouts and green onions, toss to combine and heat through, about 1 minute. Remove from heat, toss in ½ cup peanuts and transfer to serving plate. Garnish with chopped parsley, chopped peanuts and lime wedges.

> "My warrior name is Beyoncé Pad Thai."
>
> Mindy Kaling

SERVES 6–8
PREP 15 minutes
COOK 30 minutes

1 package (16 oz/1 lb) dried rice noodles

PAD THAI SAUCE
⅓ cup chicken broth
6 tbsp brown sugar
2 tbsp fresh lime juice
2 tbsp tamarind paste
1 tbsp soy sauce
1 tbsp fish sauce
1 tsp Sriracha sauce

2 tbsp vegetable oil
1 package (12 oz) firm tofu, pressed dry between paper towels, cut into bite-sized pieces
½ cup chopped shallots
2 large garlic cloves, minced
3 eggs, lightly whisked
1 lb raw, medium-sized shrimp, peeled and deveined
¼ tsp kosher salt
3 cups bean sprouts
6 green onions, finely chopped
½ cup chopped roasted peanuts

¼ cup chopped fresh flat-leaf parsley, for garnish
2 limes, cut into wedges for serving, for garnish
¼ cup chopped roasted peanutes, for garnish

MAKES   6 burgers
PREP   20 minutes
COOK   35 minutes

. . . .

LEMON & CUMIN SAUCE

½ cup mayonnaise
½ cup Greek yogurt
1 tbsp fresh lemon juice
1 tbsp minced fresh basil
1 tbsp minced fresh flat-leaf parsley
¼ tsp ground cumin
¼ tsp kosher salt
⅛ tsp cayenne pepper
⅛ tsp freshly ground black pepper

QUINOA CHICKPEA BURGERS

½ cup uncooked quinoa, rinsed well
1 cup vegetable broth
1 cup canned chickpeas, rinsed and drained
½ cup panko (Japanese breadcrumbs)
½ cup old-fashioned oats
1 small garlic clove, minced
1 tbsp minced shallot
1 tbsp chopped fresh flat-leaf parsley
1 tbsp chopped fresh basil
½ cup crumbled feta cheese
1 egg, lightly whisked
2 tbsp fresh lemon juice
1 tsp lemon zest
1 tsp ground cumin
½ tsp kosher salt
¼ tsp freshly ground black pepper
⅛ tsp cayenne pepper

6 crusty rolls
1 large ripe avocado, thinly sliced
1½ cups watercress

Calling all hardcore carnivores—we've got a beauty of a burger for you that's protein-rich *and* filling. While we have no beef with meat (bring it on!), we love that this firm, nutrient-packed veggie burger satisfies us with its nutty quinoa, healthy chickpeas, fresh herbs and feta filling. Baked and served with a lemon and cumin–flavored spread, watercress and sliced avocado, this mouthwatering, meatless Mediterranean burger is 100% grade-A goodness.

QUINOA BURGERS WITH ZESTY LEMON SAUCE

1. PREHEAT OVEN to 400°F.

2. FOR THE SAUCE, in a small bowl, combine mayonnaise, yogurt, lemon juice, basil, parsley, cumin, salt, cayenne and pepper. Whisk until blended. Refrigerate, covered, until ready to assemble.

3. TO PREPARE THE QUINOA, in a small saucepan, combine quinoa and vegetable broth. Bring to a boil over medium heat. Lower heat to a gentle simmer, cover and let cook for 15 minutes. Remove from heat and let stand for 5 minutes. Fluff with a fork, place in a large mixing bowl and let cool slightly.

4. USING A FOOD PROCESSOR, combine chickpeas, panko, oats, garlic, shallot, parsley and basil. Process until the mixture is well blended, 4–5 quick pulses. Transfer mixture to large bowl and toss with quinoa. Stir in feta, egg, lemon juice, lemon zest, cumin, salt, pepper and cayenne. Mix everything together until well combined. Form into 6 patties and place on a parchment-lined baking sheet. Lightly coat the tops of each burger with cooking spray. Bake 8 minutes, flip and continue to bake 8 minutes more. Remove from oven.

5. TO ASSEMBLE, spread lemon cumin sauce on both the top and bottom buns. Top bottom bun with burger, followed by avocado slices and a small handful of watercress. Finish with top bun and serve immediately.

. . . .

> "You know I love to talk about food I'm going to eat while I'm already eating."
>
> Grace Adler, *Will & Grace*

RULE THE ROOST

SERVES 4–6
MAKES 1¼ cups avocado dip
PREP 15 minutes
  (+1–2 hour marinade and
  skewer soak)
COOK 20 minutes

. . . .

Kebab skewers (metal, wood or
  bamboo)

DIJON LIME MARINADE
3 tbsp fresh lime juice
2 tbsp olive oil
2 tsp Dijon mustard
1 tsp lime zest
1 large garlic clove, minced
¼ tsp kosher salt
¼ tsp freshly ground black
  pepper

CREAMY AVOCADO DIP
1 large ripe avocado
¼ cup Greek yogurt
¼ cup mayonnaise
2 tbsp fresh lime juice
1 small garlic clove, minced
¾ tsp kosher salt
½ tsp honey
¼ tsp freshly ground black
  pepper
⅛ tsp cayenne pepper

4 boneless skinless chicken
  breasts, cut into 1½-inch
  cubes
2 tbsp chopped fresh flat-leaf
  parsley

While we may not know why the chicken crossed the road, we're most definitely chicken connoisseurs, able to elevate the sometimes-blah bird from dry and tasteless to moist and mouthwatering. Fire up the grill because you too can be a chicken champ with these amazingly easy (to cook, serve and eat) Lime Chicken Kebabs. Marinated in lime juice and Dijon mustard, chunks of chicken are threaded on skewers, grilled to juicy perfection and then dipped in a creamy avocado and lime dip. Now that you're a poultry pro, maybe you can tell us what came first: the chicken or the egg?

LIME CHICKEN KEBABS WITH CREAMY AVOCADO DIP

1. FOR THE MARINADE, in a small bowl, whisk lime juice, olive oil, Dijon mustard, lime zest, garlic, salt and pepper. Place chicken in a large resealable plastic bag. Add marinade and shake to coat. Refrigerate, marinating for 1–2 hours.

2. FOR THE AVOCADO DIP, combine avocado, yogurt, mayonnaise, lime juice, garlic, salt, honey, pepper and cayenne pepper in a food processor or blender and pulse until creamy and smooth. Store, covered and refrigerated, until ready to use.

3. PREHEAT GRILL to medium-high heat and oil the grill grate. If using wood or bamboo skewers, make sure to soak them in water for 30 minutes before skewering chicken. Discard marinade and thread chicken onto skewers. Grill the skewers for 10–15 minutes, or until cooked through, occasionally turning the skewers. Place on a serving plate, sprinkle with chopped parsley and serve with avocado dip.

. . . .

 Try with Mexican Couscous, page 133.

 Leftovers can be rolled in a wrap for the perfect midday meal.

Monday is movie night chez Lisa, a time when she gets inspired by the silver screen. Wasn't thrilled when she watched *Duck Soup*, but gotta say, *Casablanca* was a win-win. Not only did she get misty watching this quintessential love story (she looks funny when she cries), but she also drew on the magic of Morocco for this zesty chicken with chickpeas and olives. Quick and easy, an exotic, earthy spice mix is combined with juicy chicken, creamy chickpeas and tangy olives, a mealtime masterpiece guaranteed to captivate diners. Make it again, Lisa.

6   boneless skinless chicken breasts
2   tsp olive oil
¼   tsp ground cumin
¼   tsp smoked paprika
¼   tsp kosher salt
¼   tsp freshly ground black pepper
1   tbsp olive oil

SPICE MIX
1   tsp ground cumin
1   tsp smoked paprika
½   tsp ground ginger
¼   tsp crushed red pepper flakes
¼   tsp turmeric

1   tbsp olive oil
1   large yellow onion, cut in half and thinly sliced
2   large garlic cloves, minced
1   tbsp tomato paste
1   can (15.5 oz) diced tomatoes
1½ cups chicken broth
1¼ cups canned chickpeas, rinsed and drained
½   cup pitted green olives, halved (we love Spanish Manzanilla)
1   tbsp fresh lemon juice
1   tsp lemon zest
2   tbsp chopped fresh flat-leaf parsley

ZESTY MOROCCAN CHICKEN WITH CHICKPEAS & OLIVES

1. IN A LARGE BOWL, toss chicken breasts with 2 teaspoons of olive oil, cumin, paprika, salt and pepper. In a large skillet, heat 1 tablespoon of olive oil over medium-high heat. Add chicken and brown 3 minutes per side, until golden. Remove and set aside.

2. TO PREPARE SPICE MIX, in a small bowl, combine cumin, paprika, ginger, red pepper flakes and turmeric. Set aside.

3. FOR THE SAUCE, using the same large skillet, heat 1 tablespoon olive oil over medium heat. Add onion and cook, stirring, for 2 minutes. Add garlic and continue cooking 1 minute more. Add spice mixture, cooking for 30 seconds. Stir in tomato paste until incorporated. Add tomatoes and chicken broth and bring to a boil. Lower heat and simmer sauce for 5 minutes. Return chicken to skillet, cover and simmer 15 minutes or until the chicken is cooked through. Remove cover and stir in chickpeas, olives, lemon juice, lemon zest and parsley. Serve over cooked couscous.

Try with Parmesan Roasted Cauliflower, page 97.

"Everything I learned I learned from the movies."

Audrey Hepburn

SERVES 6
MAKES 1¼ cups barbecue sauce
PREP 10 minutes
     (+1–6 hour marinade)
COOK 20 minutes for chicken
     breasts; 50 minutes for
     drumsticks

MARINADE

6 boneless skinless chicken breasts or 12 drumsticks
2 tbsp olive oil
2 tbsp fresh lemon juice
1 large garlic clove, minced
1 tsp smoked paprika

BARBECUE SAUCE

1 cup ketchup
2 tbsp maple syrup
2 tbsp honey
1 tbsp Worcestershire sauce
1 tbsp apple cider vinegar
1 tbsp fresh lemon juice
1 tbsp Dijon mustard
1 tsp smoked paprika
¼ tsp garlic powder
¼ tsp kosher salt
¼ tsp freshly ground black pepper
1 tbsp butter

½ tsp kosher salt
½ tsp freshly ground black pepper
1 tbsp olive oil

> "My doctor told me to stop having intimate dinners for four. Unless there are three other people."
>
> Orson Welles

Winner, winner, weeknight chicken dinner. This prize poultry recipe for Saucy Oven-Baked Barbecue Chicken is foolproof, fantastic and guaranteed to become your go-to. Marinated in a zesty mixture that takes minutes to pull together, the chicken becomes tender even before getting baked in a ribbon-worthy homemade barbecue sauce. Striking the perfect balance between sweet and tangy, this speedy sauce (only 8 minutes to make) is amazing, and, when baked up, becomes literally finger-licking great. Time after time, this saucy and sticky chicken dinner wins, hands down.

SAUCY OVEN-BAKED BARBECUE CHICKEN

1. PLACE CHICKEN in a large glass baking dish. In a small bowl, combine olive oil, lemon juice, garlic and paprika. Rub over chicken, cover and refrigerate for 1–6 hours.

2. FOR THE BARBECUE SAUCE, in a medium saucepan, combine ketchup, maple syrup, honey, Worcestershire sauce, apple cider vinegar, lemon juice, Dijon mustard, paprika, garlic powder, salt and pepper over medium heat. Simmer gently for 8 minutes, stirring occasionally. Remove from heat and stir in butter. Set aside ¼ cup of the barbecue sauce to use for basting chicken before baking.

3. PREHEAT OVEN to 375°F. Remove chicken from dish and season with salt and pepper. In a large skillet, heat olive oil over high heat. Add chicken and cook 2 minutes per side. Transfer to a baking sheet lined with parchment paper and baste with barbecue sauce. Place in oven and cook chicken breasts for 10 minutes or drumsticks for 40 minutes (turning halfway through cooking). Turn broiler to high and place chicken under broiler for 3 minutes for a sticky, glazed finish. Watch chicken carefully, as the sauce will burn easily if left too long. Serve with extra barbecue sauce.

Try with Pesto & Roasted Red Pepper Pasta Salad, page 55.

SERVES 6–8

PREP 15 minutes

(+2–8 hour marinade and
30 minutes skewer soak)

COOK 45 minutes

. . . .

Kebab skewers (metal, wood or
bamboo)

MARINADE

1 cup plain Greek yogurt
2 tbsp fresh lemon juice
2 tsp grated fresh ginger
1 tsp ground cumin
½ tsp kosher salt
¼ tsp turmeric powder
¼ tsp cayenne pepper
5 boneless skinless chicken
breasts, cut into chunks

MASALA SAUCE

2 tbsp butter
1 small white onion, cut in half
and thinly sliced
2 small garlic cloves, minced
2 tbsp tomato paste
1 fresh serrano chili, seeds
removed, finely chopped
1 tsp garam masala
1 tsp ground cumin
½ tsp turmeric powder
1 can (28 oz) crushed tomatoes
1 tsp sugar
½ tsp kosher salt
½ cup heavy cream
¼ cup chopped fresh flat-leaf
parsley

I watch lots of *Jeopardy!* When Alex Trebek said, "Britain's most popular dish," I yelled out "Spice Girls!" While my earnings plummeted, it seems I wasn't far off. Full of spice and fantastic flavor, the UK has a full-on love affair with Chicken Tikka Masala. It's no wonder—chunks of chicken are marinated in tenderizing yogurt and fragrant spices, grilled to smoky perfection and finished in an Indian-spiced tomato cream sauce. Short of Lisa and me in Union Jack short shorts, what could be tastier?

GRILLED CHICKEN TIKKA MASALA

1. IF THE KEBAB SKEWERS are wood or bamboo, soak them in water for 30 minutes before threading chicken and vegetables.

2. IN A LARGE BOWL, whisk together yogurt, lemon juice, ginger, cumin, salt, turmeric and cayenne. Stir in cut-up chicken, cover and refrigerate 2–8 hours.

3. TO COOK CHICKEN, preheat grill to medium-high heat. Discard marinade and thread chicken onto skewers. Grill 5 minutes per side, until just cooked through. Remove chicken from skewers and set aside.

4. FOR THE MASALA SAUCE, heat butter in a large skillet over medium heat. Add the onion and cook 3–4 minutes, until softened. Add garlic, tomato paste, serrano chili, garam masala, cumin and turmeric. Cook, stirring continuously, for 1 minute. Add crushed tomatoes, sugar and salt. Bring to a boil, reduce heat to low and simmer for 20 minutes. Stir in cream and cooked chicken, simmering for 10 minutes. Remove from heat and stir in parsley. Serve with basmati rice or naan bread.

. . . .

 Try with Sugar Snap, Green Bean & Mint Couscous Salad, page 68.

"We're the Spice Girls, yes indeed/Just Girl Power is all we need/
We know how we got this far/Strength and courage in a Wonderbra"

Spice Girls, "Sound Off"

Lisa didn't have to go to Le Cordon Bleu to figure out how to bring fantastic French flair to dinner. Creator of this fuss-free recipe, our very own *enfant terrible* brings us an easy and elegant chicken recipe that can be served up in less than 30 minutes. Rubbed with creamy Dijon mustard and then browned until golden crusted, chicken is braised in a garlic, thyme, grain mustard and white wine sauce. Moist, healthy, simple and quick to prepare, this intensely flavorful dish most definitely cuts *la moutarde*.

SAUTÉED CHICKEN WITH DIJON & WHITE WINE SAUCE

1. IN A LARGE BOWL, combine chicken breasts with Dijon mustard, salt and pepper, and rub over both sides. In a large skillet, heat 2 tablespoons olive oil over medium-high heat. Add chicken breasts and cook until a deep golden crust forms, 2–3 minutes per side. Remove from skillet and set aside. Add remaining 1 tablespoon olive oil. Add onion and cook over medium heat until softened, about 4–5 minutes. Add garlic, mustard, thyme and salt and cook, stirring, for 1 minute. Increase heat to high, add wine and reduce for 1–2 minutes. Stir in chicken broth, reduce heat to low and return browned chicken to the skillet. Cover and cook 15 minutes, or until cooked through. Remove from heat and stir in butter.

2. TO SERVE, slice chicken, top each chicken breast with sauce and garnish with thyme.

 Try with Fusilli with Sun-Dried Tomatoes, Spinach & Kale, page 117.

SERVES 4
PREP 5 minutes
COOK 25 minutes

- 4   boneless skinless chicken breasts
- 2   tbsp Dijon mustard
- ¼   tsp kosher salt
- ¼   tsp freshly ground black pepper
- 3   tbsp olive oil
- 1   medium yellow onion, halved and thinly sliced
- 1   large garlic clove, minced
- 1   tbsp whole grain Dijon mustard
- 1   tsp chopped fresh thyme
- ¼   tsp kosher salt
- ¾   cup dry white wine
- ½   cup chicken broth
- 1   tbsp butter

Fresh thyme, for garnish

> "Boy, those French! They have a different word for everything."
>
> Steve Martin

Lisa's a hit-maker. Here, she's taken two of our most-loved chicken recipes (juicy chicken Parmesan and tangy lemon chicken) and married them to become major mealtime magic. This Parmesan-Crusted Lemon Chicken is a recipe for success, a quick and delicious weeknight meal of chicken marinated in lemon juice and olive oil, coated in buttermilk, Parmesan cheese and breadcrumbs and then finished in a skillet of lemon juice and chicken broth. With cheesy goodness, pucker-up fresh flavor and foolproof results, this chart-topping chicken is going to have everyone at your table singing your praises.

SERVES 6
PREP 15 minutes
(+1 hour marinade)
COOK 25 minutes

. . . .

6	boneless skinless chicken breasts
¼	cup fresh lemon juice
¼	cup olive oil
1	garlic clove, crushed
½	cup flour
1	tsp lemon zest
½	tsp kosher salt
¼	tsp freshly ground black pepper
2	eggs
¼	cup buttermilk
1	cup dry breadcrumbs
1	cup freshly grated Parmesan cheese
2	tsp lemon zest
½	tsp kosher salt
¼	cup olive oil
1	cup chicken broth
⅓	cup fresh lemon juice

Freshly grated Parmesan cheese, for topping
Lemon slices, for garnish

PARMESAN-CRUSTED LEMON CHICKEN

1. IN A LARGE GLASS BOWL, combine chicken, ¼ cup lemon juice, ¼ cup olive oil and garlic. Cover and refrigerate for 1 hour. Remove chicken from marinade and discard marinade. Pat chicken breasts dry with paper towel.

2. IN A LARGE RESEALABLE PLASTIC BAG, combine flour, 1 teaspoon lemon zest, ½ teaspoon salt and black pepper. In a medium bowl, whisk eggs and buttermilk. In a large bowl, combine breadcrumbs, Parmesan, lemon zest and salt. Place chicken breasts in flour mixture one at a time. Seal bag and shake to coat well. Shake off any excess flour, dip in egg mixture and then into breadcrumb mixture. Coat both sides, pressing well to adhere. Repeat with remaining chicken breasts.

3. IN A LARGE SKILLET, heat 2 tablespoons olive oil over medium heat. Add 3 of the breadcrumb-coated chicken breasts and cook 2 minutes per side, until golden brown. Remove from skillet and heat remaining 2 tablespoons olive oil. Add remaining chicken breasts until browned. Remove from skillet. Add chicken broth and lemon juice to skillet. Bring to a gentle simmer over low heat. Return chicken to skillet, cover and cook for 15 minutes, until chicken is cooked through. Remove cover and sprinkle each chicken breast with generous amount of Parmesan cheese. Replace lid and let cook 1 minute more. Remove from heat and garnish chicken with lemon slices.

. . . .

Try with Caesar Asparagus, page 101.

This chicken is great when cut into a salad or as a sandwich.

We love Mexican cuisine, and while we appreciate the "authentic" recipes out there, we don't have the time or special ingredients to pull it off. With that in mind, Lisa created these simple Slow Cooker Chicken Carnitas that satisfy our needs for Mexican munchies. In a healthy twist, Lisa has replaced traditional fried pork with chicken that has been browned and then braised in a citrus and salsa combination until it's fall-apart tender. Placed on a tortilla along with melted cheese, avocado, lime juice and jalapeños, these healthy *carnitas de pollo* are a far cry from Taco Bell's drive-thru.

MAKES 10 chicken carnitas
PREP 15 minutes
COOK 6 hours

5	boneless skinless chicken breasts
1	tbsp olive oil
1	tsp chili powder
1	tsp ground cumin
1	tsp kosher salt
½	tsp freshly ground black pepper
½	tsp dried oregano
1	tbsp olive oil
1	large yellow onion, chopped
1	red bell pepper, chopped
1	green bell pepper, chopped
1	jalapeño pepper, finely chopped
1	large garlic clove, minced
½	cup orange juice
½	cup mild salsa
2	tbsp fresh lime juice

10	(6-inch) corn tortillas
2½	cups shredded cheddar cheese
1¼	cups salsa
2	medium ripe avocados, chopped
2	small jalapeños, seeded and finely chopped
3	tbsp chopped fresh flat-leaf parsley or fresh cilantro
1	lime, to squeeze over each finished carnita

Lime wedges, for garnish

SLOW COOKER CHICKEN CARNITAS

1. IN A LARGE BOWL, rub chicken breasts with 1 tablespoon olive oil. Sprinkle with chili powder, cumin, salt, pepper and oregano. Rub mixture over both sides of chicken breasts.

2. IN A LARGE SKILLET, heat 1 tablespoon olive oil over high heat. Add chicken breasts and brown, 2 minutes per side. Remove from heat and set aside. Place chopped onion, red pepper, green pepper, jalapeño and minced garlic on the bottom of your slow cooker. Lay browned chicken over top of vegetables and pour orange juice, salsa and lime juice evenly over top. Cook on low setting for 6 hours, until chicken is tender and easily pulls apart.

3. ONCE THE CHICKEN IS DONE, remove from slow cooker and shred the chicken using 2 forks. Pour some of the remaining cooking liquid and vegetables over the chicken. Cover and keep warm.

4. TO ASSEMBLE CARNITAS, heat a large griddle or skillet over medium heat. Place 2 corn tortillas at a time flat on the griddle. Top each with ¼ cup shredded cheese and cook about 2 minutes, until bottom is golden and cheese begins to melt. Remove and top with remaining ½ cup shredded chicken, a few spoonfuls of salsa, chopped avocado, a sprinkle of jalapeños and chopped parsley. Finish with a generous squeeze of lime juice and garnish with lime wedges. Repeat with remaining tortillas.

Try with Cornbread Panzanella Salad, page 52.

Use this chicken in tacos, burritos, quesadillas or enchiladas, or on nachos.

Lisa watched a lot of TV growing up. In fact, for a short while, she would only answer to the name Snuffy and insisted on calling me Oscar. That said, it's no surprise she dreamed up this Sesame Chicken, a crowd-pleasing dish that sweeps the "What's for dinner?" clouds away. As easy as ABC and cooked up in 1-2-3, chicken is marinated until tender, stir-fried (a healthier choice than the usual battering and deep-frying) and then coated in a sweet, sticky and savory glaze. Serve this over rice and expect the whole neighborhood to come and play (and eat) when you make this super delicious and kid-friendly meal.

SERVES 4
PREP 10 minutes
(+30 minute marinade)
COOK 10 minutes

. . . .

MARINADE
2 egg whites
¼ cup cornstarch
1 tbsp sherry wine
½ tsp kosher salt
4 boneless skinless chicken breasts, cut into bite-sized pieces

SWEET & STICKY SAUCE
¼ cup ketchup
¼ cup honey
3 tbsp cider vinegar
2 tbsp brown sugar
2 tbsp soy sauce
1 small garlic clove, minced
1 tbsp cornstarch
3 tbsp cold water

2 tbsp vegetable oil

2 tsp sesame seeds, for garnish
2 chopped green onions, for garnish

SWEET & STICKY SESAME CHICKEN

1. FOR THE MARINADE, in a large bowl, whisk egg whites, cornstarch, sherry wine and salt. Toss bite-sized chicken pieces in the mixture and marinate, covered, for 30 minutes.

2. FOR THE SAUCE, in a small bowl, whisk ketchup, honey, cider vinegar, brown sugar, soy sauce and garlic. In another small bowl, dissolve cornstarch in water.

3. TO COOK THE CHICKEN, remove from marinade and reserve the remaining marinade. Heat 1 tablespoon vegetable oil in a wok or large skillet over medium-high heat. Add half the chicken to the wok and cook 6–8 minutes, stirring occasionally, until just cooked. Remove, set aside and repeat with remaining 1 tablespoon vegetable oil and remaining chicken. Remove chicken from wok. Add the sauce to the wok over medium-high heat and bring to a boil. Stir in reserved marinade and continually stir until sauce thickens. Reduce heat to low, return chicken to wok and stir to coat well. Remove from heat and sprinkle chicken with sesame seeds and green onions. Serve over rice.

"Getting a degree, being on *Sesame Street* . . . those were like real accomplishments to me."

Chaka Khan

Confucius said, "You cannot open a book without learning something." Thus, I feel it my duty to impart some wisdom. Here it is: Lisa. Lifesaver Lisa knows everything there is to know about serving up quick and easy dinnertime solutions, as evidenced by this fast and foolproof Hoisin Peanut Chicken with Rice Noodles. Marinated in the sweet and salty combination of hoisin and peanut butter, chicken is sautéed with snow peas and then tossed with tender rice noodles for a most delicious and healthy meal in a bowl. How's that for a lightning-fast lesson?

SERVES 6
PREP 10 minutes
(+20 minute marinade)
COOK 15 minutes

· ·

HOISIN PEANUT SAUCE

¼ cup hoisin sauce
¼ cup smooth peanut butter
¼ cup soy sauce
¼ cup water
2 tbsp rice vinegar
2 tbsp fresh lime juice
2 tbsp honey
1 tbsp vegetable oil
1 tsp grated fresh ginger
¼ tsp crushed red pepper flakes

4 boneless skinless chicken breasts, thinly sliced
12 oz rice noodles
1 tbsp vegetable oil
2 garlic cloves, minced
2 tsp grated fresh ginger
2 cups snow peas, trimmed

½ cup chopped roasted peanuts, for garnish
¼ cup chopped green onions, for garnish

HOISIN PEANUT CHICKEN WITH RICE NOODLES

1. FOR THE HOISIN PEANUT SAUCE, in a medium bowl, whisk hoisin, peanut butter, soy sauce, water, rice vinegar, lime juice, honey, vegetable oil, ginger and crushed red pepper flakes until well combined. Set aside.

2. IN A LARGE BOWL, toss sliced chicken with ¼ cup hoisin peanut sauce. Set aside for 20 minutes to marinate.

3. TO PREPARE RICE NOODLES, bring a large pot of water to a boil. Cook rice noodles for 3 minutes until tender or according to package directions. Drain and set aside.

4. IN A LARGE SKILLET, heat oil over medium heat and add garlic and ginger. Cook, stirring, for 30 seconds. Raise heat to medium-high and add chicken slices. Cook until just cooked through, 4–5 minutes. Lower heat to medium and add snow peas, noodles and remaining hoisin peanut sauce to the skillet. Cook 2–3 minutes, tossing to coat until well combined and heated through. Top with roasted peanuts and green onions.

· ·

Using a small spoon to scrape the thin peel from ginger makes it easy to get into the bumpy parts and gnarled knobs.

Ever hear of a "Shangri-La Sandwich"? Didn't think so. I made it up. I needed a phrase to describe the height (mile-high), breadth (ample) and flavor (bursting) of this majorly magical Miso Chicken Sandwich with Crunchy Slaw. From the crusty bun slathered with spicy ginger mayo to the marinated chicken baked in miso ginger sauce, from the juicy cucumbers and creamy avocado to the crunchy miso slaw, this Asian-inspired sandwich has it all. So the next time you're hungry, take yourself to paradise with this exotic, easy and satisfying sandwich.

MISO CHICKEN SANDWICH WITH CRUNCHY SLAW

1. FOR THE MARINADE, in a medium bowl, whisk miso paste, chicken broth, vegetable oil, sugar, soy sauce and ginger. Place chicken in a large resealable plastic bag, pour marinade over chicken and refrigerate for 1 hour.

2. PREHEAT OVEN to 375°F. Place chicken and marinade in a 13- × 9-inch baking dish. Bake until cooked through, about 18–20 minutes. Remove from oven and once cool enough to handle, thinly slice chicken and set aside.

3. FOR THE GINGER MAYO, in a small bowl, whisk mayonnaise, rice vinegar, soy sauce, ginger and cayenne. Set mixture aside until ready to assemble sandwich.

4. FOR THE MISO SLAW, in a medium bowl, whisk miso paste, water, orange juice, vegetable oil, rice vinegar and honey. Add coleslaw mix, tossing until well combined.

5. TO ASSEMBLE SANDWICHES, spread ginger mayo on both sides of the sandwich roll. Layer cucumber slices, avocado slices, sliced chicken and about ¼–½ cup of the coleslaw mixture. Repeat with remaining sandwich rolls.

 Try with Tomato Quinoa Soup, page 28.

SERVES 6
PREP 10 minutes (+1 hour marinade)
COOK 20 minutes

MISO MARINADE
¼ cup yellow miso paste
¼ cup chicken broth
¼ cup vegetable oil
2 tbsp sugar
1 tbsp soy sauce
2 tsp grated fresh ginger
6 boneless skinless chicken breasts

GINGER MAYO
½ cup mayonnaise
1 tbsp rice vinegar
1 tbsp soy sauce
1 tsp grated fresh ginger
Pinch cayenne pepper

MISO SLAW
1 tbsp yellow miso paste
1 tbsp water
1 tbsp orange juice
1 tbsp vegetable oil
2 tsp rice vinegar
1 tsp honey
3 cups coleslaw mix

6 crusty sandwich buns
1 small English cucumber, thinly sliced
2 small ripe avocados, thinly sliced

"Too few people understand a really good sandwich."

James Beard

. . . .

MARINADE

½   cup pineapple juice

2   tbsp soy sauce

2   tbsp vegetable oil

1   tbsp honey

6   boneless skinless chicken
    breasts

TERIYAKI SAUCE

⅔   cup soy sauce

⅓   cup sake

⅓   cup mirin

⅓   cup sugar

3   tbsp water

2   tbsp cornstarch

1   tbsp orange juice

½   cup flour

½   tsp kosher salt

½   tsp freshly ground black
    pepper

¼   tsp garlic powder

2   eggs

2   cups panko (Japanese
    breadcrumbs)

3   tbsp olive oil

Fresh green onions, for garnish
Sesame seeds, for garnish

Despite its reputation as a healthy choice, Japanese cuisine, with an abundance of tempura-coated, spicy-mayo-drenched food, is inching away from wellness. With her light and healthy version of chicken katsu, a Japanese-style deep-fried chicken, Lisa's on a mission to stop this slippery slide. Marinated in pineapple juice (to tenderize and add flavor), chicken is crusted in panko, baked until golden and then topped with a super easy, sweet and lustrous homemade teriyaki sauce. Served over white or brown rice, this delicious, good-for-you grub will have you saying "Domo arigato, Lisa Roboto" in no time.

CRUNCHY BAKED CHICKEN KATSU WITH TERIYAKI SAUCE

1. FOR THE MARINADE, in a small bowl, whisk together pineapple juice, soy sauce, vegetable oil and honey. Using a mallet, gently pound the chicken breasts to a uniform thickness, about ½ inch. Add chicken to a large resealable plastic bag, pour marinade over top and set aside for 30 minutes.

2. FOR THE TERIYAKI SAUCE, in a small saucepan, combine soy sauce, sake, mirin and sugar. Bring to a boil over medium heat, reduce heat to low and simmer 4 minutes. In a small bowl, combine water, cornstarch and orange juice. Slowly whisk cornstarch mixture into soy sauce mixture and simmer, whisking, for 3–4 minutes, until slightly thickened. Remove from heat; sauce will thicken more as it cools.

3. PREHEAT OVEN to 425°F. Place a wire cooling rack over a baking sheet and spray the rack with nonstick cooking spray. Place flour, salt, pepper and garlic powder in a large resealable plastic bag. Whisk eggs in a medium bowl. Place panko in another medium bowl. Remove chicken from marinade and discard the marinade. Gently pat chicken dry with paper towel and place in bag of flour. Shake to coat the chicken. Dip each chicken breast into whisked eggs and coat in panko crumbs, pressing well to adhere. Place chicken on cooling rack, drizzle with 3 tablespoons of olive oil and bake 15 minutes, until cooked through. Remove from oven and let sit 5 minutes. Slice chicken, drizzle with teriyaki sauce and garnish with green onions and sesame seeds.

. . . .

 Try with Crispy Tofu Fried Rice, page 132.

Want to know what takes the biscuit? All y'all might not know this, but I'm a wannabe Southern belle and my dream is to have Lisa call me Juniper Julie while serving me juleps on the veranda. Despite her steadfast refusal to do so, Lisa, bless her heart, has indulged my Dixie devotedness with this downright delicious Chicken & Buttermilk Biscuit Casserole. Perfect for a Southern (or Northern, in my case) feast, this comfort food classic is filled with chunks of chicken, loads of vegetables and creamy gravy, all topped with crunchy-on-the-outside, airy-on-the-inside buttermilk biscuits. I reckon that this here piping hot, savory and creamy casserole will have y'all coming back for more.

CHICKEN & BUTTERMILK BISCUIT CASSEROLE

1. PREHEAT OVEN to 400°F. Coat a 13- × 9-inch baking dish with nonstick cooking spray.

2. MELT BUTTER in a large skillet over medium heat. Add onion, celery, carrots, garlic and mushrooms. Cook 8 minutes, until vegetables are tender. Stir in peas, thyme, salt, pepper and cayenne pepper. Cook 2 minutes more. Remove from heat, stir in cubed roasted chicken and set aside.

3. FOR THE GRAVY, in a large saucepan, melt butter over medium-low heat. Add flour, stirring continuously to incorporate. Gradually add chicken broth and cream while constantly whisking. Cook 5–6 minutes to thicken slightly, and then whisk in salt. Remove from heat and stir into chicken and vegetable mixture. Transfer to prepared baking dish and set aside.

4. FOR THE BISCUITS, in a large mixing bowl, combine flour, cornstarch, baking powder, baking soda, salt and Parmesan cheese. Add cold butter and cut in with a pastry blender or your fingers. Work in until mixture is crumbly. Stir in 1 cup buttermilk, mixing just until flour is incorporated. Drop large spoonfuls evenly over filling, leaving a few gaps for steam to escape. Brush biscuit tops with remaining 1 tablespoon of buttermilk. Bake 25 minutes until the biscuits are golden. Remove from oven and let stand 5 minutes before serving.

SERVES	8
PREP	15 minutes
COOK	45 minutes

- 2   tbsp butter
- 1   large yellow onion, chopped
- 3   celery stalks, chopped
- 3   carrots, peeled and chopped
- 2   garlic cloves, minced
- 2   cups quartered fresh white mushrooms
- 1   cup frozen peas, thawed
- ½   tsp dried thyme
- ½   tsp kosher salt
- ¼   tsp freshly ground black pepper
- ¼   tsp cayenne pepper
- 4   cups cooked, cubed rotisserie chicken breasts

GRAVY
- ¼   cup butter
- ½   cup flour
- 3½ cups chicken broth
- ½   cup heavy cream
- ½   tsp kosher salt

BUTTERMILK BISCUITS
- 2   cups flour
- 2   tsp cornstarch
- 2   tsp baking powder
- 1   tsp baking soda
- ½   tsp kosher salt
- ½   cup freshly grated Parmesan cheese
- ½   cup cold butter, cubed
- 1   cup + 1 tbsp buttermilk

Photo on next page →

"I come from a family where gravy is considered a beverage."

Erma Bombeck

Chicken & Buttermilk Biscuit Casserole, page 157

Do you crave Thanksgiving but sweat at the thought of military-like planning, rigorous refereeing and schnapps-soaked relatives? We're here to rescue you from holiday horrors and make every day Turkey Day with this year-round Thanksgiving meal in a bun. Juicy thyme- and sage-studded turkey burgers are enveloped in quick and easy homemade bread stuffing, topped with hearty gravy and nestled between buns slathered in a cranberry citrus spread. Stress-free and scrumptious, the only thing missing from this festive meal is a slice of pumpkin pie.

TURKEY, STUFFING & CRANBERRY BURGERS

1. FOR THE BREAD STUFFING, preheat oven to 325°F. Coat an 11- × 7-inch baking dish with nonstick cooking spray. In a medium skillet, melt butter over medium heat. Add onion and celery and cook 4–5 minutes, until softened. Remove from heat. In a large bowl, toss onion mixture with bread, salt, thyme and chicken broth. Transfer to baking dish and pour 2 tablespoons melted butter over top. Cover and bake 20 minutes, uncover and continue to bake 15 minutes more, until top is golden.

2. WHILE THE STUFFING BAKES, prepare the gravy. In a small saucepan, melt butter over medium heat. Whisk in flour to combine. Gradually whisk in broth. Bring to a boil, lower heat to a gentle simmer and cook for 10 minutes to reduce. Remove from heat and season to taste with salt if necessary. Remove stuffing from oven and pour ½ cup gravy over top. Set aside.

MAKES 6 turkey burgers
PREP 20 minutes
COOK 1 hour, 5 minutes

BREAD STUFFING
2   tbsp butter
1   small white onion, chopped
1   celery stalk, chopped
5   cups ½-inch cubes day-old bread
½   tsp kosher salt
¼   tsp dried thyme
½   cup chicken broth
2   tbsp melted butter

GRAVY
2   tbsp butter
2   tbsp flour
2   cups turkey or chicken broth
Kosher salt, to taste

You're not done yet . . . see next page →

CRANBERRY SPREAD

½ cup mayonnaise
¼ cup cranberry sauce
1 tbsp fresh lemon juice
1 tsp orange zest
Pinch kosher salt

TURKEY BURGER

1 tbsp butter
½ cup finely chopped yellow
onion
¼ cup finely chopped celery
½ tsp dried sage
½ tsp dried thyme
½ tsp kosher salt
¼ tsp freshly ground black pepper
1½ lb ground turkey
¼ cup breadcrumbs
1 egg
1 tbsp vegetable oil
½ tsp kosher salt

6 hamburger rolls or buns

3. FOR THE CRANBERRY SPREAD, in a small bowl, whisk mayonnaise, cranberry sauce, lemon juice, orange zest and salt. Refrigerate, covered, until ready to assemble.

4. FOR THE TURKEY BURGERS, melt butter in a small skillet over medium heat. Add onion and celery and cook 3-4 minutes, until tender. Stir in sage, thyme, salt and pepper. Cook 1 minute more. Remove from heat and transfer to a large mixing bowl. Add ground turkey, breadcrumbs and egg. Form into 6 patties. Preheat a grill pan or large skillet over medium-high heat. Brush patties with vegetable oil, sprinkle with ½ teaspoon salt and cook 6-8 minutes per side, until internal temperature reaches 165°F–170°F.

5. TO ASSEMBLE, cover both the top and bottom buns with cranberry spread. Place turkey burger on bottom bun and add a generous spoonful of stuffing. Cover with the top bun. Serve immediately and repeat with remaining burgers. Use leftover gravy as a dip for the burgers.

· ·

 Try with Sweet Potato Soup, page 31.

"Thanksgiving is an emotional holiday. People travel thousands of miles
to be with people they only see once a year. And then discover
once a year is way too often."

Johnny Carson

Let's talk turkey. Do you avoid cooking it because you fear the result will be desert dry or revoltingly raw? Are you scared stiff of lumpy gravy? Well, here's an easy and foolproof recipe guaranteed to quell any turkey trepidation and transform turkey from holiday fare to an everyday dinner option. Generously seasoned with a flavorful rub, a boneless turkey breast is slow-cooked for 6 hours along with sautéed vegetables and chicken broth. Not only does this low-and-slow method ensure you get juicy, moist meat, but it also makes its own silky smooth gravy while cooking. Delicious and perfect for all weeknight warriors, this tender turkey breast and genius gravy prove that bird, is in fact, the word.

SLOW COOKER TURKEY BREAST & GRAVY

1. IN A MEDIUM SKILLET, melt butter over medium-high heat. Add onion, celery and carrots, stirring for 5 minutes until softened. Stir in white wine and cook for 1 minute. Gradually stir in flour until well combined. Add garlic, thyme, salt and pepper. Continue cooking for 1 minute, stirring continuously. Add to slow cooker along with chicken broth.

2. PAT THE TURKEY BREAST dry with paper towel. In a small bowl, combine Italian seasoning, garlic powder, paprika, salt and pepper. Coat turkey breast with olive oil and rub spice mixture over both sides. Place turkey breast skin side up in slow cooker on top of onion mixture. Cover and cook on low setting for 6 hours, or until the internal temperature reaches 160°F–165°F. Carefully transfer the turkey to a large cutting board and let rest for 10 minutes before slicing.

3. FOR THE GRAVY, strain the liquid from the slow cooker through a fine mesh sieve, skim fat from the surface and season with salt and pepper if needed. Carve turkey slices and serve with warm gravy.

 Try with Sweet Butternut Squash & Carrot Bake, page 93.

SERVES 4–6
PREP 10 minutes
COOK 6–7 hours

- 2 tbsp butter
- 1 medium yellow onion, chopped
- 2 celery stalks, chopped
- 1 carrot, peeled and chopped
- ½ cup dry white wine
- ¼ cup flour
- 2 large garlic cloves, minced
- ½ tsp dried thyme
- ½ tsp kosher salt
- ¼ tsp freshly ground black pepper
- 2 cups chicken broth
- 3½–4 lb boneless turkey breast, trimmed with skin on
- 2 tsp Italian seasoning
- 1 tsp garlic powder
- 1 tsp paprika
- 1 tsp kosher salt
- ½ tsp freshly ground black pepper
- 1 tbsp olive oil

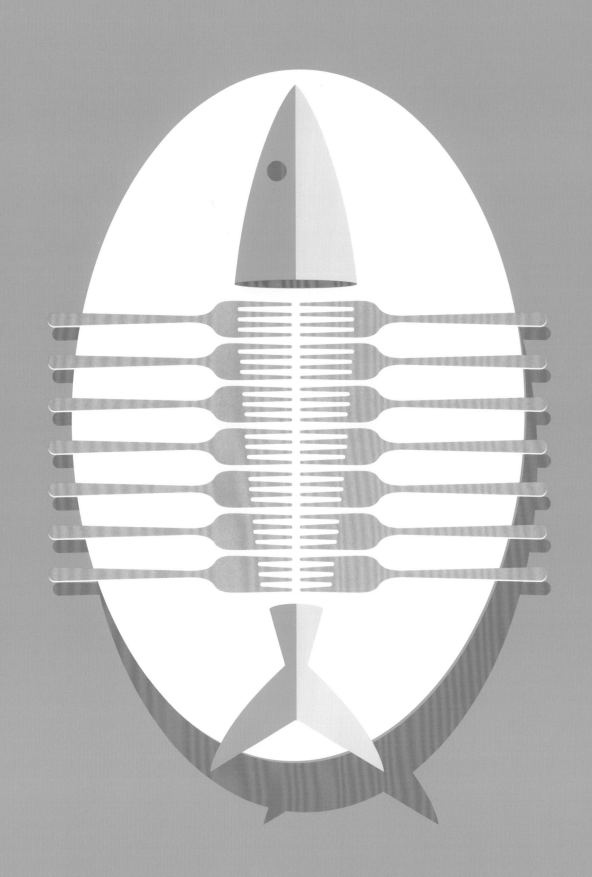

NO BONES ABOUT IT

Lisa runs a tight ship. No crystal-coated ice cream, half-melted popsicles or glacial mystery meat in her freezer. You know what else you won't find? Frozen bricks of fat-laden fish sticks. Thanks to this super-fast and simple recipe, fresh and homemade fish sticks are within our reach. Coated in a tasty panko-Parmesan mixture, mild white fish is baked until golden, moist on the inside, crunchy on the outside. Served with a flavorful tartar dipping sauce, these from-scratch, scrumptious oven-baked fish sticks have me (and my kids) thanking Captain Lisa Liner for thinking outside the box.

SERVES 4–6
PREP 15 minutes
COOK 10 minutes

CRISPY BAKED PARMESAN-CRUSTED FISH STICKS

TARTAR DIP

½ cup mayonnaise
1 tbsp fresh lemon juice
1 tbsp chopped dill pickles
1 tbsp chopped fresh flat-leaf parsley
¼ tsp kosher salt
¼ tsp freshly ground black pepper

½ cup flour
¼ tsp kosher salt
2 eggs
¾ cup panko (Japanese breadcrumbs)
¾ cup freshly grated Parmesan cheese
½ tsp kosher salt
¼ tsp dried oregano
¼ tsp dried Italian seasoning
1½ lb cod (or other firm white fish) fillet, cut into long strips
3 tbsp melted butter

1. FOR THE TARTAR DIP, using a blender, combine mayonnaise, lemon juice, dill pickles, parsley, salt and pepper. Pulse 2–3 times to combine. Cover and refrigerate until ready to use.

2. FOR THE FISH STICKS, preheat oven to 425°F. Line a baking sheet with parchment paper. In a small bowl, combine flour and salt. Place eggs in another bowl and gently whisk. In a third bowl, combine panko, Parmesan cheese, salt, oregano and Italian seasoning. Dip each fish strip in the flour, shaking off excess. Dip in egg and then dredge in panko-Parmesan mixture, pressing to adhere. Place on prepared baking sheet, drizzle with melted butter and bake 5 minutes. Flip the strips and bake 5 minutes more, until cooked and crisp on the outside. Serve with tartar dip.

Try with Cheesy Lemon Roasted Broccoli, page 96.

Wrap these fish sticks with some slaw in a tortilla for a portable feast.

SERVES 4
PREP 20 minutes
COOK 40 minutes

. . . .

EGGPLANT CAPONATA

2 tbsp olive oil
1 lb eggplant, cut into 1-inch
   pieces
1 tsp kosher salt
2 tbsp olive oil
1 medium red onion, chopped
1 celery stalk, chopped
2 garlic cloves, minced
1 tsp dried oregano
¼ tsp freshly ground black
   pepper
3 tbsp red wine vinegar
6 plum tomatoes, chopped
¼ cup halved, pitted green
   olives
2 tbsp small capers, rinsed and
   drained
1 tbsp tomato paste
1 tbsp sugar
¼ tsp crushed red pepper flakes
Kosher salt and freshly ground
   black pepper, to taste
3 tbsp chopped fresh flat-leaf
   parsley

HALIBUT

4 halibut fillets (6 oz each)
¼ tsp kosher salt
¼ tsp freshly ground black
   pepper
2 tbsp olive oil
1 tbsp butter

¼ cup slivered almonds, toasted

Caponata. Sounds like something you'd have to perform on one of those reality dance competition shows, right? While caponata takes a few simple steps to perfect, that's where the similarities end. A Sicilian-style sauce that's both sweet and sour, caponata is a combination of tender eggplant, celery, tomatoes, olives, capers and garlic, a mixture that is perfect atop grilled bread, tossed with pasta or served over polenta. Here, we're smothering pan-seared halibut with this rustic relish and topping it off with toasted slivered almonds. No fancy footwork here—this simple-to-prepare, elegant halibut will have you (and your family and friends) doing the happy dance.

GOLDEN PAN-SEARED HALIBUT WITH EGGPLANT CAPONATA

1. FOR THE CAPONATA, in a large skillet, heat 2 tablespoons olive oil over high heat. Add eggplant and cook 4–5 minutes, stirring occasionally, until eggplant is golden. Season with ½ teaspoon of the salt. Remove from skillet and set aside.

2. HEAT 2 TABLESPOONS OLIVE OIL over medium heat. Add onion, celery, garlic, oregano, remaining ½ teaspoon of salt and pepper. Cook until vegetables have softened, about 4–5 minutes. Add red wine vinegar and cook until it evaporates. Stir in cooked eggplant, tomatoes, olives, capers, tomato paste, sugar and red pepper flakes. Cook over low heat for 20 minutes, stirring occasionally. Remove from heat, season with salt and pepper and stir in chopped parsley. Can be served at room temperature or warmed. Set aside until fish is prepared.

3. FOR THE HALIBUT, season both sides of each fillet with salt and pepper. Heat olive oil and butter in a large skillet over medium-high heat. Add halibut and cook until golden brown, about 4 minutes. Flip and continue cooking 3–4 minutes more, until golden and cooked through. Top each halibut serving with caponata and sprinkle with toasted almonds. Serve immediately.

. . . .

Try with Mediterranean Orzo Salad, page 54.

Buy medium-sized, heavy-feeling eggplants that have smooth skin and bright-green stems. Avoid eggplants that have tan patches, bruises, wrinkles or are really big (over 6 inches in diameter) as it's likely they'll be tough and bitter.

While some make lemonade when life gives them lemons, we run to make this Roasted Halibut with Lemon, White Wine & Shallot Sauce. From start to finish in less than 30 minutes, you too can serve up a lemony, light and delectable dish, one that transforms mild halibut into a fantastically flavorful fish. Baked in a simple combination of lemon, olive oil and oregano, this healthy halibut is served with a tart and fragrant lemon, white wine and shallot sauce. While it likely won't replace lemonade at the stand (50 cents a fillet?), this pucker-up halibut will have them lined up around the block.

ROASTED HALIBUT WITH LEMON, WHITE WINE & SHALLOT SAUCE

1. PREHEAT OVEN to 400°F. Place fillets on a baking sheet lined with parchment paper. Drizzle with lemon juice and olive oil, and then sprinkle with oregano, salt, pepper and paprika. Bake until fish is just firm to the touch, about 15 minutes. While fish cooks, prepare the sauce.

2. FOR THE SAUCE, in a medium saucepan, heat olive oil over medium heat. Add shallots and garlic and stir for 1–2 minutes until softened. Turn heat to high and add white wine, cooking 2 minutes until slightly reduced. Lower heat and stir in lemon juice and butter until melted. Remove from heat and stir in lemon zest, salt and pepper. Spoon sauce over cooked fish and garnish with chopped parsley.

 Try with Pasta Primavera, page 112.

 To get the most out of your lemon (1 lemon yields 3–4 tablespoons of juice), microwave it for 30 seconds and then roll it on the counter before squeezing.

SERVES 4
PREP 5 minutes
COOK 20 minutes

HALIBUT
4   halibut fillets (6 oz each), patted dry
2   tbsp fresh lemon juice
1   tbsp olive oil
¼   tsp dried oregano
¼   tsp kosher salt
¼   tsp freshly ground black pepper
⅛   tsp paprika

LEMON SHALLOT SAUCE
1   tbsp olive oil
1   large shallot, finely minced
1   small garlic clove, minced
½   cup dry white wine
2   tbsp fresh lemon juice
2   tbsp butter
½   tsp lemon zest
¼   tsp kosher salt
¼   tsp freshly ground black pepper

Chopped fresh flat-leaf parsley, for garnish

SERVES 4
PREP 15 minutes
(+15 minute marinade)
COOK 10 minutes

. . . .

MARINADE

1 tbsp cornstarch
1 tbsp soy sauce
1 tbsp sherry wine
1½ lb halibut fillet, cut into 2-inch pieces

STIR-FRY SAUCE

¼ cup chicken broth
2 tbsp rice vinegar
2 tbsp soy sauce
2 tbsp brown sugar
1 tbsp sherry wine
1 tbsp cornstarch
2 tbsp water

2 tbsp vegetable oil
1 small white onion, cut into 1-inch pieces
1 small green bell pepper, cut into strips
1 small red bell pepper, cut into strips
2 small fresh red chili peppers, seeds removed, julienned
2 small garlic cloves, minced

½ cup chopped roasted peanuts

Knowing that the dinnertime routine can be simultaneously chaotic ("It's already six o'clock?") and deadly boring ("I can't eat *that* again"), we're serving up a win-win with this Kung Pao Halibut Stir-Fry. Not only can you whip up our healthy Chinese food favorite in no time, but with the substitution of halibut for chicken, this delicious dish is also sure to thrill your taste buds. Topped with roasted peanuts, sweet and spicy sauce coats halibut, onions, peppers and red chilies, delivering major ka-pow in every bite of this kickin' Kung Pao.

KUNG PAO HALIBUT STIR-FRY

1. FOR THE MARINADE, in a large bowl, whisk cornstarch, soy sauce and sherry wine. Add cubed fish, toss to coat and marinate 15 minutes.

2. FOR THE STIR-FRY SAUCE, in a small bowl, whisk chicken broth, rice vinegar, soy sauce, brown sugar and sherry wine. In another small bowl, combine cornstarch and water, mixing to dissolve. Whisk cornstarch mixture into sauce and set aside.

3. HEAT 1 TABLESPOON of the vegetable oil in a wok or skillet until very hot. Place fish in wok, cook 2 minutes until golden, flip pieces and continue to cook 2 minutes more. Remove and set aside. Add remaining 1 tablespoon vegetable oil over high heat. Add onion, green pepper, red pepper and chili peppers. Stir-fry 2 minutes, stirring continuously. Add the minced garlic and cook 30 seconds. Add the stir-fry sauce and mix until slightly thickened. Reduce heat to low, place fish back in wok and gently stir with sauce. Remove from heat and sprinkle each serving with roasted peanuts.

Mr. Wilhelm: "You're a terrible liar, George.
Look at you, you're a wreck! You're sweating bullets."
George: "It's the Kung Pao. George likes his chicken spicy."

Seinfeld, "The Jimmy"

SERVES 6

PREP 15 minutes
(+20 minute
refrigeration of fish)

COOK 10 minutes

. . . .

LIME PEACH SALSA

2 firm, ripe peaches, chopped
½ cup chopped red bell peppers
1 small jalapeño, seeded and
finely chopped
2 tbsp fresh lime juice
2 tbsp chopped fresh flat-leaf
parsley
¼ tsp sugar
¼ tsp lime zest
Pinch kosher salt

COCONUT-CRUSTED RED SNAPPER

½ cup flour
½ tsp kosher salt
¼ tsp freshly ground black
pepper
1 egg
1 tbsp fresh lime juice
¾ cup panko (Japanese
breadcrumbs)
¾ cup unsweetened shredded
coconut
¼ tsp kosher salt
6 red snapper fillets (6 oz each)
2 tbsp olive oil

Despite the fact that Lisa and I both get huge (we're talking Roseanne Roseannadanna) hair in humid weather, we think we could become seriously great Caribbean Queens. How so? While Lisa could fish for red snapper and shinny up coconut trees, I could hold down the fort and practice my merengue (the dance, not the white fluffy stuff) while waiting for her to return and make this tropically delicious Coconut-Crusted Red Snapper with Lime Peach Salsa. Crusted in coconut and panko, the mild and flaky white fish is sautéed to a golden crisp and topped with a sweet peach, spicy jalapeño and zesty lime salsa. Don't worry (this fantastic fish topped with refreshing salsa is a crowd-pleaser), be happy.

COCONUT-CRUSTED RED SNAPPER WITH LIME PEACH SALSA

1. FOR THE PEACH SALSA, in a small bowl, combine peaches, red peppers, jalapeño, lime juice, parsley, sugar, lime zest and salt. Cover and chill in refrigerator for 30 minutes while preparing fish.

2. FOR THE FISH, place flour, salt and pepper in a shallow medium bowl. In another bowl, whisk egg and lime juice. In a third bowl, combine panko, coconut and salt. Pat fish dry with paper towels and dredge in flour on both sides, shaking off excess. Dip in egg mixture and then place in panko-coconut mixture, pressing well to adhere to both sides. Place coated fish in the refrigerator, covered, for 20 minutes to firm up coating.

3. IN A LARGE SKILLET, heat olive oil over medium-high heat. Add coated fish and cook 3–4 minutes per side, or until fish flakes easily with a fork. Serve with chilled peach salsa.

. . . .

 Try with Spring Vegetable Minestrone, page 35.

"I really love your peaches/Want to shake your tree"

The Steve Miller Band, "The Joker"

There are plenty of fish in the sea, but really, who wants to dish up dogfish or four-eyed fish? While we might enjoy some humu-humunukuapua'a (only because we'd love saying it), we think the big catch is salmon, a perfectly pink source of omega-3s, quality protein, essential amino acids and vitamins A through E. Marinated in lime juice, ginger and honey, baked until flaky and then topped with a honey Sriracha glaze, this recipe is healthy, foolproof and as effortless to prepare as shooting fish in a barrel. Once again, Largemouth Lisa has hooked a winner.

"I'm sorry I ate your fish, okay?"

Otto West, *A Fish Called Wanda*

SIMPLE HONEY SRIRACHA SALMON

1. FOR THE MARINADE, in a small bowl, whisk soy sauce, olive oil, lime juice, honey, garlic, ginger and lime zest. Place salmon and marinade in a large resealable plastic bag. Seal and refrigerate 1 hour.

2. FOR THE HONEY SRIRACHA SAUCE, in a small saucepan, melt butter over low heat. Whisk in flour until combined. Add honey, Sriracha, soy sauce and lime juice. Whisk continuously for 1 minute. Remove from heat and set aside.

3. PREHEAT OVEN to 425°F. Line a baking sheet with parchment paper. Remove salmon from bag and discard marinade. Bake for 10 minutes, or until the fish flakes easily. Remove from oven and turn broiler to high. Brush the top of the salmon with half of the honey Sriracha sauce and place under broiler for 1 minute, watching carefully to ensure it doesn't burn. Remove from oven, serve with remaining sauce and garnish with a lime wedge.

 Try with Asian Vegetable Stir-Fry, page 105.

SERVES 4
PREP 5 minutes
(+1 hour marinade)
COOK 15 minutes

MARINADE
2 tbsp soy sauce
1 tbsp olive oil
1 tbsp fresh lime juice
1 tbsp honey
1 small garlic clove, minced
½ tsp grated fresh ginger
½ tsp lime zest
4 salmon fillets (6 oz each), skin removed

HONEY SRIRACHA SAUCE
¼ cup butter
1 tbsp flour
2 tbsp honey
1 tbsp Sriracha sauce
1 tbsp soy sauce
1 tbsp fresh lime juice

Lime wedges, for garnish

If you feel like you're swimming upstream in an effort to liven up your fish repertoire, we've got the recipe for you. This Spice-Rubbed Salmon with Zucchini Avocado Salsa is bursting with flavor. After marinating in a homemade mixture of cumin, paprika and garlic, salmon is topped with a zesty jalapeño-lime sauce, baked until flaky and then served with an uncooked salsa of fresh zucchini, corn, avocado and lime. Healthy, easy and intensely tasty, this savory roasted salmon will have you going with the (flavorful) flow.

SPICE-RUBBED SALMON WITH ZUCCHINI AVOCADO SALSA

1. PLACE SALMON in a shallow dish and rub each fillet with olive oil. In a small bowl, combine salt, cumin, paprika, pepper and garlic powder. Rub spice mixture over salmon, cover and refrigerate 30–60 minutes.

2. WHILE THE SALMON MARINATES, prepare the jalapeño-lime sauce. Using a small food processor or blender, combine olive oil, lime juice, parsley, jalapeño, lime zest and minced garlic. Blend until well combined.

3. PREHEAT OVEN to 400°F. Line a baking sheet with parchment paper. Place salmon on baking sheet and spread jalapeño-lime sauce over each fillet. Bake 13–15 minutes, until cooked through. Remove from oven and serve with salsa.

4. FOR THE SALSA, in a medium bowl, combine corn, zucchini, avocado, jalapeño, parsley, lime juice, salt and pepper. Cover until ready to use.

. . . .

Try with Green Beans, page 102.

What's the hottest part of the jalapeño? The white membrane where the seeds are attached to the pepper has 16 times as much heat as the rest of the pepper.

SERVES 4
PREP 20 minutes
(+30–60 minute marinade)
COOK 15 minutes

. . . .

SPICE MIXTURE
4   salmon fillets (8 oz each), skin removed
1   tbsp olive oil
1   tsp kosher salt
½   tsp ground cumin
½   tsp paprika
½   tsp freshly ground black pepper
¼   tsp garlic powder

JALAPEÑO-LIME SAUCE
2   tbsp olive oil
2   tbsp fresh lime juice
2   tbsp chopped fresh flat-leaf parsley
½   jalapeño pepper, seeded and diced
1   tsp lime zest
1   small garlic clove, minced

ZUCCHINI-AVOCADO SALSA
2   small ears corn, kernels removed
1   small zucchini, chopped
1   small avocado, chopped
½   jalapeño pepper, seeded and finely chopped
¼   cup chopped fresh flat-leaf parsley
2   tbsp fresh lime juice
¼   tsp kosher salt
⅛   tsp freshly ground black pepper

> "Life's pretty good, and
> why wouldn't it be? I'm
> a pirate, after all."
>
> Johnny Depp

As much as she'd like to, the Captain of the Kitchen (aka Lisa, of course), isn't going to get me to walk the plank anytime soon. However, she's most definitely going to get me dancing a jig all the way to my back deck to fire up the barbecue for this Grilled Cedar-Planked Salmon. Now, mateys, don't fear the plank—a simple one-hour soak of the cedar and you're ready to get cooking. Not only is this scrumptious salmon infused with a subtle and smoky cedar flavor, but it's also brightened by the addition of a fresh and zesty orange (no scurvy for you!) glaze, guaranteed to have you serving up some seriously delicious barbecue booty.

SERVES 4
PREP 5 minutes
(+1 hour cedar plank soak)
COOK 20 minutes

. . . .

1   untreated cedar plank (large enough to hold 4 pieces salmon not touching)

ORANGE GLAZE
¼   cup maple syrup
2   tbsp orange juice
1   tbsp soy sauce
1   tsp orange zest

4   salmon fillets (6 oz each)
1   tbsp olive oil
¼   tsp kosher salt
¼   tsp freshly ground black pepper

1   tbsp minced chives, for garnish
Orange slices, for garnish

GRILLED CEDAR-PLANKED SALMON WITH ORANGE GLAZE

1. IN A LARGE ROASTING PAN, soak cedar plank in water for at least 1 hour, making sure it's submerged. Remove cedar plank from water, set aside and preheat grill to medium.

2. FOR THE ORANGE GLAZE, in a small bowl, whisk maple syrup, orange juice, soy sauce and orange zest together. Set aside.

3. PLACE THE PLANK on the grill, allowing it to preheat for 3–4 minutes. Flip the plank over before placing salmon on it. Brush each salmon fillet with olive oil and sprinkle with salt and pepper. Place the salmon on the plank, skin side down, brushing each piece with orange glaze. Close the lid and cook 10–15 minutes, brushing with more glaze every 3 minutes, cooking until salmon flakes easily. Transfer plank to a serving platter and serve directly off the plank. Garnish with minced chives and orange slices.

. . . .

 Try with Quinoa, Spinach & Berry Salad, page 61.

It's crunch time, folks. The dinner bell has rung and there's no dinner to speak of. What to do? The game plan is simple—nip those hunger pangs in the bud with this Crunchy Almond Cod with Lemon Spinach. Baked under a crunchy almond crumb topping, golden-crusted cod is served atop lemony sautéed spinach in this 25-minute recipe. So easy, healthy and impressive, no one will know you didn't break a sweat solving your dinner-time dilemma.

CRUNCHY ALMOND COD WITH LEMON SPINACH

SERVES 4
PREP 10 minutes
COOK 15 minutes

1. PREHEAT OVEN to 425°F. Line a baking sheet with parchment paper and set aside.

2. IN A FOOD PROCESSOR, pulse almonds until slightly coarse. In a large bowl, combine chopped almonds, panko, basil, lemon zest, paprika, cayenne pepper and salt. Toss olive oil into almond mixture.

3. PAT FISH DRY, season with salt and pepper and place on prepared baking sheet. Spread Dijon on the top of each fillet. Press almond mixture on top of the fish. Bake 10–12 minutes, until just cooked through.

4. FOR THE SPINACH, heat olive oil in a large skillet over medium heat. Add spinach, stir to coat with oil and cook 2–3 minutes, until wilted. Remove from heat and drain any excess liquid from the pan. Season with lemon juice, salt and pepper. Serve immediately with almond crusted cod.

ALMOND CRUSTED COD

½   cup almonds
½   cup panko (Japanese breadcrumbs)
1   tbsp chopped fresh basil
1   tsp lemon zest
¼   tsp paprika
¼   tsp cayenne pepper
¼   tsp kosher salt
2   tbsp olive oil
4   cod fillets (6 oz each)
¼   tsp kosher salt
¼   tsp freshly ground black pepper
1   heaping tbsp Dijon mustard

LEMON SPINACH

1   tbsp olive oil
1   package (16 oz) fresh baby spinach
1   tsp fresh lemon juice
¼   tsp kosher salt
¼   tsp freshly ground black pepper

Try with Roasted Fingerling Potatoes & Brussels Sprouts, page 90.

Did you know that chocolate makers use 40% of the world's almonds?

En papillote. Such a fussy name for such a simple method: cooking in parchment. A popular practice in fancy restaurants across the country, wrapping fish in its own little packet is a no-fuss, super-healthy and tasty way to cook. In this two-step recipe, mild cod is baked in parchment paper and steamed to moist perfection along with tomatoes, Kalamata olives, fresh herbs, spices and white wine. Elegant and easy, in 30 minutes you'll be able to wrap up (and serve) a delicious dinner.

BAKED MEDITERRANEAN COD PACKETS

SERVES 4
PREP 5 minutes
COOK 25 minutes

. . . .

4 cod fillets (6 oz each)
¼ tsp kosher salt
¼ tsp freshly ground black pepper
1 cup halved cherry tomatoes
½ cup pitted Kalamata olives, halved
2 tbsp chopped oil-packed sun-dried tomatoes
2 tbsp chopped fresh flat-leaf parsley
1 small garlic clove, thinly sliced
1 tsp lemon zest
½ tsp dried oregano
Pinch crushed red pepper flakes
2 tbsp olive oil
2 tbsp dry white wine
1 tbsp fresh lemon juice

Lemon wedges, for garnish

1. PREHEAT OVEN to 425°F. Cut 4 large sheets of parchment paper or aluminum foil, enough to tightly enclose fish. Place one fillet centered on each sheet. Sprinkle both sides of the fish with salt and pepper. In a medium bowl, toss tomatoes, olives, sun-dried tomatoes, parsley, garlic, lemon zest, oregano and red pepper flakes. Divide tomato-olive mixture evenly over each piece of fish. In a small bowl, whisk olive oil, wine and lemon juice. Drizzle over each fish packet. To seal packets, bring the sides of the parchment paper or aluminum foil up and crimp tightly to create an enclosed pouch for the fish.

2. PLACE PACKETS on a baking sheet and bake 16–18 minutes. Remove from oven and let rest 5 minutes before opening. Carefully open packets, garnish with lemon wedges and serve.

. . . .

Fish packets can be assembled in advance and baked off just before serving.

Now before you get all, "I don't like black licorice," and dismiss this recipe because of fennel, read on. One of the most delicious and underused vegetables, fennel is the "What's in this? It's so delicious" secret ingredient you've been waiting for. Roasted until sweet, fennel bumps up the flavor of meaty and mild sea bass big time. Covered in a mixture of sautéed tomato, onion, oregano, fennel seed and parsley, sea bass is roasted atop fennel until tender. Finished with lemon zest and feathery fennel fronds, this healthy and delicious fish dish can be prepared in advance and baked off just before serving. Aren't you glad you didn't turn the page?

ROASTED SEA BASS, FENNEL & TOMATOES

1. PREHEAT OVEN to 450°F. In a large bowl, toss sliced fennel with 1 tablespoon olive oil, salt, pepper, oregano and crushed red pepper flakes. Place in a 13- × 9-inch baking dish and roast for 15 minutes. Stir and continue to cook until tender, 5–8 minutes more.

2. WHILE FENNEL IS ROASTING, heat 1 tablespoon olive oil in a large skillet over medium heat. Add onion and cook, stirring, 4–5 minutes until tender. Add garlic, fennel seeds, oregano, sugar, salt and pepper. Cook, stirring, for 1 minute. Increase heat to high, add wine and let reduce for 1 minute. Stir in tomatoes, reduce heat to low, cover and simmer for 10 minutes. Remove from heat and stir in parsley and lemon zest.

3. REMOVE FENNEL from oven and lower temperature to 400°F. Pat fish dry with paper towel and season fish with salt and pepper. Place the fish over the fennel, top with tomato-onion mixture and place in oven for 10–15 minutes, until cooked through. Garnish with fennel fronds and lemon zest.

SERVES 6
PREP 20 minutes
COOK 35 minutes

- 1 large fennel bulb, cored and thinly sliced, about 4–5 cups sliced
- 1 tbsp olive oil
- ½ tsp kosher salt
- ¼ tsp freshly ground black pepper
- ¼ tsp dried oregano
- Pinch crushed red pepper flakes

- 1 tbsp olive oil
- 1 large yellow onion, cut in half and thinly sliced
- 2 large garlic cloves, minced
- 1 tsp fennel seeds
- ½ tsp dried oregano
- ½ tsp sugar
- ½ tsp kosher salt
- ¼ tsp freshly ground black pepper
- ½ cup dry white wine
- 1 can (28 oz) whole tomatoes, drained (liquid discarded) and coarsely chopped
- 2 tbsp chopped fresh flat-leaf parsley
- 1 tsp lemon zest

- 6 sea bass fillets (6 oz each)
- ¼ tsp kosher salt
- ¼ tsp freshly ground black pepper

Fennel fronds, for garnish
Lemon zest, for garnish

4-6
10 MINUTES (+20-30 MINUTE
TUNA MARINADE AND SLAW
REFRIGERATION)
10 MINUTES

. . . .

¼ cup finely chopped fresh
flat-leaf parsley

3 tbsp olive oil

2 tbsp fresh lime juice

1 jalapeño pepper, seeded and
finely chopped

1 small garlic clove, minced

1 tsp grated fresh ginger

½ tsp ground coriander

4 (6 oz) tuna steaks

4 cups thinly sliced napa
cabbage

¼ cup chopped fresh flat-leaf
parsley

½ jalapeño pepper, seeded and
minced

2 tbsp fresh lime juice

1 tbsp olive oil

¼ tsp kosher salt

¼ tsp freshly ground black
pepper

¼ cup black sesame seeds

¼ cup white sesame seeds

¼ tsp kosher salt

¼ tsp freshly ground black
pepper

1 cup coarsely chopped roasted
peanuts

Hear that? That's the siren song of the barbecue, begging for tuna, a meaty and marvelous fish. Inspired and unable to ignore the enticing call, lured-in-Lisa has taken tuna, the steak of the sea, to new grilling heights. Marinated in a fresh mixture of lime juice, ginger, garlic and jalapeños, the firm fish is encrusted in black and white sesame seeds, quickly seared on the barbecue, thinly sliced and served atop zingy napa and peanut slaw. Healthy, satisfying and scrumptious, this superb sesame tuna will have everyone singing your praises.

GRILLED SESAME TUNA OVER NAPA CABBAGE SLAW

1. FOR THE MARINADE, in a medium bowl, whisk parsley, olive oil, lime juice, chopped jalapeño, garlic, ginger and coriander. Place tuna steaks in a flat dish and add marinade. Cover and marinate no longer than 20–30 minutes.

2. FOR THE NAPA CABBAGE SLAW, in a large bowl, toss sliced cabbage, parsley, jalapeño, lime juice, olive oil, salt and pepper. Cover and chill 30 minutes before serving.

3. PREHEAT BARBECUE to medium-high heat and oil grill grates. Place both black and white sesame seeds together on a plate. Remove tuna from marinade and discard marinade. Season tuna with salt and pepper and coat on all sides in the sesame seeds. Grill tuna 1–2 minutes per side. Remove from heat and let rest 5 minutes before thinly slicing.

4. TOSS HALF THE CHOPPED PEANUTS in the napa cabbage mixture. Place grilled tuna slices over the cabbage and garnish with remaining chopped peanuts.

. . . .

 Try with Soba Noodle Miso Soup, page 48.

"Is this chicken, what I have, or is this fish?
I know it's tuna, but it says 'Chicken of the Sea.'"

Jessica Simpson

Tacos? Pshaw. They're child's play when you're starving for something sizable. Instead, make a beeline for these Mega Grande Shrimp Burritos and get ready to really chow down. A Tex-Mex meal that's second to none, these bountiful burritos are created when flour tortillas are loaded with chipotle and lime marinated shrimp, spiced rice and beans, creamy avocado sauce and grated cheddar cheese. So simple, you'll be able to stuff, roll and wrap your way to a cheesy, gooey and hearty hand-held meal and still have time for a siesta.

MAKES	6 burritos
PREP	15 minutes (+30 minute marinade)
COOK	45 minutes

. . . .

SHRIMP

1½ lb (about 30) medium-large shrimp, shells and tails removed
1 canned chipotle pepper in adobo sauce, seeds removed
2 tbsp olive oil
2 tbsp fresh lime juice
1 small garlic clove
1 tsp honey

RICE & BEANS

1 tbsp olive oil
½ cup chopped yellow onion
1 small garlic clove, minced
½ tsp ground cumin
½ tsp chili powder
¼ tsp kosher salt
1 cup long-grain white rice
2 cups chicken broth
1 cup canned black beans, rinsed and drained

AVOCADO SAUCE

2 medium ripe avocados
½ cup sour cream
2 tsp canned adobo sauce
¼ tsp kosher salt

1 tbsp olive oil
6 (10-inch) flour tortillas
2 cups shredded cheddar cheese

MEGA GRANDE SHRIMP BURRITOS

1. PLACE SHRIMP in a medium bowl. Using a mini food processor or blender, purée chipotle pepper, olive oil, lime juice, garlic and honey until smooth. Add marinade to shrimp, toss and refrigerate for 30 minutes. While the shrimp marinates, prepare the rice.

2. FOR THE RICE, heat olive oil in a medium saucepan over medium heat. Add onion, garlic, cumin, chili powder and salt. Cook, stirring, for 2 minutes. Add rice and continue stirring for 1 minute. Stir in chicken broth and bring to a boil. Cover, reduce heat to low and simmer 15 minutes, until liquid has been absorbed. Remove from heat and keep covered for 10 minutes. Stir in black beans and set aside.

3. FOR THE AVOCADO SAUCE, in a medium bowl, mash avocados with sour cream, adobo sauce and salt. Set aside.

4. TO COOK THE SHRIMP, heat 1 tablespoon olive oil in a large skillet over medium-high heat. Remove shrimp from marinade and add shrimp in 2 or 3 batches, cooking 2 minutes per side.

5. TO ASSEMBLE BURRITOS, place scant ½ cup rice down the center of each tortilla. Top with a few spoonfuls of avocado sauce, lay about 5 shrimp over sauce and top with shredded cheddar cheese. Roll by folding 2 sides in, then roll and tuck as you go. Press each burrito in a panini press or place in a dry skillet over medium-high heat to give the outside a golden toasty crust.

. . . .

To tell if an avocado is ripe, flick off the dry stem. If it comes off easily and you see green underneath, it's ripe.

SERVES 4

PREP 20 minutes
(+30 minute
refrigeration)

COOK 20 minutes

. . . .

CRAB CAKE BURGER

1 lb lump crabmeat, shell pieces
removed

1 egg, lightly whisked

1 cup panko (Japanese breadcrumbs)

½ cup mayonnaise

1 tbsp chopped shallots

2 tsp Creole seasoning

1 tsp Dijon mustard

½ tsp freshly ground black
pepper

RÉMOULADE SAUCE

½ cup mayonnaise

2 tbsp ketchup

1 tbsp horseradish

1 tbsp fresh lemon juice

1 tsp Dijon mustard

1 tsp Creole seasoning

½ cup panko (Japanese
breadcrumbs)

2 tbsp butter

1 tbsp olive oil

4 soft hamburger buns

2 large tomatoes, sliced

1 cup sprouts, pea shoots,
sunflower greens or alfalfa
sprouts

Forget the beads and beignets. We've brought you home something even better from our jaunt to Mardi Gras. With a frosty
hurricane in hand, let-the-good-times-roll-Lisa was struck with
the genius idea of this Cajun Crab Cake Burger, a brilliantly tasty
twist on the traditional crab cake and a hearty homage to New
Orleans. A veritable party between the buns, tender lumps of
sweet crab are mixed with Creole seasonings, crisp-coated in
panko crumbs and layered with spicy rémoulade sauce, tomatoes
and sprouts. This celebration-of-the-South sandwich once again
proves what I've been saying all along—Lisa's a girl gone wild.

CAJUN CRAB CAKE BURGERS

1. IN A LARGE BOWL, combine crabmeat, egg, panko, mayonnaise,
shallots, Creole seasoning, Dijon mustard and black pepper. Gently
fold all ingredients together until well combined. Cover and refrigerate
mixture for 30 minutes.

2. TO PREPARE RÉMOULADE SAUCE, in a small bowl, whisk mayonnaise,
ketchup, horseradish, lemon juice, Dijon mustard and Creole seasoning.
Cover and refrigerate until burgers are ready to assemble.

3. PLACE ½ CUP PANKO on a small plate and remove crab mixture from
refrigerator. Make the crab burgers by dividing mixture into 4 parts and
shaping them into patties. Press both sides of each patty into panko.

4. IN A LARGE SKILLET, heat butter and olive oil over medium heat. Add
patties and cook 4 minutes per side, until golden brown and heated
through.

5. TO ASSEMBLE, spread a generous amount of rémoulade sauce over each
burger bun. Add tomato, crab burger and sprouts. Serve immediately.

. . . .

 Try with Spiced Red Lentil Soup, page 38.

GRADE-A

[**MEAT**]

Whenever I have a yen for Chinese food (Sunday night staple of my youth), I remember my deep-fried days are behind me. What's a middle-aged gal to do? Wok this Way and whip up this healthy and easy version of Saucy Beef and Broccoli. Quickly cooked at high heat, tender steak and fresh vegetables get caramelized, making this simple, sizzling stir-fry a family favorite that trumps greasy, fat-laden takeout, every time.

SAUCY BEEF & BROCCOLI STIR-FRY

SERVES 4-6
PREP 10 minutes
(+20 minute marinade)
COOK 10 minutes

. . . .

MARINADE
2 tbsp oyster sauce
1½ tbsp cornstarch
1½ lb sirloin steak, thinly sliced

SAUCE
¼ cup beef broth
2 tbsp soy sauce
2 tbsp sherry wine
1 tsp brown sugar
¼ tsp crushed red pepper flakes
1 tsp grated fresh ginger
1 tbsp cornstarch
2 tbsp water

3 tbsp vegetable oil
6 cups broccoli florets
1 medium yellow onion, thinly sliced
1 small garlic clove, minced
1 yellow pepper, cut in strips
1 red bell pepper, cut in strips

1. FOR THE MARINADE, in a medium bowl, combine oyster sauce, cornstarch and sliced steak. Toss well and set aside for 20 minutes to marinate.

2. FOR THE SAUCE, in a small bowl, whisk beef broth, soy sauce, sherry wine, brown sugar, red pepper flakes and ginger. In another small bowl, dissolve cornstarch into water and whisk into sauce. Set aside.

3. HEAT A LARGE WOK over high heat. Add 1 tablespoon vegetable oil and let it get very hot. Add broccoli, onions, garlic and yellow and red peppers. Stir-fry until vegetables are tender but still crisp, continuously tossing the vegetables, 2–3 minutes. Remove from heat and transfer to a plate. Heat 1 tablespoon vegetable oil over high heat, add half the steak slices and stir-fry until no longer pink, about 2 minutes. Remove from wok and heat remaining 1 tablespoon vegetable oil to cook the rest of the uncooked steak. Once the remainder of the steak is cooked, return first batch of steak, vegetables and reserved sauce to the wok. Toss to coat and cook a few minutes, until sauce comes to a boil and thickens. Serve immediately.

. . . .

A single cup of broccoli has over 200% of your daily vitamin C needs.

As the expression goes, we're all "as busy as popcorn on a skillet." With that in mind, we're grabbing our skillet, our steak and just a half hour to cook up a delectable dinner. Juicy strips of sirloin steak are quickly seared and mixed in with a chunky, sweet and tangy tomato onion sauce. A crowd-pleaser for sure, this fast and flavorful dish delivers the steak *and* the sizzle in no time at all.

SIZZLING SWEET & SOUR SIRLOIN STEAK

1. SEASON SLICED STEAK with salt and pepper. In a large skillet, heat oil over high heat. Add half the steak, making sure not to crowd the pan. Cook 1 minute per side, remove and cook remaining steak. Set aside while preparing the sauce.

2. FOR THE SAUCE, in the same skillet, heat olive oil over medium heat. Add onion and cook 3 minutes, stirring frequently. Add garlic, ginger and cayenne and cook 1 minute. Stir in tomato paste until combined. Add tomatoes, water, rice vinegar, sugar and soy sauce. Increase heat to medium-high and bring to a boil. Reduce heat to medium and simmer 10 minutes, stirring occasionally. Reduce heat to low, add steak to skillet and stir until coated with sauce. Season to taste with freshly ground black pepper.

· ·

 Try with Balsamic Roasted Carrots, Parsnips & Beets, page 94.

 Place leftover steak with bell peppers, mushrooms, tomato sauce and provolone cheese in a crusty bun for a satisfying sandwich.

SERVES 4–6
PREP 10 minutes
COOK 20 minutes

· ·

STEAK

1½ lb sirloin steak, thinly sliced
½ tsp kosher salt
½ tsp freshly ground black pepper
1 tbsp olive oil

TOMATO ONION SAUCE

1 tbsp olive oil
1 large white onion, halved and thinly sliced
2 garlic cloves, minced
1 tsp grated fresh ginger
¼ tsp cayenne pepper
2 tbsp tomato paste
6 plum tomatoes, cut in half, seeded and coarsely chopped
1 cup water
¼ cup rice vinegar
¼ cup sugar
2 tbsp soy sauce
Freshly ground black pepper, to taste

SERVES 6
PREP 10 minutes
(+2–24 hour marinade)
COOK 15 minutes

. . . .

CRUNCHY PEANUT SAUCE

½ cup chunky peanut butter
¼ cup chicken broth
1 tbsp fresh lime juice
1 tbsp soy sauce
1 tbsp vegetable oil
1 tbsp brown sugar
1 small garlic clove, minced
1 tsp fish sauce
¼ tsp cayenne pepper
¼ cup chopped roasted peanuts

LEMONGRASS MARINADE

2 stalks lemongrass, inner core
   only, finely chopped
2 large garlic cloves, minced
2 tbsp soy sauce
2 tbsp olive oil
1 tbsp brown sugar
1 tbsp fresh lime juice
1 tbsp fish sauce
½ tsp ground cumin
½ tsp ground ginger

2 lb flank steak

Chopped green onions, for
   garnish

You may know all about sirloins, rib eyes and roasts, but are you flummoxed by flank steak? We're here to help decode this flavorful and inexpensive cut of meat, an oft-overlooked but delicious way to satisfy your meat tooth. The secret to transforming flank steak from tough to tender is all in the marinade—here, we let the lean steak sit in an aromatic blend of sweet lemongrass, lime juice, garlic, soy and fish sauce. After readily absorbing the Vietnamese-inspired marinade, the flank steak is grilled until crusty on the outside and juicy on the inside, thinly sliced and served with a crunchy peanut sauce. No confusion here—flank is one scrumptious, sizzling steak.

GRILLED LEMONGRASS FLANK STEAK WITH PEANUT SAUCE

1. FOR THE PEANUT SAUCE, in a blender, combine peanut butter, chicken broth, lime juice, soy sauce, vegetable oil, brown sugar, garlic, fish sauce and cayenne. Blend until almost smooth. Transfer to a small bowl, stir in chopped roasted peanuts, cover and refrigerate until serving.

2. FOR THE MARINADE, in a small bowl, whisk lemongrass, garlic, soy sauce, olive oil, brown sugar, lime juice, fish sauce, cumin and ginger. Pour into a wide, shallow dish, add flank steak and toss to coat well. Cover and refrigerate at least 2 hours or overnight. Let flank steak come to room temperature before cooking.

3. PREHEAT GRILL to medium-high heat and lightly oil grill grates. Remove meat from marinade and place on grill. Grill 6 minutes, flip and cook 5 minutes more, until cooked through. Transfer meat to a cutting board and let rest 5 minutes. Slice flank steak thinly against the grain. Top steak slices with peanut sauce and chopped green onions.

. . . .

Try with Thai Coconut & Ginger Chicken Soup, page 45.

To cut against the grain, look which way the muscle fibers run in the meat and cut perpendicular to them.

"showboat *n.* A person, especially an athlete, who performs in an ostentatiously sensational manner calculated to draw attention; show-off."

Dictionary.com

Clearly, "showboat" is not a description of Lisa—while she's a gold-medaler in cooking, she's humble and understated. I, on the other hand, am all about the razzle-dazzle, and this recipe is my showstopper. Not only is this rosemary and thyme–crusted beef tenderloin tender (as its name suggests) and delicious, but it's also super-simple to make while off-the-charts impressive. Perfectly paired with a hearty red wine and mushroom sauce, this tenderloin is as flawless and crowd-pleasing as my touchdown dance.

SERVES	6
MAKES	2 cups mushroom sauce
PREP	10 minutes
COOK	45 minutes

BEEF TENDERLOIN

2½ lb center-cut beef tenderloin
½ tsp kosher salt
2 tbsp olive oil
2 tbsp Dijon mustard
2 tsp finely chopped fresh rosemary
2 tsp finely chopped fresh thyme
½ tsp freshly ground black pepper

MUSHROOM RED WINE SAUCE

2 tbsp butter
1 large shallot, minced
1 package (8 oz) sliced mushrooms
1 garlic clove, minced
1 tsp finely chopped fresh rosemary
¼ tsp kosher salt
¼ tsp freshly ground black pepper
1 tbsp flour
½ cup dry red wine
1 cup beef broth

HERB-CRUSTED BEEF TENDERLOIN WITH MUSHROOM RED WINE SAUCE

1. PREHEAT OVEN to 400°F. Line a baking sheet with aluminum foil and coat with nonstick cooking spray. Season the tenderloin on both sides with salt and place on baking sheet. In a small bowl, combine olive oil, Dijon mustard, rosemary, thyme and black pepper. Rub tenderloin with the mustard mixture. Roast tenderloin for 35 minutes until an instant-read thermometer reads 130°F–135°F for medium rare. Remove from oven and let rest on a cutting board for 10 minutes. Cut beef into slices and serve with mushroom red wine sauce.

2. WHILE THE BEEF IS ROASTING/RESTING, PREPARE THE SAUCE, in a large saucepan, melt butter over medium-high heat. Add shallot and mushrooms, cooking for 3 minutes. Add garlic, rosemary, salt and pepper, cooking 1 minute more. Sprinkle flour and continue to stir. Add the red wine and cook for 2 minutes, stirring. Add beef broth and once mixture comes to a boil, reduce heat to a low simmer for 6 minutes. Serve over cooked tenderloin.

Try with The Perfect Scalloped Potatoes, page 89.

The tenderloin can be covered with mustard-herb mixture, refrigerated and roasted just before serving for even quicker prep.

SERVES 6-8

PREP 10 minutes (+30 minute seasoning)

COOK 1 hour, 30 minutes

. . . .

ROAST BEEF

1   eye of round roast (3 lb)
1   tsp kosher salt
1   tsp freshly ground black pepper
½   tsp onion powder
½   tsp garlic powder
½   tsp sugar
½   tsp paprika
1   tbsp olive oil

RICH ONION SAUCE

2   tbsp butter
1   large yellow onion, thinly sliced
1   small garlic clove, minced
1   tbsp sherry vinegar
1   tsp sugar
½   tsp dried thyme
1   bay leaf
⅓   cup port wine, or bold red wine
4   cups beef broth
1   tbsp Worcestershire sauce
Kosher salt and freshly ground black pepper, to taste

6-8 soft hoagie rolls

The French dip is the Holy Grail of sandwich lovers everywhere, a dreamy combination of beef, bread and a license to double-dip. Popular across the country (Palm Beach Grill is our fave restaurant dip), the classic French dip is a spectacularly snazzy hot beef sandwich that's so simple it can be replicated at home. Tender and juicy roast beef (the eye of round cut is lean and inexpensive but ends up as succulent as prime rib) is sliced thin, piled atop a soft bun and repeatedly dunked in a rich homemade onion sauce, making this one magnificent, mile-high and sacred sandwich.

THE ULTIMATE FRENCH DIP SANDWICH

1. TO PREPARE THE ROAST BEEF, preheat oven to 375°F. Place roast beef in a shallow baking pan. In a small bowl, combine salt, pepper, onion powder, garlic powder, sugar, paprika and olive oil. Rub herb mixture over the entire roast. Let stand at room temperature for 30 minutes before baking.

2. FOR THE ROAST, bake for 1 hour or until a cooking thermometer inserted in the thickest part registers 135°F. Remove from oven and let stand 15 minutes before slicing.

3. WHILE THE ROAST COOKS, prepare the sauce. In a medium saucepan, melt butter over medium heat. Add onion and cook until golden, 6-8 minutes. Add garlic and sherry vinegar and cook for 1 minute, stirring continuously. Stir in sugar, thyme and bay leaf. Deglaze saucepan with port wine. Add beef broth and Worcestershire sauce and bring to a boil. Reduce heat to low and simmer 35-40 minutes. Remove from heat, strain and reserve onions. Return sauce to saucepan and keep warm until serving. Season to taste with salt and pepper.

4. TO ASSEMBLE SANDWICHES, slice beef thinly and pile on sandwich rolls. Spoon sauce over beef, top with onions and serve individual dishes of sauce for dipping.

. . . .

 Try with Cajun Oven Fries, page 92.

 When cooking roast beef at 375°F, allow 20 minutes per pound.

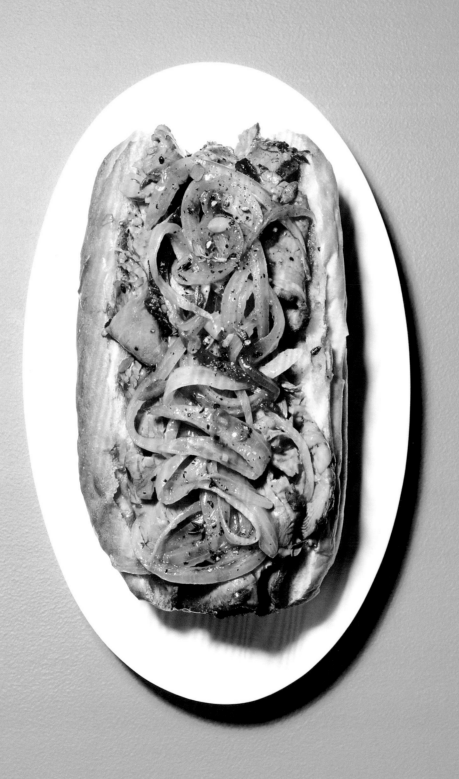

This isn't your average Joe. It isn't the cafeteria classic from a can. It isn't made from a preservative-laden spice packet. This sloppy Joe is exceptional and easy. Healthy and hearty, sweet and tangy sloppy Joe mixture is piled high on toasted buns and topped with creamy and crunchy Memphis coleslaw. One (albeit messy) bite and you'll already start asking for some scrumptious sloppy seconds.

SERVES 6
PREP 20 minutes
COOK 45 minutes

SAUCY SLOPPY JOES WITH MEMPHIS SLAW

1. FOR THE SLAW, place coleslaw mix in a large bowl. In a small bowl, whisk mayonnaise, Dijon, cider vinegar, sugar, celery seeds, salt and pepper. Pour over coleslaw mix and toss well to coat. Cover and let stand while preparing sloppy Joes.

2. FOR THE SLOPPY JOES, in a large skillet, brown beef and onion over medium heat. Cook 6–8 minutes, stirring frequently. Drain off any fat. Add green peppers, celery, garlic, oregano, salt, pepper and red pepper flakes. Cook 4 minutes more. Add crushed tomatoes, water, ketchup, brown sugar, apple cider vinegar, Dijon mustard and Worcestershire sauce. Bring to a boil, reduce heat to low and simmer for 30 minutes, stirring occasionally.

3. TO ASSEMBLE, toast hamburger buns under the broiler. Top with a generous scoop of sloppy Joe mixture followed by coleslaw. Serve immediately.

Try with Creamy Corn & Butternut Squash Chowder, page 30.

MEMPHIS SLAW

5	cups coleslaw mix
¾	cup mayonnaise
1	tbsp Dijon mustard
1	tbsp cider vinegar
1	tbsp sugar
½	tsp celery seeds
¼	tsp kosher salt
¼	tsp freshly ground black pepper

SLOPPY JOES

1½	lb lean ground beef
1	small yellow onion, chopped
1	green bell pepper, chopped
2	celery stalks, chopped
1	large garlic clove, minced
½	tsp dried oregano
½	tsp kosher salt
½	tsp freshly ground black pepper
¼	tsp crushed red pepper flakes
2	cups canned crushed tomatoes
½	cup water
½	cup ketchup
1	tbsp brown sugar
1	tbsp apple cider vinegar
2	tsp Dijon mustard
1	tsp Worcestershire sauce
6	hamburger buns

"Have some more sloppy Joes. I made 'em extra sloppy for youse. I know how youse kids like 'em sloppy."

Lunch Lady, *Billy Madison*

MAKES 6 burgers
PREP 10 minutes
COOK 40 minutes

. . . .

CARAMELIZED ONIONS

1 tbsp butter
1 tbsp olive oil
2 large yellow onions, halved
    and thinly sliced
½ tsp sugar
½ tsp kosher salt
¼ tsp dried thyme

CREAMY LEMON THYME SPREAD

½ cup mayonnaise
1 tbsp fresh lemon juice
2 tsp Dijon mustard
1½ tsp chopped fresh thyme
½ tsp lemon zest
¼ tsp kosher salt

BURGERS

1½ lb lean ground beef
2 tbsp onion soup mix
¼ tsp freshly ground black
    pepper
½ tsp kosher salt

6 slices Gruyère cheese
6 hamburger buns or rolls
Large handful of baby arugula
    leaves

Lisa has always been the doyenne of deliciousness, so it comes as no surprise that she's taken the classic soup-and-sandwich combo to soaring (and scrumptious) heights. This French Onion Soup Cheeseburger, a most creative and cheesy comfort food collision, serves up the best bistro bites between buns. A juicy, onion-flavored hamburger is covered with Gruyère cheese, piled high with sweet caramelized onions and nestled between two toasted buns slathered with zesty lemon thyme spread. A true pairing pro, Lisa's mash-up of a melty crock of onion soup and a hearty burger is turning all of us into chowing-down champs.

FRENCH ONION SOUP CHEESEBURGERS

1. FOR THE CARAMELIZED ONIONS, heat the butter and olive oil in a large skillet over medium heat. Add the onion slices and cook 3 minutes, stirring occasionally. Reduce heat to low and add sugar, salt and thyme. Continue cooking 15–20 minutes, until onions are golden and tender.

2. FOR THE LEMON THYME SPREAD, in a small bowl, whisk mayonnaise, lemon juice, Dijon mustard, thyme, lemon zest and salt. Cover and refrigerate until ready to assemble.

3. FOR THE BURGERS, in a medium bowl, combine ground beef, onion soup mix and pepper. Form beef mixture into 6 patties and sprinkle burgers with kosher salt. Heat a grill pan or griddle over medium heat and cook burgers 4 minutes per side for medium-rare. Top each burger with 1 slice of cheese and cook 1 minute longer until cheese melts.

4. TO ASSEMBLE, toast the buns on the grill pan or under a broiler until golden. Spread lemon thyme sauce on top and bottom buns. Place arugula leaves on the bottom of each bun. Place cooked burger over arugula, a generous serving of caramelized onions and the top bun. Serve immediately.

. . . .

Try with Balsamic Roasted Carrots, Parsnips & Beets, page 94.

To ensure juicy burgers, don't compress or overwork the meat, don't press on the patty as it grills (you'll lose juice) and let burgers rest for 5 minutes before serving to seal in juices.

We did a little experiment with word association, and when we said "brisket," responses included "shoe" and "leather." While we aren't meat marketers, we're prepared to sell the heck out of brisket, an inexpensive cut of beef that gets a bad rap. Tough? Nothing could be further from the truth with this incredible and easy recipe, a Beer-Braised Brisket that's so meltingly tender, it's like cutting through butter. Cooked low and slow (four hours), brisket is braised in beer, surrounded by flavor-packed vegetables and then put in the refrigerator overnight to allow all the richness and succulence to develop. Once sliced, the brisket is smothered in rich braising liquid, resulting in some serious meat magic. Now, when we say "brisket," you say "tender."

TENDER BEER-BRAISED BRISKET

SERVES 8–10
PREP 10 minutes
COOK 5 hours (+overnight refrigeration)

. . . .

3   tbsp olive oil
1   flat cut brisket (5 lb), trimmed, leaving a thin layer of fat
1   tbsp kosher salt
2   tsp freshly ground black pepper
2   large yellow onions, sliced
2   large carrots, peeled, cut into large chunks
2   celery stalks, cut into large chunks
½   tsp kosher salt
3   cups light beer (we love Stella Artois)
2   cups beef broth

1. PREHEAT OVEN to 325°F. In a heavy-bottomed pot or large Dutch oven, heat olive oil over medium-high heat. Season both sides of the brisket with salt and pepper. Add brisket to pot, fat side down, and sear 4–5 minutes, until browned. Flip and cook the other side until browned, 4–5 minutes more. Remove from pot and set aside. Add onions, carrots, celery and salt to the same pot and set over medium heat. Cook, stirring often, until vegetables are golden brown, 8–10 minutes. Add beer and beef broth, bringing to a boil. Remove from heat and return brisket to the pan. Cover tightly with aluminum foil and place in oven until brisket is tender, about 4 hours. Remove from oven, keeping covered, and cool to room temperature. Refrigerate overnight.

2. TO SLICE AND REHEAT, preheat oven to 350°F. Trim fat cap from beef and discard. Thinly slice beef across the grain and lay the slices in a 13- × 9-inch baking dish. Strain braising liquid into a large saucepan, removing and discarding vegetable pieces. Let liquid reduce over medium-high heat for 10 minutes. Adjust seasoning if necessary. Pour over sliced brisket, cover with aluminum foil and place in oven until heated through, about 20 minutes.

. . . .

 Try with Buttermilk Ranch Mashed Potatoes, page 84.

 You can buy brisket either point cut or flat cut. Point cut is thick and marbled with fat, while flat cut, the easy-to-slice cut used here and when making corned beef, has only a thin layer of fat along the bottom to keep the brisket moist.

It may be called a "slow cooker," but the prep time for this easy dish is anything but. Not only does it take less than 10 minutes to get all the ingredients prepared for this tasty beef chili, but with a quick turn of the dial, you can run away while it spends hours developing a rich and intense flavor. In this classic game-day (and everyday) delight, chipotle chili peppers lend a spicy kick while molasses adds sweetness, making this hearty beef chili perfect in a bowl, topping a baked potato, blanketing a hot dog . . .

SLOW COOKER BEEF CHILI

1. IN A LARGE SKILLET, heat olive oil over medium-high heat. Add onion and green and red peppers and cook, stirring, for 4–5 minutes. Add garlic, chipotle pepper, adobo sauce, chili powder, cumin, oregano, salt and pepper. Cook 1 minute longer. Transfer to slow cooker. In the same skillet, add beef over medium-high heat and cook, stirring occasionally, until the beef has browned. Drain fat and add beef to slow cooker, along with beef broth, tomato purée, diced tomatoes, red kidney beans, apple cider vinegar and molasses. Cook 6–8 hours on low setting. Serve warm, topped with shredded cheese, sour cream and crushed tortilla chips.

For less heat in your chili, remove the seeds and white membranes from the chipotle pepper.

SERVES	6–8
PREP	15 minutes
COOK	6–8 hours

1   tbsp olive oil
1   large yellow onion, chopped
1   green bell pepper, chopped
1   red bell pepper, chopped
2   large garlic cloves, minced
1   canned chipotle pepper in adobo sauce, chopped
1   tsp adobo sauce
2   tbsp chili powder
2   tsp ground cumin
1   tsp dried oregano
1   tsp kosher salt
½   tsp freshly ground black pepper
2   lb lean ground beef
2   cups beef broth
2   cups tomato purée
1   (15 oz) can diced tomatoes
1   (15 oz) can red kidney beans, rinsed and drained
2   tbsp apple cider vinegar
1   tbsp molasses

TOPPINGS
Shredded cheddar cheese
Sour cream
Crushed tortilla chips

When I complain about a bad hair day, Lisa often humors me by reminding me, "It's what's inside that counts." While I know she utters this cliché to quiet me, what I didn't know was that she takes this expression quite literally. I mean, how else would she have conceived the greatest surprise of all, juicy meatballs stuffed with melty mozzarella cheese? In a superb twist, these meatballs stuffed with mozzarella are baked until tender and finished in a rich red wine tomato sauce. *Mamma mia*, this easy recipe takes the Italian classic (and inner beauty) to new heights.

MOZZARELLA-STUFFED MEATBALLS IN RED WINE TOMATO SAUCE

1. FOR THE TOMATO SAUCE, in a large pot, heat olive oil over medium heat. Add onion and garlic, cooking for 3 minutes, until softened. Add wine and cook for 2–3 minutes to reduce. Stir in tomato paste, sugar, salt and pepper until well combined. Add beef broth and tomatoes, breaking up tomatoes with a wooden spoon. Bring to a boil, reduce heat to low and simmer, partially covered, for 20 minutes.

2. FOR THE MEATBALLS, preheat oven to 400°F and line 2 baking sheets with parchment paper. Set aside.

MAKES 20 large meatballs
PREP 20 minutes
COOK 1 hour, 10 minutes

. . . .

RED WINE TOMATO SAUCE
1   tbsp olive oil
1   small red onion, chopped
2   garlic cloves, minced
½   cup dry red wine
3   tbsp tomato paste
1   tsp sugar
½   tsp kosher salt
½   tsp freshly ground black pepper
1   cup beef broth
2   cans (28 oz) San Marzano whole tomatoes

You're not done yet . . . see next page ➜

MOZZARELLA-STUFFED MEATBALLS

1   cup panko (Japanese breadcrumbs)
1   cup freshly grated Parmesan cheese
1   cup ricotta cheese
2   eggs
1   tsp dried Italian seasoning
1   tsp kosher salt
½   tsp freshly ground black pepper
1   large garlic clove, minced
1½ lb lean ground beef
1   lb ground veal
4   oz mozzarella cheese, cut into bite-sized cubes

Fresh basil leaves, for garnish

3. IN A LARGE BOWL, combine panko, Parmesan cheese, ricotta, eggs, Italian seasoning, salt, pepper and garlic, mixing well to combine. Add ground beef and ground veal, mixing thoroughly by hand. Scoop out ¼ cup of the meat mixture and roll into a ball. Press one mozzarella cube in the center and roll again to seal in the cheese. Repeat and place meatballs on prepared baking sheets. Bake for 12 minutes, flip meatballs and bake 12 minutes more. Remove from oven, place meatballs in sauce and simmer for 20 minutes more. Serve with spaghetti and garnish with fresh basil leaves.

. . . .

 Create the ultimate Italian meatball sub by placing warmed meatballs with sauce in a hoagie roll topped with cheese and basil.

Want to know the hardest thing about veal scaloppini? The divide between spelling it "scaloppini" or "scallopini." We fall into the double p camp—scaloppini is both palatable and perfect. In this amazingly reliable recipe, the delicate, thin veal cooks quickly (three minutes total), yet remains super-tender and tasty, especially when paired with earthy mushrooms and sweet sautéed apples. Finished with a sherry and cider-infused cream sauce, this elegant and easy dish is impressively fancy without being fussy.

VEAL SCALOPPINI WITH MUSHROOMS & APPLE CREAM SAUCE

SERVES 4–6
PREP 10 minutes
COOK 20 minutes

1. FOR THE VEAL, heat butter and olive oil in a large skillet over medium heat. Season both sides of veal with salt and pepper. Dust each side lightly with flour, shaking off excess. In 2 batches, brown veal in skillet, about 1–1½ minutes per side. Remove from skillet and set aside.

2. FOR THE SAUCE, using the same skillet, melt 2 tablespoons of butter over medium heat. Add shallots, mushrooms and apple slices, sauté 5 minutes and season with salt and pepper. Turn heat to high and deglaze pan with sherry. Add apple cider and cook, stirring occasionally, for 4 minutes. Reduce heat to low, stir in cream and add veal back to skillet. Cook 2 minutes more. Garnish with fresh chives.

Try with Winter Couscous Salad, page 64.

To keep mushrooms from getting slimy, store them in their original packaging. If you're buying loose ones, place them in a small container and instead of a lid, cover with plastic wrap with a few tiny holes poked through it to let mushrooms "breathe" and cool air circulate.

VEAL

2 tbsp butter
1 tbsp olive oil
1½ lb veal scaloppini
¼ tsp kosher salt
¼ tsp freshly ground black pepper
2 tbsp flour

APPLE CREAM SAUCE

2 tbsp butter
2 medium shallots, minced
8 oz sliced white mushrooms
2 Granny Smith apples, peeled and sliced
½ tsp kosher salt
¼ tsp freshly ground black pepper
½ cup sherry wine
1 cup apple cider
¼ cup heavy cream

Fresh chives, for garnish

> "My tongue is smiling."
>
> Abigail Trillin

SERVES 4

PREP 10 minutes
(+6–24 hour marinade)

COOK 20 minutes

. . . .

MARINADE

4 veal chops, each about 1 inch thick

3 tbsp olive oil

3 tbsp fresh lemon juice

2 tbsp chopped fresh flat-leaf parsley

1 tbsp lemon zest

1 large garlic clove, minced

1 tsp dried oregano

¼ tsp kosher salt

¼ tsp freshly ground black pepper

HERB GREMOLATA

3 tbsp chopped fresh flat-leaf parsley

2 tbsp olive oil

1 tbsp chopped fresh mint

1 tbsp lemon zest

1 tbsp fresh lemon juice

1 small garlic clove, minced

¼ tsp kosher salt

Lemon wedge, for garnish

What's the first thing you should do after you brew your morning coffee? Quickly answer the "What's for dinner?" question by getting a jump-start on these fantastic Grilled Tuscan Veal Chops with Herb Gremolata. In mere minutes, you can get these veal chops marinating in a savory and zesty combination of olive oil, parsley, garlic and lemon. Then, you can go about your day knowing that at the end of it, you'll be able to grill up these tasty marinated chops to perfection, smother them in a fresh herb, garlic and lemon gremolata, and put an incredible meal on the table in 20 minutes or less. How's that for a glory day (and dinner)?

GRILLED TUSCAN VEAL CHOPS WITH HERB GREMOLATA

1. FOR THE MARINADE, place veal chops in a glass baking dish. In a small bowl, whisk olive oil, lemon juice, parsley, lemon zest, garlic and oregano and pour over veal chops. Turn chops to coat well, cover and refrigerate, turning occasionally, for 6–24 hours.

2. REMOVE VEAL CHOPS from marinade and season with salt and pepper. Preheat barbecue to medium-high heat and lightly oil grill grate. Grill veal chops 6–8 minutes per side for medium doneness. Remove from grill and let rest 5 minutes before serving.

3. FOR THE GREMOLATA, in a small bowl, combine parsley, olive oil, mint, lemon zest, lemon juice, garlic and salt. Once the veal chops are cooked, transfer to a serving platter and top each chop with a spoonful of gremolata. Serve with a wedge of lemon.

. . . .

 Try with Sweet Potato Risotto, page 110.

What's elegant and easy and straight from Milan? No, not that little black dress but something just as glamorous—this Classic Veal Milanese with Arugula Salad. In this classic Italian dish, veal chops are pounded thin, coated in Parmesan breadcrumbs, lightly sautéed until a crisp crust forms and topped with a fresh arugula and tomato salad. Tender and super-tasty, this delicious dish can be done pronto, making it perfect for casual yet impressive entertaining that'll never go out of style.

CLASSIC VEAL MILANESE WITH ARUGULA SALAD

1. FOR VEAL MILANESE, in a shallow bowl, combine flour, salt and pepper. In a second medium-sized bowl, whisk eggs and Dijon mustard together. In a third bowl, combine breadcrumbs, Parmesan cheese, oregano, basil, salt and pepper. Dredge veal chops in the flour and shake off excess. Dip in egg mixture, allowing excess to drip off. Coat in breadcrumb mixture and press gently to adhere. Place coated veal chops on a large plate, cover and refrigerate for 20 minutes.

2. IN A LARGE SKILLET, heat olive oil and butter over high heat. Add 2 veal chops and cook 2 minutes per side. Transfer to a serving plate and repeat with remaining 2 veal chops. Top each veal chop with arugula salad and serve immediately.

3. FOR THE SALAD, in a large bowl, toss arugula, tomatoes, lemon juice, olive oil, salt and pepper. Garnish with Parmesan cheese shavings.

 Try with Spaghetti with Chunky Marinara, page 113.

SERVES 4
PREP 15 minutes (+20 minute refrigeration)
COOK 10 minutes

VEAL MILANESE
¼ cup flour
½ tsp kosher salt
¼ tsp freshly ground black pepper
2 eggs
1 tbsp Dijon mustard
1 cup plain breadcrumbs
½ cup freshly grated Parmesan cheese
½ tsp dried oregano
¼ tsp dried basil
½ tsp kosher salt
¼ tsp freshly ground black pepper
4 veal chops, pounded to ¼-inch thickness
2 tbsp olive oil
1 tbsp butter

ARUGULA SALAD
2 cups baby arugula
12 cherry tomatoes, halved
1 tbsp fresh lemon juice
1 tbsp olive oil
¼ tsp kosher salt
¼ tsp freshly ground black pepper

Fresh Parmesan cheese shavings, for garnish

"You may have the universe if I may have Italy."

Giuseppe Verdi

Lisa's a meat martyr. While she knew she'd have to endure endless wisecracks about frenching lamb, she also knew that the benefits and beauty of these Pistachio-Crusted Lamb Chops far outweighed having to ignore her sister. Instead of fussing with a rack of lamb, Lisa has taken tender chops and coated them in zesty Dijon mustard and a pistachio, honey, thyme and lemon crust. Taking only a few minutes to cook, this flavor-packed, succulent and superb meat on a stick is guaranteed to rack up some major dinnertime kudos.

PISTACHIO-CRUSTED LAMB CHOPS

MAKES 12 lamb chops; serves 4–6
PREP 10 minutes
COOK 15 minutes

. . . .

PISTACHIO CRUST

1 cup shelled unsalted pistachio nuts
⅓ cup olive oil
2 tbsp fresh lemon juice
1 tbsp honey
1 large garlic clove
1 tsp chopped fresh thyme
1 tsp lemon zest
¼ tsp kosher salt

2 tbsp olive oil
12 lamb rib chops, trimmed, about 1 inch thick
¼ tsp kosher salt
¼ tsp freshly ground black pepper
2 tbsp Dijon mustard

1. PREHEAT OVEN to 400°F. Line a baking sheet with parchment paper.

2. FOR THE PISTACHIO CRUST, in a food processor, combine pistachios, olive oil, lemon juice, honey, garlic, thyme, lemon zest and salt. Process until it combines and forms a paste. Set aside.

3. IN A LARGE SKILLET, heat 2 tablespoons of olive oil over high heat. Season the lamb chops with salt and pepper. Add to skillet and sear 2 minutes per side. Remove from skillet and place on baking sheet. Rub Dijon mustard over one side of each chop and pat with 1 table-spoon of pistachio crust. Bake 4 minutes for medium-rare. Turn broiler to high and broil lamb chops for 1½ minutes, until crust is golden, watching carefully to make sure crust doesn't burn. Remove from oven and let lamb chops rest 5 minutes before serving.

. . . .

 Try with Twice-Baked Sweet Potatoes, page 86.

"Always remember: If you're alone in the kitchen and you drop the lamb, you can always just pick it up. Who's going to know?"

Julia Child

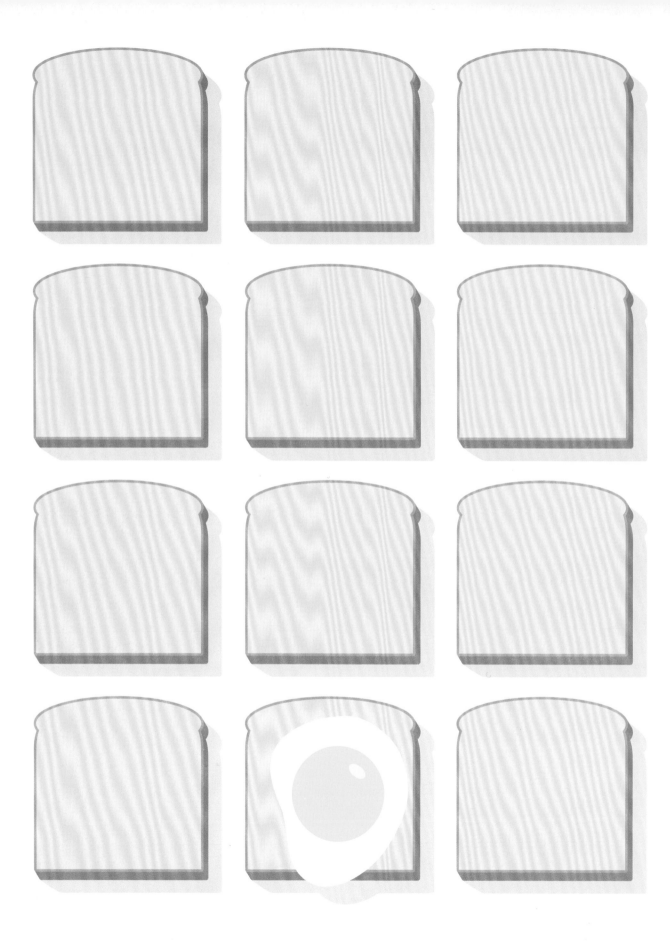

RISE & SHINE

Not a breakfast person? I bet the ranch you will be after trying these Huevos Rancheros, a marvelous medley of spices, beans, tortillas and eggs. In our fast and easy version of this tried-and-true Tex-Mex mishmash, crunchy corn tortillas are topped with creamy black beans, melted sharp white cheddar, a soft-yolk fried egg, tangy salsa, creamy avocado and fresh lime. What are you waiting for? Wake up, smell the southwestern spices and devour these hearty huevos.

SPEEDY & SATISFYING HUEVOS RANCHEROS

SERVES 6
PREP 5 minutes
COOK 15 minutes

• •

CREAMY BLACK BEANS

2½ cups canned black beans, rinsed and drained
½ cup water
¼ cup sour cream
1 small garlic clove, minced
1 tsp ground cumin
½ tsp kosher salt
½ tsp freshly ground black pepper

6 (6-inch) corn tortillas
¾ cup shredded sharp white cheddar cheese
2 tsp olive oil
6 eggs
¾ cup salsa
¼ cup chopped fresh flat-leaf parsley

Ripe avocado slices, for garnish
Lime wedges, for garnish

1. FOR THE BLACK BEANS, in a medium saucepan, combine black beans, water, sour cream, garlic, cumin, salt and pepper. Mash bean mixture with a potato masher or a handheld immersion blender until it has a chunky, thick consistency. Bring to a gentle boil over medium heat. Reduce heat to low and simmer for 5 minutes, stirring frequently. Turn off heat, cover and keep warm.

2. PREHEAT OVEN on the broil setting. Place tortillas on a baking sheet 3 at a time and spray one side with cooking spray. Place tortillas under broiler and toast for 1½–2 minutes. Remove from oven and flip tortillas over. Spread a heaping ¼ cup of black bean mixture over each tortilla and top each tortilla with 2 tablespoons of shredded cheddar. Place under the broiler for 1 minute more. Meanwhile, in a large skillet, heat olive oil over medium-high heat. Gently crack eggs in the pan and cook for 2 minutes. Cover and cook 1–2 minutes more, until desired doneness. Place 1 egg on each tortilla over melted cheese. Top each serving with 2 tablespoons of salsa, sprinkle with chopped parsley and garnish each serving with avocado slices and a wedge of lime. Repeat with remaining ingredients.

• •

Why should you always store eggs in their cartons? With over 17,000 tiny pores on their shells, eggs can absorb flavors and odors in the refrigerator.

Growing up, my sister longed to be Julia Child. I, on the other hand, had my sights set on Flo, the sassy Texan dame on *Alice* who got to sling hash and tell people to kiss her grits. Now Lisa's making all my dreams come true—I get to make hash (and sling it too), with this delicious combo of roasted Yukon Gold and sweet potatoes, sautéed onions, apples, thyme, maple syrup and a small kick of spice. To top it all off, eggs are cooked in the same skillet, making this hash an easy, healthy and delicious addition to any brunch. Is Lisa ever going to realize her dream of becoming Julia Child? As Flo would say, "You bet your sweet patoot."

DOUBLE POTATO HASH WITH SUNNY-SIDE-UP EGGS

1. PREHEAT OVEN to 400°F. Line a baking sheet with parchment paper. In a large bowl, toss chopped sweet and Yukon Gold potatoes with olive oil, ½ teaspoon kosher salt and ½ teaspoon freshly ground black pepper. Place on baking sheet and bake 18–20 minutes, until potatoes are just tender. Remove from oven and set aside.

2. IN A LARGE SKILLET, melt butter over medium heat. Add onion and cook until tender and lightly browned, 4 minutes. When potatoes are out of the oven, add to the onions and continue to cook for 2 minutes more. Add apples, lemon juice, thyme, maple syrup, Tabasco, salt and pepper, cooking for 2 minutes. Turn heat to low and make wells in the potato-apple mixture. Crack an egg into each well, cover and cook until eggs are set, 4–5 minutes for soft and runny centers or 6 minutes for firmer yolks. Finish with salt and pepper to taste. Serve immediately.

> "I know family comes first, but shouldn't that mean after breakfast?"
>
> Jeff Lindsay

SERVES 4
PREP 15 minutes
COOK 35 minutes

. . . .

1½ lb (approximately 3) sweet potatoes, peeled and cut into ½-inch cubes
1 lb (approximately 2) Yukon Gold potatoes, scrubbed and cut into ½-inch cubes
1 tbsp olive oil
½ tsp kosher salt
½ tsp freshly ground black pepper
2 tbsp butter
1 large yellow onion, chopped
2 Gala or Honeycrisp apples, cored and chopped
1 tbsp fresh lemon juice
2 tsp chopped fresh thyme
1 tsp maple syrup
1 tsp Tabasco sauce
¼ tsp kosher salt
¼ tsp freshly ground black pepper
4 eggs
Kosher salt and freshly ground black pepper, to taste

If I'm the fancy, fussy and fattening quiche of the egg world, Lisa's the simple, versatile and healthy frittata. A one-skillet recipe, this Caramelized Onion, Zucchini & Ricotta Frittata is a quick way to serve up an amazing meal that's long on forgiveness (no crust or custard to worry about) and short on difficulty. In 30 minutes, you can get this fantastic frittata of tender eggs, caramelized onions and zucchini, peppery arugula, creamy ricotta and sharp Parmesan, from pantry to plate. See? Easy, like Lisa.

CARAMELIZED ONION, ZUCCHINI & RICOTTA FRITTATA

SERVES 6
PREP 10 minutes
COOK 20 minutes

- 2   tbsp olive oil
- 1   large red onion, thinly sliced
- 2   small zucchinis, chopped
- 2   tbsp finely chopped, oil-packed sun-dried tomatoes
- ½   tsp Italian seasoning
- ½   tsp kosher salt
- ¼   tsp freshly ground black pepper
- 10   eggs
- ½   cup freshly grated Parmesan cheese
- 2   tbsp chopped fresh basil
- ¼   tsp kosher salt
- ¼   tsp freshly ground black pepper
- 3   cups roughly chopped arugula
- ½   cup ricotta cheese
- ¼   cup freshly grated Parmesan cheese

1. PREHEAT OVEN to 425°F. Heat olive oil in a 12-inch skillet over medium-high heat. Add onion and stir, cooking to soften for 2 minutes. Add zucchini and continue to cook for 4 minutes, stirring occasionally. Stir in sun-dried tomatoes, Italian seasoning, ½ teaspoon salt and ¼ teaspoon pepper. Cook for 1 minute more. Remove from heat.

2. IN A LARGE BOWL, whisk eggs, ½ cup Parmesan, basil, ¼ teaspoon salt and pepper. Scatter arugula over onion-zucchini mixture. Pour egg mixture evenly over vegetables. Drop dollops of ricotta cheese over top and sprinkle with ¼ cup Parmesan. Transfer to oven and bake 10–12 minutes, until golden brown and slightly firm to the touch. Let cool for a few minutes then slide out onto a cutting board. Cut in wedges and serve.

If you want a thicker frittata, use a 10-inch skillet and bake an extra 2–4 minutes.

> "Never eat spinach just before going on the air."
>
> Dan Rather

SERVES 8–10

PREP 20 minutes (+4–24 hour refrigeration)

COOK 1 hour

· ·

2 tbsp butter

1 tbsp olive oil

1 large yellow onion, thinly sliced

1 large red bell pepper, thinly sliced

2 small garlic cloves, minced

1 large shallot, minced

2 tsp Dijon mustard

1 tsp chopped fresh thyme

½ tsp kosher salt

½ tsp freshly ground black pepper

¼ cup dry white wine

10 cups loosely packed baby spinach

8 eggs

3 cups whole milk

½ tsp kosher salt

¼ tsp freshly ground black pepper

12 cups cubed French bread, 1-inch cubes

2 cups grated Gruyère cheese

2 cups grated sharp white cheddar

1 cup freshly grated Parmesan cheese

What do I do when the day after buying a French bread it hardens into a rock? I grab the somewhat lethal weapon, holler "On Guard" and challenge Lisa to a duel. What does Lisa do? She rolls her eyes and then sets about transforming the stale bread into a golden savory strata of cheese and spinach. In this make-ahead marvel (you assemble it the night before and bake it off in the morning for your brunch buffet), spinach and roasted red peppers are layered with Gruyère, white cheddar and Parmesan cheese, resulting in a flavorful, aromatic egg and bread casserole. One bite and I realize that my swashbuckling days are done—Lisa has given me the true edge, showing me how to easily turn my sword into this superb strata.

MAKE-AHEAD CHEESY SPINACH STRATA

1. COAT a 13- × 9-inch baking dish with nonstick cooking spray.

2. FOR THE SPINACH MIXTURE, heat butter and olive oil in a large skillet over medium heat. Add onion and cook 4 minutes, until softened. Add red peppers, garlic, shallots, Dijon mustard, thyme, salt and pepper. Cook, stirring, for 2 minutes. Add wine to skillet and reduce for 1 minute. Stir in spinach, just until wilted, and then remove pan from heat.

3. IN A MEDIUM BOWL, whisk eggs, milk, salt and pepper.

4. TO ASSEMBLE STRATA, spread half the bread cubes over the base of the baking dish. Top with half the spinach mixture. Sprinkle with 1 cup Gruyère cheese, 1 cup white cheddar and ½ cup Parmesan cheese. Scatter remaining bread over the cheese and top with remaining spinach mixture. Pour egg mixture evenly over strata and finish with remaining Gruyère, cheddar and Parmesan. Cover with plastic wrap and refrigerate 4–24 hours. When ready to bake, preheat oven to 350°F. Let strata sit at room temperature until oven is heated. Bake 50–55 minutes, until set and starting to brown on the top. Remove from oven and let cool 5 minutes before serving.

It's said that breakfast is the most important meal of the day, and we're treating it that way by thinking outside the preservative-laden, overpriced box and baking up our own Chunky Chocolate, Pecan & Berry Granola. There isn't a store-bought granola that can beat this scrumptious, homemade 5-minutes-from-pantry-to-oven granola—oats, pecans, pumpkin seeds and coconut are tossed with a honey cinnamon mixture and baked until golden. After baking, the crunchy, crisp clusters are mixed with dark chocolate chunks, dried cranberries and dried cherries, creating a breakfast (or snack) of champions that's going to power you through your day.

CHUNKY CHOCOLATE, PECAN & BERRY GRANOLA

1. PREHEAT OVEN to 300°F. Line a baking sheet with parchment paper.

2. IN A LARGE BOWL, combine oats, pecans, coconut and pumpkin seeds. In a small bowl, whisk together honey, melted butter, brown sugar, vanilla extract, cinnamon and salt. Pour over oat mixture and toss well to coat.

3. SPREAD GRANOLA evenly over prepared baking sheet. Bake 25–30 minutes, stirring every 10 minutes. Remove from oven, transfer to a large bowl and let cool for 10 minutes. Add chocolate chunks, dried cranberries and dried cherries, mixing to combine. Cool completely and store at room temperature in an airtight container for up to 1 week.

Feel free to use walnuts or almonds in place of the pecans, dried apricots in place of the dried cherries and white chocolate in place of the dark chocolate chunks.

MAKES 6 cups
PREP 5 minutes
COOK 40 minutes

. . . .

3   cups old-fashioned oats
1   cup coarsely chopped pecans
½   cup unsweetened flaked coconut
⅓   cup pumpkin seeds
⅓   cup honey
¼   cup melted butter
¼   cup brown sugar
1   tsp vanilla extract
½   tsp ground cinnamon
½   tsp kosher salt
1   cup dark chocolate chunks
½   cup dried cranberries
½   cup dried cherries

Photo on next page →

Chunky Chocolate, Pecan & Berry Granola, page 223

No need to grab your French–English dictionary because we're going to spell it out for you: *les crêpes sont délicieuses* (translation: "crepes are delicious"). Delicate yet satisfying, crepes are thin pancakes that can be served with either a sweet or savory filling. La Lisa, our in-*maison* crepe connoisseur, has made all our *fantaisies françaises* come true with these crepes *du jour*. Crisp and golden quick-cooking crepes are filled with a fluffy lemon ricotta and cream cheese mixture and topped with fresh citrus-flavored mixed berries. Pardon our French, but these crepes are @#$%ing *fantastique*.

MAKES 10–12 crepes
PREP 10 minutes
COOK 30 minutes

. . . .

BERRY SAUCE
2 cups mixed fresh berries, raspberries, blueberries and/or strawberries, quartered
¼ cup sugar
1 tsp cornstarch
1 tsp Grand Marnier
1 tsp fresh lemon juice
½ cup fresh blueberries

CHEESE FILLING
1 cup ricotta cheese
½ cup cream cheese, softened
¼ cup sugar
1 tsp lemon zest
½ tsp vanilla extract
¼ tsp kosher salt

CREPES
1¼ cups whole milk
1 cup flour
3 eggs
1 tbsp melted butter
¼ tsp kosher salt
Butter, for skillet

LEMON RICOTTA CREPES WITH FRESH BERRY SAUCE

1. FOR THE BERRY SAUCE, in a small bowl, toss 2 cups berries with sugar and cornstarch. Pour mixture into a small saucepan and place over medium heat. Stir until sugar melts, lower heat to a gentle simmer and cook for 5 minutes. Stir in Grand Marnier and remove from heat. Stir in lemon juice and remaining ½ cup blueberries. Transfer to a serving dish and set aside.

2. FOR THE CHEESE FILLING, using a blender, combine ricotta, cream cheese, sugar, lemon zest, vanilla and salt. Blend until smooth and set aside.

3. FOR THE CREPES, in a blender, combine milk, flour, eggs, melted butter and salt. Blend until mixture is smooth. Heat a crepe pan or a small skillet with low sides over medium heat. Generously grease pan with butter. Pour in ¼ cup crepe batter, swirl the pan to spread evenly and cook about 30 seconds per side, until the edges just start to become golden. Transfer crepe to a plate and cover with a clean dish towel to keep warm. Repeat with remaining crepe batter, greasing pan with more butter after making 2 or 3 crepes. Pile cooked crepes on top of each other.

4. TO ASSEMBLE, lay a crepe flat, spread a heaping tablespoon of cheese filling in the center, fold the crepe in half and then fold in half again. Top with berry sauce and serve.

. . . .

 To quickly soften cream cheese, seal it in a resealable plastic bag and immerse it in hot water for 10 minutes.

Want to be the apple of every eye? Batter up and get ready to make dessert-for-breakfast dreams come true with these ambrosial Apple Pie Pancakes. Flippin' great flapjacks, these fluffy, warmly spiced buttermilk pancakes are filled with chunky apples, cinnamon and graham cracker crumbs, and smothered with sweet caramelized apples. But watch out—these scrumptious stacks are going to disappear like hotcakes.

FLUFFY APPLE PIE PANCAKES

1. FOR THE APPLE PIE TOPPING, in a large bowl, toss diced apples, brown sugar, cornstarch, cinnamon and salt together. Melt butter in a large saucepan over medium heat. Add apple mixture and cook, stirring, for 2 minutes. Add water and continue to cook 4–5 minutes, until apples have softened. Set aside until pancakes are ready.

2. FOR THE PANCAKES, in a large mixing bowl, combine flour, graham cracker crumbs, baking powder, brown sugar, cinnamon and salt. Set aside. In a medium bowl, whisk eggs, milk, buttermilk, melted butter and vanilla. Stir egg mixture and chopped apples into the dry ingredients. Do not overmix—lumps are okay in the batter.

3. OVER MEDIUM HEAT pour ½ cup batter onto a lightly greased hot skillet or griddle. Cook until bubbles form, flip and cook on the other side until golden. Serve with a spoonful of apple pie topping.

 Making batches? Place finished pancakes in a single layer on a large baking sheet in a 200°F oven while cooking the rest.

MAKES	10 large pancakes
PREP	15 minutes
COOK	20 minutes

APPLE PIE TOPPING
4   Granny Smith apples, peeled and diced
⅓   cup brown sugar
2   tsp cornstarch
1   tsp ground cinnamon
¼   tsp kosher salt
¼   cup butter
½   cup water

BUTTERMILK PANCAKES
2   cups flour
2   cups graham cracker crumbs
1   tbsp baking powder
¼   cup brown sugar
2   tsp ground cinnamon
½   tsp kosher salt
2   eggs
1½   cups whole milk
1¼   cups buttermilk
¼   cup melted butter
1   tsp vanilla extract
1   Granny Smith apple, peeled and finely chopped

SERVES 8–10
PREP 30 minutes (+overnight refrigeration)
COOK 1 hour, 10 minutes

. . . .

STRAWBERRY SAUCE

4   cups fresh strawberries, hulled and halved
½   cup sugar
¼   cup water
2   tbsp fresh lemon juice
2   tbsp cornstarch
2   tbsp water

FRENCH TOAST

14   cups French bread, cut into 1-inch cubes
1½   packages (12 oz) cream cheese, room temperature
⅔   cup sugar
¼   cup whole milk
1   tbsp fresh lemon juice
1   tsp lemon zest
½   tsp kosher salt

2¼   cups whole milk
6   eggs
2   tsp vanilla extract

CRUMBLE TOPPING

1½   cups flour
½   cup sugar
¼   tsp kosher salt
½   cup cold butter, cubed

"She was so wild that when she made French toast, her tongue got caught in the toaster."

Rodney Dangerfield

Thanks to Lisa and Lionel (as in Richie), we can all be easy like Sunday morning. How so? All you have to do when you wake up is turn on the oven and get your fork and knife ready. Thanks to this overnight (it's assembled a day in advance) Strawberry Cheesecake French Toast Soufflé, you can pull together the most jaw-dropping brunch in no time. French bread is cubed, slathered with a smooth cream cheese filling and a fresh strawberry sauce. Topped with a buttery crumble before going in the oven, this perfect-for-every-French-toast-fanatic dish comes out golden and filled with a creamy strawberry cheesecake layer that's sure to have everyone dancing on the ceiling.

STRAWBERRY CHEESECAKE FRENCH TOAST SOUFFLÉ

1. FOR THE STRAWBERRY SAUCE, in a medium saucepan, combine strawberries, sugar, water and lemon juice over medium heat. Bring to a boil, stirring frequently. In a small bowl, mix cornstarch and water until smooth. Stir into strawberry mixture and simmer over low heat for 3 minutes to thicken. Set aside to cool slightly before covering and refrigerating.

2. COAT A 13- Q 9-INCH BAKING DISH with nonstick cooking spray. Add ½ the bread cubes. Using an electric mixer, beat cream cheese and sugar on medium speed until well combined and smooth. Add ¼ cup milk, lemon juice, lemon zest and salt, beating until smooth and well combined. Drop spoonfuls of cream cheese mixture over bread cubes in the baking dish. Spread as best you can. Top with strawberry sauce, pouring evenly over cream cheese. Top with remaining bread cubes.

3. IN A LARGE BOWL, whisk 2¼ cups milk, eggs and vanilla. Pour egg mixture over top, while creating small pockets for the egg mixture to fall through to the bottom bread. Cover tightly and refrigerate overnight.

4. PREHEAT OVEN to 350°F. Remove French toast baking dish from the refrigerator. For the crumble, in a small bowl, combine flour, sugar and salt. Cut in butter using your fingertips until the butter is in pea-sized pieces. Sprinkle crumble topping over French toast and bake 50–55 minutes, until topping is golden. Allow to rest out of the oven for 10 minutes before serving.

Forget midnight—it's usually 11 o'clock (in the morning) when I turn into a pumpkin. Thanks to my fairy godsister, these light and fluffy Spiced Pumpkin Waffles fill my mornings with magic. With a bibbidi-bobbidi-boo, Lisa has transformed the flavors of pumpkin pie into quick and easy waffles, a sweet and spicy mix of pumpkin, cinnamon, ginger and nutmeg. The writing is on the plate—these wondrous waffles, topped with a fluffy cloud of whipped cream, are spellbinding.

SPICED PUMPKIN WAFFLES

1. FOR THE WAFFLES, in a large mixing bowl, combine flour, cinnamon, baking powder, baking soda, ginger, salt and nutmeg. Set aside.

2. USING A BLENDER, combine milk, pumpkin purée, brown sugar, melted butter, egg and vanilla extract until smooth. Stir pumpkin mixture into flour mixture just until combined. Lumps in the batter are okay.

3. BRUSH A WAFFLE IRON lightly with vegetable oil and spoon batter into waffle iron, spreading quickly. Close lid and let cook 4–5 minutes, until the waffle is golden brown. Repeat with remaining batter and serve with a dollop of whipped cream and maple syrup.

MAKES	12 (4-inch) waffles
PREP	10 minutes
COOK	20 minutes

2¼ cups flour
2   tsp ground cinnamon
2   tsp baking powder
½   tsp baking soda
½   tsp ground ginger
½   tsp kosher salt
¼   tsp ground nutmeg
1¾ cups whole milk
1   cup canned pumpkin purée
½   cup brown sugar
¼   cup melted butter
1   egg
1   tsp vanilla extract

Vegetable oil, for waffle iron

Whipped cream, for topping
Maple syrup, for topping

If you don't have a waffle iron, you can make 18 large pancakes from the batter.

When morning has broken, so have I. After I deal with my irreparable bed head, all I've got time to grab is the kid's left-over crusts and dregs of juice. Until now. Thanks to Lively Lisa (a truly irritating morning person), I'll be eating cookies for breakfast. Yes, cookies. These hearty, healthy and delicious Oatmeal Almond Breakfast Cookies are chock-full of nutritious nuts, fiber-rich oats, bananas and dried fruit. A snap to pull together and perfect to bake in batches (refrigerate or freeze them for future on-the-run meals), these convenient and satisfying cookies may do little for my hair, but boy oh boy, they definitely make my day.

OATMEAL ALMOND BREAKFAST COOKIES

1. PREHEAT OVEN to 350°F. Line a baking sheet with parchment paper and set aside.

2. IN A LARGE BOWL, combine oats, almond flour, cinnamon, baking soda and salt. In a medium bowl, whisk mashed bananas, almond butter and honey. Pour into oat mixture and stir in chopped almonds, dried cranberries, semisweet chocolate and pumpkin seeds. Mix until ingredients are well combined.

3. DROP DOUGH by ¼ cup scoop onto prepared baking sheet. Bake 12–14 minutes, until the edges are golden.

You can replace almond butter with peanut butter and use pecans, walnuts or pistachios instead of almonds.

MAKES 16 breakfast cookies

PREP 10 minutes

COOK 15 minutes

· ·

1½ cups old-fashioned oats

1½ cups almond flour

1 tsp ground cinnamon

½ tsp baking soda

½ tsp kosher salt

1 cup mashed ripe bananas (2 small bananas)

½ cup almond butter

⅓ cup honey

½ cup coarsely chopped toasted almonds

½ cup dried cranberries

½ cup semisweet chocolate chips

¼ cup shelled pumpkin seeds

Want to know my favorite four-letter word? No, not that. This is a family book. It's cake. Yes, c-a-k-e. Thanks to Lisa, I eat it for breakfast, lunch and dinner, and this Chocolate Chunk Banana Coffee Cake, the perfect collision between sweet bananas and rich chocolate, is no exception. With a chunky chocolate cinnamon streusel layered between (and atop) moist banana sour cream cake, every bite is a winner. Simple and quick to throw in the oven, this perfect-for-brunch coffee cake is my favorite eight-letter word: heavenly.

CHOCOLATE CHUNK BANANA COFFEE CAKE

SERVES 10–12
PREP 15 minutes
COOK 40 minutes

. . . .

CHOCOLATE STREUSEL

1½	cups coarsely chopped semisweet chocolate
½	cup brown sugar
1	tbsp cocoa powder
1	tsp ground cinnamon

BANANA CAKE

½	cup butter, room temperature
¾	cup sugar
1	egg
1	tsp vanilla extract
¼	cup sour cream
½	tsp baking soda
1¼	cups mashed ripe bananas (about 2 large)
1½	cups flour
1	tsp baking powder
½	tsp kosher salt

1. PREHEAT OVEN to 350°F. Coat an 8-inch square baking pan with non-stick cooking spray. Line the bottom of the pan with parchment paper for easier removal.

2. FOR THE CHOCOLATE STREUSEL, in a medium bowl, combine chocolate, brown sugar, cocoa powder and cinnamon until well blended. Set aside.

3. FOR THE CAKE, using an electric mixer, cream butter and sugar on medium speed until light and fluffy. Add egg and vanilla, mixing until well incorporated. In a small measuring cup, combine sour cream and baking soda. Allow mixture to sit for 1 minute and then add to mixer. On low speed, add mashed bananas, flour, baking powder and salt. Mix just until flour disappears.

4. SPREAD HALF THE BATTER into prepared baking pan. Sprinkle with half the chocolate streusel. Cover with remaining batter and finish on top with remaining streusel. Bake 40–42 minutes, until springy to the touch.

. . . .

 To quickly ripen bananas, put them in a paper bag with apples, tomatoes or pears.

When asked to describe Lisa in food terms, the phrases tossed around are "sweet as sugar" and "such a peach." Not that I'm jealous or anything (me it's "bad apple" and "sour grapes"), but it's super-nice to see that Lovely Lisa is living up to her name with these marvelous Sweet Peach Cobbler Muffins. Chunks of fresh and juicy peaches are baked into moist cinnamon vanilla muffins and finished with a buttery brown sugar crumble topping. A summer staple, these scrumptious cobbler-flavored muffins once again prove that when Lisa's at the helm, everything turns out just peachy.

SWEET PEACH COBBLER MUFFINS

1. PREHEAT OVEN to 400°F. Coat 12-cup muffin tin with nonstick cooking spray and lightly dust cups with a pinch of flour, shaking out excess.

2. FOR THE CRUMB TOPPING, in a small bowl, combine flour, sugar, brown sugar and cinnamon. Add butter and mix using your fingers or a fork until mixture resembles course crumbs. Set aside.

3. FOR THE PEACH MUFFINS, using an electric mixer, cream butter and sugar on medium speed until well combined. Add egg and vanilla and continue mixing for 1 minute, until light and fluffy. Add sour cream, mixing to combine. Fold in flour, baking powder, baking soda, cinnamon, salt and chopped peaches. Stir just until blended. Do not overmix.

4. SPOON BATTER evenly into prepared muffin tins. Press crumb topping over muffins and bake 20–22 minutes, until muffins are golden and spring back when gently pressed. Remove from oven and transfer muffins to wire rack to cool completely.

If peaches aren't in season, use strawberries or blueberries instead.

MAKES 12 muffins
PREP 10 minutes
COOK 20 minutes

CRUMB TOPPING
¾ cup flour
3 tbsp sugar
2 tbsp brown sugar
⅛ tsp ground cinnamon
⅓ cup butter, softened

PEACH MUFFINS
½ cup butter, room temperature
¾ cup sugar
1 egg
1 tsp vanilla extract
1 cup sour cream
2 cups flour
1 tsp baking powder
1 tsp baking soda
½ tsp ground cinnamon
½ tsp kosher salt
1½ cups chopped fresh ripe peaches

When Lisa told me to brace myself for a brunch bombshell, I promptly pulled my spoon out of the Nutella jar, paused my poetry writing (Sweet and darling Nutella/I love you more than any fella) and readied myself. Good thing, because she was serving up these one-in-a-million moist chocolate chip muffins oozing with melty Nutella centers and glistening with Nutella-glazed tops. Using the heavenly hazelnut chocolate spread and her breathtaking baking skills, Lisa has performed a muffin miracle.

MAKES 12 muffins
PREP 15 minutes
COOK 20 minutes

. . . .

CHOCOLATE CHIP MUFFINS

1   cup Greek vanilla yogurt
¾   cup sugar
½   cup butter, melted
1   egg
1   tsp vanilla extract
2   cups flour
1   cup mini chocolate chips
1   tsp baking powder
1   tsp baking soda
½   tsp kosher salt

½   cup Nutella

NUTELLA GLAZE

¼   cup icing sugar
1   tbsp Nutella
2   tsp whole milk

NUTELLA-STUFFED CHOCOLATE CHIP MUFFINS

1. PREHEAT OVEN to 375°F. Line 12 muffin cups with paper liners and lightly coat with nonstick cooking spray. Set aside.

2. IN A LARGE BOWL, whisk yogurt, sugar, melted butter, egg and vanilla until well combined. Fold in flour, chocolate chips, baking powder, baking soda and salt. Mix just until flour disappears.

3. PLACE A LARGE SPOONFUL of batter into each muffin cup. Spoon 1 heaping teaspoon Nutella in the center of each muffin and top with remaining batter to fill the muffin cup. Bake for 20–22 minutes, until muffin springs back when gently touched. Cool completely before drizzling with glaze.

4. FOR THE GLAZE, in a small bowl, whisk icing sugar, Nutella and milk until smooth. Drizzle over cooled muffins.

"Your body is not a temple, it's an amusement park. Enjoy the ride."

Anthony Bourdain

If you haven't figured it out yet, I love my sister. She's got my back and more important, she's supportive of my stomach. With these Double Cranberry & White Chocolate Scones, Lisa has taken my favorite cookie (our signature White Chocolate Cranberry from our first cookbook, *Bite Me*) and transformed it into a superb scone. Fresh, tart cranberries are balanced with creamy white chocolate, chewy dried cranberries and a sweet and tart lemon glaze, resulting in a most flavorful, flaky scone. Thanks to Loyal Lisa, you too can have brunch in the bag with a batch of these buttery beauties.

DOUBLE CRANBERRY & WHITE CHOCOLATE SCONES

1. PREHEAT OVEN to 400°F and line a baking sheet with parchment paper. In a large bowl, combine flour, sugar, baking powder, lemon zest and salt. Cut in butter using your fingers until the butter is in pea-sized crumbs. Stir in fresh cranberries, dried cranberries and white chocolate. In a small bowl, whisk cream, egg and vanilla. Add to flour mixture, stirring with a wooden spoon until moistened.

2. PLACE DOUGH onto a lightly floured surface and knead 4 times. Do not overwork the dough. Form into a flat circle, about 6–8 inches round. Cut into 8 large wedges and place on prepared baking sheet, leaving 1 inch between scones. Bake scones until golden on the bottom, 16–18 minutes. Remove from oven and cool before glazing.

3. FOR THE GLAZE, in a small saucepan, heat white chocolate and corn syrup over low heat. Stir constantly until melted and stir in cream. Remove from heat and stir in lemon zest. Drizzle over scones before glaze hardens.

 Fresh cranberries can last a year in the freezer and up to 2 months tightly wrapped in the fridge.

MAKES	8 large scones
PREP	20 minutes
COOK	20 minutes

2	cups flour
¼	cup sugar
1	tbsp baking powder
2	tsp lemon zest
½	tsp kosher salt
½	cup cold butter, cut into pieces
1	cup roughly chopped fresh cranberries
½	cup dried cranberries
½	cup white chocolate chips
½	cup heavy cream
1	egg
½	tsp vanilla extract

WHITE CHOCOLATE LEMON GLAZE

3	oz white chocolate, chopped
2	tbsp light corn syrup
1	tbsp heavy cream
½	tsp lemon zest

We aren't math mavens, but we've come up with a winning equation for when life gives you lemons: 12 buns in the oven + 1 sticky situation = countless oohs and aahs. Yes, siree, in this perfect citrus twist on the cinnamon classic, we've baked up sweet and tart sticky buns—world-class, soft and ambrosial dough is surrounded by fresh and fantastic lemon filling and glaze. So the next time you're stumped, remember this finger-licking formula for a delectable dessert.

> "We are in the stickiest situation since Sticky the stick insect got stuck on a sticky bun."
>
> Rowan Atkinson

LUSCIOUS LEMON STICKY BUNS

1. FOR THE DOUGH, in a medium bowl, combine warm milk and ½ teaspoon sugar. Sprinkle yeast over top and let sit 5–10 minutes until foamy. In the bowl of an electric mixer, combine flour, sugar, butter, lemon zest and salt. Using a dough hook, mix on low speed. Add eggs, vanilla and yeast mixture. Continue to mix on low speed until incorporated. Turn mixer to medium speed, allowing it to knead dough for 4–5 minutes. Remove dough from mixer, and on a lightly floured surface, roll into a large ball. Place in a large bowl that has been lightly coated with nonstick cooking spray. Cover with plastic wrap and let rise in a warm place until doubled in size, about 1 hour.

2. FOR THE LEMON FILLING, in a small bowl, combine sugar, lemon zest and vanilla extract. Set aside.

3. FOR THE LEMON GLAZE, in a medium bowl, whisk sugar, corn syrup, lemon juice, melted butter and lemon zest. Pour half the lemon glaze in a lightly greased 13- × 9-inch baking dish. Set remaining lemon glaze aside.

MAKES	12 sticky buns
PREP	20 minutes (+2 hours rising time)
COOK	35 minutes

SWEET DOUGH

1	cup whole milk, warmed
½	tsp sugar
1	package (¼ oz) active dry yeast (not rapid rise)
4	cups flour
½	cup sugar
½	cup butter, softened
1	tsp lemon zest
1	tsp kosher salt
2	eggs, room temperature
1	tsp vanilla extract

You're not done yet . . . see next page →

LEMON FILLING

¾   cup sugar
1   tbsp lemon zest
½   tsp vanilla extract

LEMON GLAZE

¾   cup sugar
6   tbsp corn syrup
1½ tbsp fresh lemon juice
1½ tbsp melted butter
2   tsp lemon zest

¼   cup butter, softened

4. ON A LIGHTLY FLOURED SURFACE, roll dough into a ¼-inch-thick rectangle that measures around 14 × 20 inches. Brush softened butter on the surface of the dough and sprinkle with lemon filling. Roll the dough into a fairly tight cylinder and press along the edges to seal. Cut into 12 equal pieces and place in prepared baking dish. Pour remaining glaze evenly over rolls, cover with a cloth and let rise in a warm area for 1 hour.

5. PREHEAT OVEN to 350°F. Bake sticky buns for 28–30 minutes, until golden. Remove from oven and let sit for 5 minutes before flipping buns out. Note: Don't let them sit too long in the pan or the gooey goodness in the bottom of the pan will firm up too much.

Before you start wondering, let me explain why this luscious loaf is hanging out in the brunch section. While it is cake, it's shaped like a loaf, which is otherwise known as bread. Who doesn't eat bread at breakfast? We do. And, while this super-moist loaf is loaded with creamy, rich white chocolate, it's also bursting with fresh raspberries, one of the healthiest fruits around. Who doesn't like fruit for breakfast? We do. Finally, this beautiful brunch bread is a dessert lover's dream, perfect for beginner bakers, quick and simple to get from pantry to oven. Who doesn't love quick and simple? We do. See? Perspective is everything.

WHITE CHOCOLATE RASPBERRY LOAF

1. PREHEAT OVEN to 325°F. Coat a 9- × 5-inch loaf pan with nonstick cooking spray.

2. IN AN ELECTRIC MIXER, cream butter and sugar on medium speed until well blended. Add the eggs one at a time, beating well after each addition. On low speed, add vanilla, lemon juice and sour cream and mix until combined. Add flour, baking powder, baking soda and salt, mixing just until flour disappears.

3. IN A SMALL BOWL, toss raspberries with 1 teaspoon flour. Fold into batter with white chocolate chips. Pour into prepared loaf pan and bake for 70–75 minutes, until golden around the edges. Let cool in pan for 10 minutes before removing. Once cool, drizzle with melted white chocolate.

 Dusting raspberries with flour keeps them from sinking in the batter.

MAKES 10–12 slices
PREP 15 minutes
COOK 1 hour, 10 minutes

½ cup butter, room temperature
1 cup sugar
2 eggs
1 tsp vanilla extract
2 tbsp fresh lemon juice
¾ cup sour cream
2 cups flour
1 tsp baking powder
½ tsp baking soda
¼ tsp kosher salt
1¼ cups fresh raspberries
1 tsp flour
1 cup white chocolate chips

2 oz white chocolate, melted, for drizzling

Spoiler alert. There's no Easter Bunny and this coffee cake loaf has no coffee in it. Baking blasphemy? Nope. In keeping with other sour cream coffee cakes, this perfect-for-brunch loaf serves up a moist sour cream cake layered and topped with a crunchy cinnamon and brown sugar streusel. A slice of this simply spectacular sweet bread is guaranteed to perk up any coffee break, tea time or snack attack.

SOUR CREAM COFFEE CAKE LOAF

SERVES 10
PREP 20 minutes
COOK 1 hour, 5 minutes

. . . .

STREUSEL FILLING & TOPPING

1   cup flour
½   cup brown sugar
1   tsp ground cinnamon
¼   tsp kosher salt
½   cup cold butter, cut into
     pieces

1¼   cups sugar
¾   cup butter, room temperature
2   eggs
1   tsp vanilla extract
1   cup sour cream
2¼   cups flour
1   tsp baking powder
½   tsp baking soda
½   tsp kosher salt

1. FOR THE STREUSEL FILLING and topping, in a medium bowl, combine flour, brown sugar, cinnamon and salt. Cut in butter with a fork until mixture is crumbly and set aside.

2. PREHEAT OVEN to 350°F. Coat a 10-inch loaf pan with nonstick cooking spray. Using an electric mixer, cream sugar and butter on medium speed until well combined. Add eggs one at a time, beating until light and fluffy. Add vanilla and sour cream, mixing until combined. On low speed, add flour, baking powder, baking soda and salt, mixing just until flour disappears.

3. POUR HALF THE BATTER into prepared loaf pan. Sprinkle with ¾ cup of streusel and top with remaining batter. Finish by evenly sprinkling remaining streusel over top. Bake for 65–70 minutes. Remove from oven and let cool for 10 minutes before removing from pan.

"In Seattle you haven't had enough coffee
until you can thread a sewing machine
while it's running."

Jeff Bezos

As our tradition goes, we break bread with our loved ones on Friday nights, when candles are lit, nectar of the gods (aka Manischewitz wine) is poured (I take a double of this splendidly syrupy adult grape juice) and warm challah (pronounced HAH-luh) bread is cut. While our dad often tries to save some of the braided bread for Saturday morning French toast, with this challah, there's no hope. No matter how you slice it, there isn't a crumb left of this golden and aromatic (so intoxicating, the scent should be bottled) egg bread, with its sweet honey-infused center and lacquer-like crust topped with crunchy streusel. Can I get an amen?

CHALLAH WITH SWEET CRUMBLE TOPPING

1. PLACE WARM WATER in a medium bowl and stir in 1 tablespoon sugar. Sprinkle yeast on top, cover and leave for 10 minutes. In a small bowl, whisk eggs, honey, vegetable oil and salt. Place 3 cups flour in the bowl of an electric mixer. Once the yeast mixture doubles in volume, stir and add to flour on low speed. Add egg mixture and combine well on low speed. Add ½ cup more of flour until dough starts to come together in a ball. Add flour as needed. Knead dough on medium speed for 4–5 minutes, until the dough is smooth and no longer sticky. Place dough in a lightly greased bowl and cover with a damp, clean cloth. Let it rise in a warm, draft-free place for 1 hour.

2. LINE A BAKING SHEET with parchment paper and set aside. After the dough has risen, punch it down to deflate it and remove air bubbles. Divide it into 3 equal pieces and roll into long ropes, about 20 inches long. Pinch the ends of the 3 ropes together firmly, braid them and tuck the ends under the loaf. Transfer to prepared baking sheet, cover with a dish towel and let rise 1 hour.

3. PREHEAT OVEN to 350°F. For the crumble topping, in a medium bowl, combine flour, sugar and margarine, mixing with your fingertips until crumbly. In a small bowl, whisk egg and salt together. Gently brush challah with beaten egg mixture and cover with crumble topping. Bake 35–38 minutes until the crust is golden and the bread has a hollow sound when tapped on the bottom. Cool before slicing.

MAKES	1 large challah
PREP	25 minutes (+2 hours rising time)
COOK	35 minutes

1 cup warm water
1 tbsp sugar
1 package (¼ oz) active dry yeast (not rapid rise)
2 eggs
¼ cup honey
¼ cup vegetable oil
1 tsp kosher salt
3½–4 cups flour

CRUMBLE TOPPING
½ cup flour
½ cup sugar
¼ cup margarine
1 egg, lightly beaten
¼ tsp kosher salt

 Hot water kills yeast. One way to tell if the temperature is right is to test a few drops on your forearm—if it doesn't feel hot or cold, it's the correct temperature.

MAKES 10–12 slices
PREP 25 minutes
COOK 1 hour

. . . .

CREAM CHEESE FILLING

6	oz cream cheese, room temperature
⅓	cup sugar
1	egg
½	tsp vanilla extract
2	tbsp heavy cream
1	tbsp flour

CARROT BREAD

1	cup sugar
¾	cup vegetable oil
⅓	cup brown sugar
2	eggs
1	tsp vanilla extract
½	cup buttermilk
2	cups flour
1	tsp baking powder
1	tsp baking soda
1	tsp ground cinnamon
½	tsp kosher salt
2	cups coarsely grated carrots

CREAM CHEESE GLAZE

2	tbsp butter, softened
2	oz cream cheese, softened
½	cup icing sugar
1	tbsp whole milk
½	tsp vanilla extract
½	cup chopped toasted walnuts (optional topping)

I can be lazy, but Lisa knows how to mobilize me. She either feigns a Donny Osmond sighting (watch me move!) or she uses the tried-and-true carrot-and-stick trick (she's the driver and I'm the mule), baking up this luscious Cream Cheese Swirled Carrot Bread (yes, there's an icing-like cream cheese swirl running through it) that's topped with a cream cheese glaze. One whiff of this cinnamon-spiced loaf and I'm off to the races, hoofing it to the nearest fork and plate. Moist and overrun with grated carrots, this delicious cream cheese-swirled-and-glazed quick bread tastes like carrot cake but is perfect for rise and shine time.

CREAM CHEESE SWIRLED CARROT BREAD

1. PREHEAT OVEN to 350°F. Coat a 10-inch loaf pan with nonstick cooking spray.

2. FOR THE CREAM CHEESE FILLING, using an electric mixer, combine cream cheese and sugar on medium speed. Scrape down sides of the bowl and add the egg and vanilla, mixing until combined. Add cream and flour, mixing until smooth. Set aside.

3. FOR THE CARROT BREAD, in a large mixing bowl, whisk sugar, vegetable oil, brown sugar, eggs and vanilla extract until well combined. Whisk in buttermilk until smooth. Gently stir in flour, baking powder, baking soda, cinnamon, salt and grated carrots. Do not overmix.

4. POUR HALF THE BATTER into prepared loaf pan. Spread cream cheese mixture evenly on top. Top with remaining batter and bake 60–65 minutes until a wooden skewer inserted in the center comes out with only a few moist crumbs (not wet). Remove from oven and let cool 10 minutes before removing from pan. Let cool completely before glazing.

5. FOR THE GLAZE, using an electric mixer, cream together butter, cream cheese, icing sugar, whole milk and vanilla until smooth. Pour glaze over cooled loaf and sprinkle with toasted walnuts, if desired.

"I've heard that hard work never killed anyone, but I say why take the chance?"

Ronald Reagan

Warning: you're going to go wild for this Graham Cracker Marshmallow Monkey Bread. Also known as sticky bread (for good reason, as you'll discover while licking your fingers) and pinch-me cake (don't know why, and please don't pinch me), monkey bread is sweet pull-apart bread that's baked in a Bundt pan. A S'mores-like delight, this brunch favorite is made of dough rolled in cinnamon sugar and sweet crumbs, piled among graham crackers and mini marshmallows and then baked to ooey gooey greatness. One bite and you'll immediately discover that we don't monkey around when it comes to serving up lip-smackin' sweets.

THE GREATEST GRAHAM CRACKER MARSHMALLOW MONKEY BREAD

SERVES 12
PREP 30 minutes
(+2 hours rising time, divided)
COOK 30 minutes

DOUGH

¼ cup warm water
1 tsp sugar
1 package (¼ oz) active dry yeast (not rapid rise)
¾ cup whole milk
¼ cup butter
¼ cup sugar
1 tsp kosher salt
2 eggs, room temperature
3½ cups flour

1. FOR THE DOUGH, in a small bowl, combine warm water and 1 teaspoon sugar. Sprinkle yeast on top, cover and set aside for 10 minutes. Combine milk and butter, and heat until butter is melted. Pour butter mixture into the bowl of an electric mixer. Using the dough hook attachment, add ¼ cup sugar, salt and eggs, mixing to combine. Stir yeast mixture and once it has doubled in volume, add to electric mixture. Add flour, mixing on low speed to combine. Once the flour is incorporated, mix on medium speed for 3 minutes to knead the dough. Remove from mixer, knead dough into a ball and place in a lightly greased bowl. Cover and let rise for 1 hour in a warm, draft-free spot.

2. GREASE the inside of a 10-inch Bundt pan.

3. FOR THE GRAHAM COATING, in a small bowl, combine graham cracker crumbs, brown sugar and cinnamon. In another small bowl, place the melted butter. Set aside.

4. TO PREPARE THE SWEET GLAZE, melt butter in a medium saucepan over medium-low heat. Whisk in brown sugar, corn syrup and salt. Whisking constantly, boil the mixture for 1 minute. Remove from heat, stir in heavy cream and pour half the glaze in the bottom of the prepared Bundt pan. Place 1 cup coarsely chopped graham crackers evenly over the glaze. Scatter 1 cup mini marshmallows over top the crackers. Set remaining glaze aside.

5. WHEN THE DOUGH HAS RISEN, punch down and lightly knead for 1 minute. Cut off golf-ball-sized pieces of dough and roll each piece into a ball. You should have about 40 balls. Lightly dip each dough ball into the melted butter and then roll in the graham crumb mixture. As you go, stack the balls of dough over the mini marshmallows in the pan. Once you have gone through about 20–22 balls, sprinkle remaining ½ cup chopped graham crackers and remaining ½ cup mini marshmallows. Continue stacking the balls until all the dough is used up. If remaining glaze has hardened, reheat gently and pour over the prepared dough balls. Cover the pan with a clean cloth and set in a warm place to rise for 1 hour.

6. PREHEAT OVEN to 350°F. Once the dough has doubled in size, bake for 28–30 minutes, or until golden brown. Remove from oven and allow to cool for 5 minutes. Run a knife around the edges for easy removal and carefully flip onto a serving plate.

. . . .

 To soften brown sugar, place it in an airtight container with a slice of white bread or slice of apple.

GRAHAM COATING

½ cup graham cracker crumbs
¼ cup brown sugar
¼ tsp ground cinnamon
⅓ cup melted butter

SWEET GLAZE

¼ cup butter
1 cup brown sugar
¼ cup corn syrup
Pinch kosher salt
2 tbsp heavy cream

1½ cups coarsely chopped graham crackers
1½ cups mini marshmallows

BE-ALL
& END-ALL

[DESSERTS]

I recently learned that cheesecake was served to athletes in the Olympics of 776 BC to give them energy. Yet another thing elite athletes and I have in common—we're both fueled by cheesecake. This rich Toffee Crunch Caramel Cheesecake is a winner. Crumbly graham cracker and toffee crust is layered with golden caramel sauce (which is also mixed into the batter) and smooth cheesecake filling and is finished with a sweet toffee and sour cream topping. Slice after luscious slice, this creamy cheesecake delivers high-octane power and gold-medal mouthfuls.

TOFFEE CRUNCH
CARAMEL CHEESECAKE

1. FOR THE CARAMEL SAUCE, in a medium saucepan, combine sugar and corn syrup over medium heat. Gently stir until all the sugar is melted. Continue to cook until caramel is a rich amber color. Remove from heat and stir in butter until melted. Add cream, return to heat, stirring, for 1 minute. Pour caramel in a glass dish to cool and set aside.

2. PREHEAT OVEN to 450°F. For the crust, in a medium bowl, combine graham cracker crumbs, brown sugar and melted butter. Press into the bottom and halfway up the sides of a 9-inch springform pan. Drizzle 6 tablespoons caramel sauce over the base of the crust and sprinkle with ¾ cup toffee bits. Place crust in freezer while preparing the filling.

3. FOR THE CHEESECAKE, using an electric mixer, combine cream cheese and sugar on medium speed for 2 minutes, until light and creamy. Add eggs one at a time, beating well after each addition. On low speed, add flour until combined. Add caramel sauce and vanilla, mixing just until incorporated.

SERVES	10–12
PREP	30 minutes
COOK	1 hour 20 minutes (+1 hour 30 minutes cooling and 3–24 hours refrigeration)

CARAMEL SAUCE

1	cup sugar
¼	cup light corn syrup
6	tbsp butter, softened
⅔	cup heavy cream, warmed

GRAHAM CRACKER CRUST

2	cups graham cracker crumbs
¼	cup brown sugar
½	cup melted butter
6	tbsp caramel sauce (recipe above)
¾	cup toffee bits

You're not done yet . . . see next page →

> "I'm gonna kill him, I swear. I'm gonna finish him like a cheesecake."
>
> Fat Amy, *Pitch Perfect*

CHEESECAKE

4   packages (8 oz each) cream cheese, room temperature
1¼ cups sugar
4   eggs
¼   cup flour
½   cup caramel sauce (recipe page 255)
1   tsp vanilla extract

TOPPING

1¼ cups sour cream
¼   cup sugar
1   tsp vanilla extract
¾   cup toffee bits

4. POUR INTO PREPARED CRUST. Bake 10 minutes in preheated oven. Without opening oven door, reduce temperature to 250°F. Continue to bake 60–65 minutes more. Remove cheesecake from oven and raise temperature to 350°F. Let cheesecake cool for 30 minutes before topping.

5. FOR THE TOPPING, in a medium bowl, whisk sour cream, sugar and vanilla extract together. Carefully run a knife around the cheesecake to loosen the sides. Spread topping evenly over cheesecake and bake for 5 minutes. Remove from oven and cool on a wire rack for 1 hour. Sprinkle the top of the cheesecake with remaining ¾ cup toffee bits and refrigerate for several hours or overnight before cutting. Serve with remaining caramel sauce.

I like to live on the edge, but thanks to my sister, my obit won't read "death by dough." Lisa, vexed by my years spent in the batter bowl knuckle-deep in raw cookie dough, has created this dessert just for me (and you), a creamy cheesecake studded with cookie dough morsels. While I devour slice after intoxicating slice of graham cracker crust topped with a cookie dough layer, followed by smooth cheesecake and decadent cookie dough bites, I know I'm sealing my fate as a gal contented by cheesecake.

DECADENT CHOCOLATE CHIP COOKIE DOUGH CHEESECAKE

1. PREHEAT OVEN to 450°F. Line the bottom of a 10-inch springform pan with parchment paper.

2. FOR THE GRAHAM CRUST, in a medium bowl, combine graham cracker crumbs, sugar and melted butter. Press into the bottom and halfway up the sides of the prepared pan. Place in the freezer until ready to use.

3. FOR THE COOKIE DOUGH, using an electric mixer on medium speed, cream the butter, sugar and brown sugar until well combined. Add vanilla extract. On low speed, add the flour, salt and mini chocolate chips. Mix just until combined.

4. PRESS 1¼ cups of the cookie dough mixture over the prepared graham crust and refrigerate. Roll remaining cookie dough into pea-sized balls and place on a baking sheet. Cover and refrigerate until ready to use.

5. FOR THE FILLING, using an electric mixer, beat the cream cheese and sugar on medium speed until smooth, making sure to scrape down the sides a few times. Add eggs one at a time, beating well after each addition. On low speed, add vanilla extract, flour and melted white chocolate, mixing just until blended.

6. POUR BATTER over graham crust and cookie dough layer. Scatter cookie dough bites over the top. Bake in preheated oven for 10 minutes. Reduce heat to 250°F and continue to bake 45–50 minutes more. The cheesecake is ready when the edges begin to brown slightly and the center is slightly wiggly. It will firm as it cools. Cool completely and then refrigerate 4 hours before serving.

SERVES 10–12
PREP 30 minutes
COOK 55 minutes
(+4 hours refrigeration)

. . . .

GRAHAM CRUST

2¼ cups graham cracker crumbs
¼ cup sugar
½ cup melted butter

COOKIE DOUGH

¾ cup butter, room temperature
½ cup sugar
½ cup brown sugar
1 tsp vanilla extract
1 cup flour
¼ tsp kosher salt
1 cup mini chocolate chips

WHITE CHOCOLATE CHEESECAKE

4 packages (8 oz each) cream cheese, room temperature
1¼ cups sugar
4 eggs
1 tsp vanilla extract
3 tbsp flour
6 oz white chocolate, melted

"I had a stick of Carefree gum, but it didn't work. I felt pretty good while I was blowing that bubble, but as soon as the gum lost its flavor, I was back to pondering my mortality."

Mitch Hedberg

> "Coffee and chocolate—
> the inventor of mocha
> should be sainted."
>
> Cherise Sinclair, *Hour of the Lion*

It's a well-known fact Lisa's a chocoholic. What is lesser known is that she's also a coffee fanatic. You (and me both) don't want to know her if she doesn't get her daily chocolate and coffee fix—she becomes a bristly bear. With that in mind, it's no wonder she came up with this cocoa and coffee collision, a Fudgy Chocolate Layer Cake with Coffee Frosting. Layers of rich, dark and moist chocolate cake are iced with a creamy coffee frosting, resulting in a decadent dessert guaranteed to satisfy all your (and her) cravings.

SERVES 10
PREP 25 minutes
COOK 25 minutes (+cooling and assembling cake)

. . . .

1   cup buttermilk
¾   cup vegetable oil
2   eggs
1   tsp vanilla extract
2   cups flour
2   cups sugar
¾   cup cocoa powder, sifted
2   tsp baking powder
1   tsp baking soda
½   tsp kosher salt
1   cup strong brewed or instant coffee, cooled slightly

COFFEE FROSTING

4   cups icing sugar
¾   cup butter, softened
2   tbsp cocoa powder, sifted
2   tbsp instant coffee granules
2   tbsp boiling water
1   tbsp whole milk

Semisweet chocolate, melted, for drizzling

FUDGY CHOCOLATE LAYER CAKE WITH COFFEE FROSTING

1. PREHEAT OVEN to 350°F. Coat two 9-inch round baking pans with non-stick cooking spray.

2. FOR THE CAKE, in an electric mixer using the whisk attachment, combine buttermilk, oil, eggs and vanilla on low speed. Add flour, sugar, cocoa powder, baking powder, baking soda and salt. Beat at medium speed for 2 minutes. On low speed, add coffee and continue to mix until batter is smooth.

3. DIVIDE BATTER EVENLY between prepared pans and bake 22–24 minutes. Remove from oven and let cool slightly before removing from pans. Let layers cool completely before frosting.

4. FOR THE FROSTING, using an electric mixer, cream icing sugar, butter and cocoa powder on low speed. In a small bowl, combine coffee and boiling water. Add coffee and milk to frosting. Increase speed to medium and beat until frosting is smooth.

5. TO ASSEMBLE, cut each layer in half, ending up with 4 thin layers. Place 1 layer on a serving plate and top with 1 cup frosting, spreading evenly. Top with a second layer and 1 cup frosting. Repeat with the third layer and 1 cup frosting. Finish the top of the cake with the final layer. Frost sides and top with remaining frosting. Drizzle melted chocolate over top to garnish.

I know I shouldn't be doing this, but we've already established I have a big mouth. Much like giving away the magician's secret (you can't bend a spoon with your mind), I'm going to tell you how my sorcerer sister has managed to Houdini a lemon cake into something so delicious it'll make you levitate. Ready? The secret ingredient is pudding. Bet you didn't see that coming. The abracadabra addition of vanilla pudding mix elevates the buttery, lemony fresh flavors to sweet and tangy heights, and, along with a smooth lemon cream cheese frosting, the result is one very spellbinding dessert. Now that I've broken the Chefs' Code, who's going to stop Lisa from sawing me in half?

FROSTED LEMON PUDDING LAYER CAKE

1. PREHEAT OVEN to 350°F. Coat 2 (8-inch) baking pans with nonstick cooking spray.

2. IN A MEDIUM BOWL, combine flour, lemon zest, baking powder, baking soda and salt. Set aside.

3. USING AN ELECTRIC MIXER, cream butter and sugar on medium speed. Add eggs one at a time, beating well after each addition. Add vanilla. On low speed, add vegetable oil and vanilla pudding powder, mixing until well combined.

4. IN A SMALL BOWL, combine milk and lemon juice. Alternate adding flour mixture and milk mixture, beginning and ending with flour mixture.

5. POUR BATTER into prepared baking pans and bake 32 minutes, or until a toothpick inserted into the center of the cake comes out clean. Allow cake layers to cool completely before frosting.

SERVES   10
PREP   25 minutes
COOK   35 minutes (+cooling and assembling cake)

. . . .

LEMON CAKE

2   cups flour
1   tbsp lemon zest
1   tsp baking powder
1   tsp baking soda
½   tsp kosher salt
½   cup butter, softened
1¼   cups sugar
3   eggs
1   tsp vanilla extract
¼   cup vegetable oil
1   package (3.4 oz) instant vanilla pudding powder
1   cup whole milk
¼   cup fresh lemon juice

You're not done yet . . . see next page →

LEMON CREAM CHEESE FROSTING

4   oz cream cheese, room
     temperature
½   cup butter, room temperature
2½   cups icing sugar
2   tbsp fresh lemon juice
1   tsp lemon zest
Pinch kosher salt

Lemon zest, for decoration

6. FOR THE FROSTING, in an electric mixer, beat cream cheese and butter on medium speed until well combined. On low speed, slowly add icing sugar, lemon juice, lemon zest and salt. Continue to mix until a smooth consistency is reached, scraping down sides of the bowl once or twice.

7. TO ASSEMBLE, place 1 layer on a serving plate and top with 1 cup frosting, spreading evenly. Top with remaining cake layer, frost top with remaining frosting and decorate with lemon zest.

Turn this into an orange pudding cake by substituting orange zest for the lemon zest and orange juice for the lemon juice.

Get ready to take the sweet-and-salty combination to new heights with this jaw-dropping Salted Caramel Pecan Layer Cake. Four layers of moist vanilla cake are filled with creamy salted caramel frosting, sprinkled with crunchy pecans and drizzled with salted caramel sauce. Sweet and nutty flavors (reminiscent of pecan pie), along with gooey homemade salted caramel sauce (a pinch of sea salt amazingly enhances the richness of caramel) make this decadent layer cake the consummate cake, the summit where sweet and salty meet.

SALTED CARAMEL PECAN LAYER CAKE

1. FOR THE CARAMEL SAUCE, place sugar in a medium saucepan over medium heat. Stir continuously until the sugar is completely melted and a deep amber color. Remove from heat and stir in butter until melted. Add cream and sea salt (mixture will bubble up) and return to heat for 1 minute, stirring constantly until smooth. Remove from heat and pour into a glass container to cool completely.

2. PREHEAT OVEN to 350°F. Coat two 8-inch round cake pans with non-stick cooking spray and cover the bottom of each pan with parchment paper.

3. FOR THE VANILLA CAKE, in a large bowl, whisk sugar and eggs until slightly thickened. Add vegetable oil, vanilla extract and sour cream. Whisk until well combined. Using a wooden spoon, stir in the flour, baking powder, baking soda and salt, mixing just until combined.

4. DIVIDE THE BATTER evenly into prepared pans. Bake 30–33 minutes, or until a toothpick inserted in the center comes out clean. Let cool for 10 minutes before removing cakes from the pans. Cool completely before frosting.

SERVES	10–12
PREP	20 minutes
COOK	30 minutes (+cooling and assembling cake)

SALTED CARAMEL SAUCE

1	cup sugar
⅓	cup butter, softened
½	cup heavy cream, warmed
½	tsp flaky sea salt

VANILLA CAKE

2	cups sugar
3	eggs, room temperature
1	cup vegetable oil
2	tsp vanilla extract
1	cup sour cream
2½	cups flour
1	tsp baking powder
½	tsp baking soda
½	tsp kosher salt

You're not done yet . . . see next page →

5. FOR THE CARAMEL FROSTING, using an electric mixer, cream butter, icing sugar, ½ cup of the caramel sauce and milk on low speed to combine. Once incorporated, turn mixer to medium speed until frosting is smooth.

6. TO ASSEMBLE, slice each cake layer in half to make 4 layers. Place 1 layer on a serving plate, spread with ½ cup frosting and drizzle with a few spoonfuls of caramel sauce. Top with the second layer, spread ½ cup frosting and ¾ cup toasted pecans and drizzle with a few spoonfuls of caramel sauce. Top with the third layer and spread with ½ cup frosting and a few spoonfuls of caramel sauce. Top with final cake layer and spread remaining frosting over the top and sides of the cake. Drizzle caramel sauce over top and sprinkle remaining ½ cup pecans around the top of the cake to garnish. Refrigerate until ready to serve.

CARAMEL FROSTING

1   cup butter, softened
4   cups icing sugar
½   cup caramel sauce (recipe page 255)
3   tbsp whole milk

1¼ cups toasted, chopped pecans

"Desserts are like mistresses.
They are bad for you. So if you are having one,
you might as well have two."

Chef Alain Ducasse

What do *The Wizard of Oz* and Lisa's pecan pie have in common? They're classics that shouldn't be remade. Like, ever. So, when Lisa said she was going to tinker with her famous pecan pie, you can imagine my displeasure. How could she possibly improve upon the perfection of her buttery, flaky crust or sweet and gooey pecan filling? Well, clearly there's no place like Lisa's kitchen, because she's done it again—she's taken her scrumptious Southern pie and made it even better with the surprise addition of creamy white chocolate blanketing the crust and drizzled atop this primo, picture-perfect pie. I'm eating my (white chocolate) words, over and over and over again.

PS: A note to all casting agents: Lisa thinks I'd be a great Wicked Witch of the West.

SERVES 8–10

PREP 30 minutes

COOK 1 hour, 5 minutes
(+3 hours to set)

. . . .

BUTTER CRUST

1½ cups flour

½ tsp kosher salt

2 tbsp sugar

½ cup butter, cold

4 tbsp ginger ale

CHOCOLATE PECAN FILLING

¼ cup melted butter

4 eggs

¾ cup corn syrup

½ cup brown sugar

1 tsp vanilla extract

¼ tsp kosher salt

1¼ cups coarsely chopped pecans

1¼ cups chopped white chocolate

1¼ cups pecan halves

2 oz white chocolate, for drizzling

GOOEY WHITE CHOCOLATE PECAN PIE

1. FOR THE CRUST, preheat the oven to 450°F. In a medium bowl, combine flour, salt and sugar. Using your fingertips, cut butter into flour mixture until it resembles coarse crumbs. Gradually drizzle ginger ale over flour mixture. Toss the mixture to moisten until dough starts to come together. Gently gather dough into a ball.

2. ON A LIGHTLY FLOURED SURFACE, roll dough out into a circle that is 1 inch larger all around than an upside-down 9-inch pie plate. Once rolled, ease dough into a 9-inch pie plate. Fold overhanging dough into itself to form a decorative rim.

3. TRANSFER TO FREEZER for 10 minutes. Bake for 6 minutes, remove from oven, reduce oven temperature to 350°F and let cool slightly.

4. FOR THE FILLING, in a medium bowl, whisk melted butter, eggs, corn syrup, brown sugar, vanilla extract and salt. Sprinkle coarsely chopped pecans and 1¼ cups chopped white chocolate evenly over the bottom of the pie crust. Pour filling mixture over top and top with pecan halves. Place on a baking sheet and bake for 55–60 minutes. Check after 45 minutes, and if the crust is getting too dark, cover with strips of foil. Remove from oven and cool completely before serving. Allow at least 3 hours for pie to set.

"I don't want to spend my life not having good food going into my pie hole. That hole was made for pies."

Paula Deen

Standing in Lisa's kitchen, I'm constantly forced to make snap decisions. Do I give her the 10 feet of space she demands or do I snuggle up close and make her cringe? Do I feign interest in the origins of the olive oil she's using or do I take a nap with my eyes open? All these dilemmas are often compounded by the do-I-eat-brownies-or-pie predicament. Now, thanks to this super-easy and decadent dessert, I get to devour both. With a buttery graham cracker crust beneath layers of fudgy brownies and gooey toasted marshmallows, the only thing I'm left wondering is how much of this delicious brownie-pie hybrid can I chow down on before Lisa cuts me off?

"I don't think I've ever seen pie advertised. That's how you know it's good. They advertise ice cream and other desserts. They advertise the bejeezus out of yogurt, but I haven't seen one pie commercial."

Adam Carolla

EASY FUDGE BROWNIE & TOASTED MARSHMALLOW PIE

1. PREHEAT OVEN to 350°F. Coat a 9-inch pie plate with nonstick cooking spray.

2. FOR THE CRUST, in a small bowl, combine graham cracker crumbs, melted butter and sugar. Press mixture into the bottom and up the sides of pie plate. Set aside.

3. FOR THE BROWNIE FILLING, in a large bowl, whisk melted butter, sugar, brown sugar, eggs and vanilla for 1–2 minutes. Stir in flour, cocoa and salt.

4. POUR BATTER over prepared crust. Bake for 38–40 minutes and remove from oven. Turn oven to broil and top brownie pie with mini marshmallows. Place pie under broiler, watching closely as marshmallows can burn quickly.

SERVES   8–10
PREP   10 minutes
COOK   40 minutes

GRAHAM CRUST
1¼ cups graham cracker crumbs
⅓   cup butter, melted
¼   cup sugar

BROWNIE FILLING
¾   cup butter, melted
¾   cup sugar
¾   cup brown sugar
2   eggs
½   tsp vanilla extract
¾   cup flour
½   cup cocoa powder, sifted
½   tsp kosher salt

2   cups mini marshmallows

SERVES 8–10

PREP 30 minutes (+1 hour soak time)

COOK 50 minutes

. . . .

BREAD PUDDING

14 cups cubed French bread or challah bread
3   cups whole milk
1   cup heavy cream
½   cup brown sugar
6   eggs
1   tbsp vanilla extract
1   tsp ground cinnamon
½   tsp kosher salt

PECAN CRUNCH

1½ cups chopped pecans
1   cup flour
¾   cup brown sugar
¼   tsp ground cinnamon
½   cup butter, softened

PRALINE SAUCE

½   cup brown sugar
½   tsp ground cinnamon
¼   tsp kosher salt
½   cup butter
½   cup heavy cream, warmed
½   cup chopped toasted pecans
1   tsp vanilla extract
½   tsp fresh lemon juice

Want to try the best thing since sliced bread? This divine Bread Pudding with Pecan Crunch & Praline Sauce is it, a superbly comforting and classic dessert. Best made using day-old loaves, cubed bread is soaked in a creamy brown sugar, vanilla and cinnamon custard, topped with crunchy pecan streusel and baked until soft in the center, golden and crusty on the outside. Served warm and finished with a buttery-sweet praline sauce (and a scoop of vanilla ice cream to boot), the proof that this is a soul-satisfying, decadent dessert is, as they say, in the pudding.

WARM BREAD PUDDING WITH PECAN CRUNCH & PRALINE SAUCE

1. FOR THE BREAD PUDDING, place cubed bread in a lightly greased 13- × 9-inch baking dish. In a large bowl, whisk milk, cream, brown sugar, eggs, vanilla, cinnamon and salt. Pour over bread cubes, toss gently and let sit at room temperature for 1 hour.

2. TO PREPARE THE PECAN CRUNCH, in a medium bowl, combine pecans, flour, brown sugar and cinnamon. Add butter and mix until crumbly. Sprinkle pecan crunch over bread pudding.

3. PREHEAT OVEN to 350°F. Bake 45–50 minutes, until set and golden on top. Serve warm with praline sauce.

4. FOR THE PRALINE SAUCE, in a medium saucepan, whisk brown sugar, cinnamon and salt. Add butter and whisk over medium heat until smooth. Whisk in cream and simmer the mixture for 4–5 minutes, stirring frequently. Remove saucepan from heat and stir in pecans, vanilla and lemon juice. Transfer mixture to a glass bowl and cool to room temperature before serving.

"Avoid those who don't like bread and children."

Swiss proverb

I'm a true middle child (or so I've been told), one whose first words were, "No likey." While I still have some trouble flying under the radar (Lisa and big bro Ken are pros and never got caught up in my 1985 attempted vodka heist from our parents' liquor cabinet, or the 1988 "Who dented the car?" fiasco), I "likey" lots these days, especially these classically Southern Red Velvet Cupcakes. How much? So much that I didn't care when I got caught red-handed digging into a dozen of these beauties, trailing crumbs of moist, vibrant, chocolate-flavored cupcakes topped with a smooth white cream cheese frosting. Seems I still can't keep my nose (or mouth) out of trouble.

MAKES 12 cupcakes
PREP   20 minutes
COOK   20 minutes
       (+cooling time)

RED VELVET CUPCAKES

1½	cups flour
2	tbsp cocoa powder
½	tsp baking powder
½	tsp baking soda
½	tsp kosher salt
½	cup butter, room temperature
1	cup sugar
2	eggs
6	tbsp vegetable oil
2	tsp white vinegar
1	tsp vanilla extract
2	tsp flavorless red food coloring
¾	cup buttermilk

CREAM CHEESE FROSTING

4	oz cream cheese, room temperature
¼	cup butter, room temperature
2	cups icing sugar
2	tbsp whole milk
1	tsp vanilla extract

RED VELVET CUPCAKES
WITH CREAM CHEESE FROSTING

1. PREHEAT OVEN to 350°F. Line 12 muffin cups with paper liners and spray with nonstick cooking spray.

2. FOR THE CUPCAKES, in a medium bowl, sift flour, cocoa powder, baking powder, baking soda and salt. Set aside.

3. USING AN ELECTRIC MIXER, cream butter and sugar on medium speed. Add eggs one at a time, beating well after each addition. Add vegetable oil, white vinegar and vanilla extract, mixing until light and fluffy. On low speed, add red food coloring. Alternate adding flour mixture and buttermilk, beginning and ending with the flour, mixing just until flour disappears. Be careful not to overmix.

4. FILL PREPARED MUFFIN CUPS ¾ full with batter. Bake 18–20 minutes, until a toothpick inserted comes out clean. Cool cupcakes before frosting.

5. FOR THE CREAM CHEESE FROSTING, in an electric mixer, combine cream cheese, butter and icing sugar on low speed. Once combined, increase to medium speed, add milk and vanilla and beat until the frosting has the desired consistency. Spread frosting on cooled cupcakes.

"Mini-cupcakes? As in the mini version of regular cupcakes? Which is already a mini version of cake? Honestly, where does it end with you people?"

Kevin, *The Office*

Folks, it's finally time to put the cupcakes-are-a-passing-fad debate to rest, OK? Really, where do you think these heavenly handheld bundles of gratifying goodness are going? Nowhere other than into our mouths. These moist banana and chocolate chip cupcakes topped with smooth and creamy banana frosting deliver a delicious duo of tastes: bananas and chocolate. So, cupcake craze naysayers, time to pack up your soap boxes and move on—we hear macaroon madness is coming to an end . . .

BANANA CHOCOLATE CHIP CUPCAKES WITH BANANA FROSTING

MAKES 18 cupcakes
PREP 20 minutes
COOK 20 minutes (+cooling time)

BANANA CHOCOLATE CHIP CUPCAKES

½ cup butter, softened
¾ cup sugar
¾ cup brown sugar
2 eggs
1 tsp vanilla extract
1 tbsp fresh lemon juice
⅓ cup sour cream
1¾ cups (about 4–5) mashed ripe bananas
2 cups flour
1 tsp baking soda
½ tsp kosher salt
1 cup mini chocolate chips

BANANA FROSTING

¼ cup butter, softened
½ cup mashed ripe bananas
1 tsp fresh lemon juice
3½ cups icing sugar

1. PREHEAT OVEN to 350°F. Line 18 muffin cups with paper liners and spray with nonstick cooking spray.

2. FOR THE CUPCAKES, using an electric mixer, cream butter, sugar and brown sugar on medium speed until light and fluffy. Add eggs one at a time, beating well after each addition. Add vanilla, lemon juice and sour cream, mixing until well combined. On low speed, add mashed bananas, flour, baking soda, salt and mini chocolate chips. Mix until all ingredients are combined.

3. SPOON BATTER into prepared cupcake liners, filling each one ¾ full. Bake 20–22 minutes, or until a toothpick inserted in the center comes out clean. Cool completely before frosting.

4. FOR THE FROSTING, in an electric mixer, combine butter, mashed bananas, lemon juice and icing sugar on low speed. Once combined, beat on medium speed until a smooth consistency. Spread frosting on cooled cupcakes.

 Did you know that mosquitoes are more likely to bite you after you've eaten a banana?

The crisp is the Dalai Lama of desserts. How so? It's the most popular and forgiving. Mess up the measurements? No problem. Scared to roll a piecrust? Crisps are crustless. Hey, you don't even need major knife skills—if you can work a peeler, you can make a crisp. While exceptional, this Golden Apple Crisp with Salted Caramel Sauce is no exception—so easy to bake, even the wannabe baker will look like a world-class chef. A base layer of sweet and tender cinnamon apples is drizzled with homemade salted caramel sauce and nestled beneath a delectably crisp and crumbly top, delivering forkful after forkful of bliss-filled bites.

> "Ducking for apples— change one letter and it's the story of my life."
> Dorothy Parker

GOLDEN APPLE CRISP WITH SALTED CARAMEL SAUCE

1. PREHEAT OVEN to 350°F and coat a 13- × 9-inch baking dish with non-stick cooking spray.

2. FOR THE SALTED CARAMEL SAUCE, place sugar in a medium saucepan over medium heat. Whisk as sugar melts, until sugar is completely melted and turns amber in color. Immediately stir in butter and whisk until melted. Remove from heat and add cream and sea salt. Transfer to a glass bowl and cool to room temperature.

3. FOR THE OAT TOPPING, in a medium bowl, combine flour, oats, brown sugar, cinnamon and salt. Cut in the butter using your fingertips or a fork, until the mixture resembles coarse crumbs. Set aside.

4. FOR THE APPLE FILLING, in a large bowl, toss apples with brown sugar, lemon juice, flour and cinnamon. Pour mixture into prepared baking dish. Drizzle ½ cup salted caramel sauce over apple slices and sprinkle with oat topping.

5. BAKE until apples are bubbling and topping is golden brown, 40–45 minutes. Allow to cool 15 minutes before serving. Serve with vanilla ice cream and remaining caramel sauce.

SERVES	8
MAKES	1¼ cups caramel sauce
PREP	30 minutes
COOK	40 minutes (+15 minute cooling time)

SALTED CARAMEL SAUCE
- 1 cup sugar
- ⅓ cup butter, cubed
- ½ cup heavy cream, warmed
- 1 tsp flaky sea salt

CRISP OAT TOPPING
- 1½ cups flour
- 1½ cups old-fashioned oats
- 1 cup brown sugar
- 1 tsp ground cinnamon
- ½ tsp flaky sea salt
- ¾ cup butter, cut into small pieces

APPLE CINNAMON FILLING
- 10 Granny Smith apples, peeled and sliced
- 2 tbsp brown sugar
- 2 tbsp fresh lemon juice
- 1 tbsp flour
- ½ tsp ground cinnamon

We've been known to amend expressions to suit our needs. Thanks to this simple recipe, forget your cake—you can have your crumble *and* your pie *and* eat them too. These Blueberry Pie Crumble Bars deliver the best of both worlds—the creamy pie-like filling is bursting with juicy blueberries, and the buttery sweet streusel topping delivers the coveted crumble cover. No tricky crust to navigate (this one has a no-brainer graham bottom), and no canned filling (fresh blueberries and lemon!), this delicious dessert is as easy as . . . bars.

EASY BLUEBERRY PIE CRUMBLE BARS

MAKES	20–24 bars
PREP	10 minutes
COOK	45 minutes (+1 hour cooling time)

GRAHAM CRUST
2   cups graham cracker crumbs
¼   cup brown sugar
½   cup melted butter

CREAMY BLUEBERRY FILLING
4   cups fresh blueberries
1   tbsp cornstarch
1½   tsp lemon zest
1   cup sour cream
¾   cup sugar
2   eggs
2   tbsp flour
½   tsp vanilla extract

CRUMBLE TOP
1   cup flour
1   cup sugar
½   cup melted butter

1. PREHEAT OVEN to 350°F. Coat a 13- × 9-inch baking pan with nonstick cooking spray. Line the bottom of the pan with parchment paper for easy removal.

2. FOR THE CRUST, in a medium bowl, combine graham crumbs and brown sugar. Mix in melted butter until well combined.

3. PRESS THE MIXTURE evenly over the bottom of the prepared baking pan. Bake crust for 8 minutes. Remove from oven and set aside to cool slightly.

4. FOR THE BLUEBERRY FILLING, in a medium bowl, toss blueberries with cornstarch and lemon zest. In a large bowl, whisk sour cream, sugar, eggs, flour and vanilla until well combined. Fold in blueberry mixture and pour into prepared crust.

5. FOR THE CRUMBLE TOP, in a medium bowl, combine flour, sugar and melted butter until streusel is crumbly. Sprinkle over blueberry filling and bake for 35 minutes until top is golden. Cool for 1 hour before serving. These bars are best stored refrigerated.

"I don't return fruit. Fruit is a gamble.
I know that going in."

Jerry Seinfeld, *Seinfeld*

I had an awesome childhood. When I wasn't forcing Lisa into mass production at her Easy-Bake Oven, I was making her whistle while eating peanut butter and crackers. Though to this day she hates whistling (and people who whistle), she learned both the beauty of baking and the pleasure of peanut butter from her big sis (thank me later), resulting in these Peanut Butter & Jam Bars. Sweet and nutty, these heavenly bars have a graham cracker and peanut butter crust that's topped with fruity strawberry jam and finished with a peanut butter crumb topping. Simple to make and even easier to devour, if this classic combo of pb & j doesn't have you whistlin' "Dixie," not sure what will.

PEANUT BUTTER & JAM BARS

1. PREHEAT OVEN to 350°F. Coat a 13- × 9-inch baking pan with nonstick cooking spray and cover the bottom of the pan with parchment paper. Using an electric mixer, cream butter and sugar on medium speed until combined. Add peanut butter and continue to mix until light and creamy. Add egg and vanilla, mixing well. On low speed, add flour, graham cracker crumbs, peanuts, baking powder and salt. Mix just until combined.

2. PRESS DOUGH over the bottom of prepared baking pan. Place in freezer for 20 minutes. Remove and bake crust for 15 minutes. Allow to cool for 5 minutes.

3. FOR THE PEANUT CRUMB TOPPING, in a medium bowl, combine flour, brown sugar, peanut butter, chopped peanuts and salt. With a pastry blender or your fingers, blend in butter until mixture is crumbly.

4. SPREAD STRAWBERRY JAM evenly over partially baked crust. Sprinkle peanut crumb topping over the jam. Bake 20 minutes, until golden. Cool, cover and refrigerate for 1 hour before cutting into bars.

It takes approximately 772 peanuts to make a 16.3 ounce jar of peanut butter.

MAKES	24 bars
PREP	20 minutes
	(+20 minutes in freezer)
COOK	40 minutes
	(+1 hour refrigeration)

PEANUT BUTTER CRUST
½	cup butter, room temperature
¾	cup sugar
¾	cup creamy peanut butter
1	egg
1	tsp vanilla extract
1	cup flour
½	cup graham cracker crumbs
½	cup chopped roasted peanuts
½	tsp baking powder
½	tsp kosher salt

PEANUT CRUMB TOPPING
1	cup flour
6	tbsp brown sugar
6	tbsp creamy peanut butter
¼	cup chopped roasted peanuts
Pinch kosher salt	
¼	cup butter, room temperature

1¾ cups strawberry jam

It's at times like this that I'm grateful that I get to employ the written, versus the spoken, word. If asked what kind of fudgy dense brownies these are, I'd likely say something about chocolaty toffee, but I'd leave out the most incredible part, the dulce de leche. Why? In the past, I've butchered the pronunciation of this sweet and delicious ingredient a million ways—doolchay-de-lesh, duuulche-de-letche, and the list goes on. Well, I'm proud to tell you that these DOOL-se de LE-che brownies are moist, awesome bites that'll leave your tongue twisted and taste buds thrilled.

DECADENT DULCE DE LECHE BROWNIES

MAKES	25–30 brownies
PREP	15 minutes
COOK	40 minutes

1   cup butter
1½   cups (12 oz) chopped semi-sweet chocolate
½   cup (4 oz) chopped unsweetened chocolate
1   cup sugar
1   cup brown sugar
4   eggs
2   egg yolks
2   tsp vanilla extract
1¼   cups flour
¼   cup unsweetened cocoa powder, sifted
½   tsp kosher salt
1¼   cups dulce de leche

1   cup mini chocolate chips
1   cup chopped Skor or Heath bar

1. PREHEAT OVEN to 325°F. Line a 13- × 9-inch baking pan with parchment paper, leaving overhang on all sides for easier removal of baked brownies.

2. FOR THE BROWNIES, place butter, semisweet chocolate and unsweetened chocolate in a microwave-safe bowl. Heat in the microwave for short intervals, stirring every 30 seconds, until completely melted. Let cool.

3. IN A LARGE BOWL, whisk sugar and brown sugar with cooled chocolate mixture. Add eggs, egg yolks and vanilla, whisking well to incorporate. Stir in flour, cocoa powder and salt until just combined.

4. POUR HALF THE BATTER into prepared pan. Spoon half the dulce de leche in large dollops over the brownie batter. Use a knife to swirl it through the batter. Pour the remaining brownie batter over top and spoon the remaining dulce de leche over the top. Swirl through with a knife again and sprinkle the brownies evenly with mini chocolate chips and chopped toffee bar. Bake 40–45 minutes.

5. ALLOW TO COOL completely. Cut around the edges to release from the side of the pan before refrigerating. Refrigerate for 2 hours for easier, cleaner cutting.

Dulce de leche, a rich, thick and decadent sauce, is a combination of milk and sugar that has been cooked until the sugars caramelize. Serve it spread on toast, with white cake, stirred in hot chocolate or sandwiched between cookies.

How do two brunettes raise the bar? We bake up a blondie bonanza, complete with these irresistible, melt-in-your-mouth Cookies & Cream Blondies. We've taken the classic blondie bar up a dreamy and delectable notch by filling it with chopped Oreo cookies, creamy white chocolate and deeply flavorful semisweet chocolate. Chewy and chunky, these blondies are bombshells: super-popular and totally beauteous.

CHUNKY COOKIES & CREAM BLONDIES

1. PREHEAT OVEN to 350°F. Coat a 13- × 9-inch baking pan with nonstick cooking spray. Line the bottom with parchment paper.

2. IN A SMALL BOWL, stir together flour, salt and baking soda. Using an electric mixer, cream together butter, sugar and brown sugar on medium speed until light and fluffy. Beat in eggs and vanilla, adding eggs one at a time until well combined. Scrape down the sides of the bowl between adding each egg. Add flour mixture, chopped Oreos and white and semisweet chocolate chips, mixing on low speed just until the flour disappears.

3. SPREAD THE BATTER evenly in the prepared pan. Press remaining ¾ cup Oreo chunks over the top of the blondies. Bake about 25 minutes, or until golden around the edges. Cool for 1 hour before removing from pan.

MAKES	20–24 blondies
PREP	15 minutes
COOK	25 minutes

- 2 cups flour
- ½ tsp kosher salt
- ¼ tsp baking soda
- ¾ cup butter, softened
- ½ cup sugar
- 1 cup brown sugar
- 2 eggs
- 1½ tsp vanilla extract
- 1½ cups chopped Oreo cookies
- ¾ cup white chocolate chips
- ¾ cup semisweet chocolate chips
- ¾ cup Oreo cookies, cut in large pieces for topping

"I'm not offended by all the dumb blonde jokes because I know I'm not dumb … and I also know that I'm not blonde."

Dolly Parton

If there was a Girl Scout badge for making more smoke than fire, I'd have it. I lack outdoorswoman skills, thus seriously limiting my opportunity to dig in to my favorite trio—golden melted marshmallows, creamy chocolate and crunchy graham crackers. Or so I thought. Troop Leader Lisa has taken my quest indoors with these unbelievable Chewy S'mores Pudding Cookies. With vanilla pudding giving an extra flavor punch and filled with graham cracker pieces, mini marshmallows and milk chocolate, these campfire-free creations have earned me my baking badge. Move aside, Thin Mints and Samoas—there's a new coveted cookie in town.

CHEWY S'MORES PUDDING COOKIES

MAKES 18 large cookies

PREP 10 minutes
(+1 hour refrigeration)

COOK 15 minutes

. . . .

1 cup butter, room temperature
1 cup brown sugar
½ cup sugar
1 package (3.4 oz) instant vanilla pudding powder
2 eggs
1 tsp vanilla extract
2¼ cups flour
½ tsp baking soda
¼ tsp kosher salt
1 cup coarsely broken graham crackers
1 cup mini marshmallows
1½ cups chopped milk chocolate

1. LINE A BAKING SHEET with parchment paper. Set aside.

2. USING AN ELECTRIC MIXER, cream butter, brown sugar and sugar on medium speed. Add vanilla pudding powder and continue to beat to combine. Add the eggs one at a time, beating until mixture is light and fluffy. Mix in vanilla extract. On low speed, add the flour, baking soda, salt, graham crackers, mini marshmallows and chopped chocolate. Mix just until flour disappears and mixture is incorporated, being careful not to overmix.

3. DROP by ¼ cup scoop on prepared baking sheet. Cover and refrigerate 1 hour before baking.

4. TO BAKE COOKIES, preheat oven to 325°F. Bake 14–15 minutes, until edges are golden. Cool cookies on a wire rack.

. . . .

To revive stale marshmallows, place a slice of white bread with the marshmallows in an airtight container.

Lisa has a lot in common with Oprah—people tell her their secrets, she's charitable and she's a mogul. However, one thing Lisa won't do is pick favorites. She loves her kids equally, she likes all 31 flavors and she'll never single out a favorite recipe. But I'm more like Ellen and I have a big mouth, so I'm going to tell you that Lisa loves these soft and spicy ginger cookies—sandwiching a sweet and tart lemon cream filling—the very most. With blackstrap molasses bringing deep color and flavor to these classic cookies and zesty lemon that makes us suckers for the pucker, this is one delectable dessert. Now, don't tell her I told you, but I'm also Lisa's favorite sister.

GINGER COOKIE SANDWICHES WITH LEMON FILLING

1. LINE 2 BAKING SHEETS with parchment paper. Using an electric mixer on medium speed, cream butter, sugar and brown sugar until light and fluffy. Add egg and vanilla, beating until well incorporated. Add molasses and mix on low speed until combined. Add flour, baking soda, cinnamon, ginger and salt, mixing on low speed just until combined.

2. TAKE 2 TABLESPOONS of dough and roll into a ball. Place 3 tablespoons sugar on a flat plate and roll dough ball into the sugar. Place ball on prepared baking sheet and continue with remaining dough. Cover both baking sheets and refrigerate for 1 hour before baking.

3. PREHEAT OVEN to 350°F. Remove baking sheets from refrigerator and using the bottom of a glass, flatten each dough ball slightly. Bake cookies 8–10 minutes, until golden around the edges. Let cookies cool completely before filling.

4. FOR THE FILLING, using an electric mixer, cream butter, icing sugar, lemon juice and lemon zest on medium speed until a spreadable consistency.

5. TO ASSEMBLE cookie sandwiches, using a small spoon, place filling in the center of a cookie bottom. Gently press another cookie bottom on top until filling spreads.

MAKES   12 cookie sandwiches
PREP   25 minutes
        (+1 hour refrigeration)
COOK   10 minutes

. . . .

GINGER COOKIES
¾   cup butter, room temperature
½   cup sugar
¼   cup brown sugar
1   egg
1   tsp vanilla extract
6   tbsp blackstrap molasses
2½ cups flour
1   tsp baking soda
1   tsp ground cinnamon
1   tsp ground ginger
¼   tsp kosher salt

3   tbsp sugar, for rolling cookie dough

LEMON FILLING
½   cup butter, room temperature
2½ cups icing sugar
2   tbsp fresh lemon juice
1   tsp lemon zest

. . . .

Baking sheets without sides let the heat circulate better, make cookies brown more evenly and make for easier removal of cookies than rimmed baking sheets.

Want to hit the chocolate trifecta? Step right up and place your bets on Hot to Trot Lisa, a baker with the inside scoop on serving up ribbon-winning cookies. These Triple Chocolate Chip Cookies are no exception—overrun with semisweet, milk and white chocolate, these chewy and moist cookies deliver a perfecta in every bite, guaranteed to get you over the finish line first. With so many trips to the winner's circle, Jockey Julie (that's me) isn't putting the nag (aka Lisa, the old horse) out to pasture just yet.

CHEWY TRIPLE CHOCOLATE CHIP COOKIES

MAKES	36 cookies
PREP	10 minutes (+30–60 minute refrigeration)
COOK	10 minutes

1   cup butter, room temperature
1   cup sugar
1   cup brown sugar
2   eggs
1½   tsp vanilla extract
3   cups flour
1   tsp baking soda
¾   tsp kosher salt
1   cup semisweet chocolate chips
1   cup milk chocolate chips
1   cup white chocolate, cut into chunks

1. PREHEAT OVEN to 350°F. Line a baking sheet with parchment paper.

2. USING AN ELECTRIC MIXER, cream butter, sugar and brown sugar on medium speed. Add the eggs one at a time, beating until incorporated. Mix in vanilla extract. On low speed, add the flour, baking soda, salt, semisweet chocolate, milk chocolate and white chocolate. Mix just until the flour disappears, being careful not to overmix.

3. DROP 2 heaping tablespoons of dough for each cookie on prepared baking sheet. Cover and refrigerate 30–60 minutes before baking. Bake 10–12 minutes, just until the edges begin to brown. Cool cookies on a wire rack.

Chilling the dough before baking off the cookies results in thick, moist and chewy coffee shop–style treats.

How do I love these cookies? Let me count the ways. First, they hit the trio of texture: crispy edges, crunchy tops *and* chewy centers. Sounds impossible, but it's a remarkable feat accomplished by our ace baker, Smart Cookie Lisa. Next, these classic cookies-with-a-twist are studded with sweet, creamy butterscotch chips and cornflakes, secret ingredients that deliver surprising, scrumptious bites. Last (but certainly not least), I have a stellar excuse when I get my hand caught in the cookie jar at breakfast—I take my oatmeal to go . . .

THE ULTIMATE OATMEAL BUTTERSCOTCH COOKIE

1. PREHEAT OVEN to 350°F. Line a baking sheet with parchment paper.

2. USING AN ELECTRIC MIXER, cream butter, brown sugar and sugar on medium speed. Add eggs one at a time, beating until fluffy. Mix in vanilla extract. On low speed, add the flour, baking soda, salt, cinnamon, oats, cornflakes and butterscotch chips, mixing just until flour disappears. Do not overmix.

3. DROP ¼ cup batter for each cookie on prepared baking sheet. Bake for 10 minutes, until edges begin to brown slightly. Cool cookies on wire rack.

MAKES	25 large cookies
PREP	10 minutes
COOK	10 minutes

1	cup butter, room temperature
1½	cups brown sugar
½	cup sugar
2	eggs
1	tsp vanilla extract
2	cups flour
1	tsp baking soda
½	tsp kosher salt
½	tsp ground cinnamon
2	cups old-fashioned oats
2	cups coarsely crushed cornflakes
2	cups butterscotch chips

"I think baking cookies is equal to Queen Victoria running an empire. There's no difference in how seriously you take the job, how seriously you approach your whole life."

Martha Stewart

When in New York, we make a beeline for Levain Bakery. Their cookies are legendary, and we've been known to eat our weight in them. That said, since we can't always brave the long lineups, Lisa has created her own version of their colossal chewy Chocolate Chip Walnut Cookies. Crunchy on the outside, gooey on the inside, these thick cookies are loaded with creamy chocolate and toasted (don't skip toasting them—it makes a huge difference in flavor) walnuts. While we're always happy to take a bite out of the Big Apple, bake up these cookies and discover the greatest thing outside of Gotham.

LISA'S LEVAIN CHOCOLATE CHIP WALNUT COOKIES

MAKES 12 large cookies

PREP 10 minutes
(+1 hour refrigeration)

COOK 15 minutes

· ·

1	cup cold butter, cubed
1	cup brown sugar
¾	cup sugar
2	eggs
3¼	cups flour
2	tbsp cornstarch
1	tsp baking powder
¼	tsp baking soda
¾	tsp kosher salt
1½	cups semisweet chocolate chips
1	cup milk chocolate chips
1	cup coarsely chopped toasted walnuts

1. LINE 2 BAKING SHEETS with parchment paper. Using an electric mixer, cream butter, brown sugar and sugar on medium speed until combined. Add eggs one at a time, beating until incorporated. On low speed, add flour, cornstarch, baking powder, baking soda, salt, semisweet chocolate, milk chocolate and walnuts. Mix just until the flour disappears, being careful not to overmix the dough.

2. PORTION OUT ½-cup mounds of dough for each cookie. Pile the dough high on the cookie sheets. Cover and refrigerate 1 hour before baking.

3. PREHEAT OVEN to 375°F. Bake cookies 15–16 minutes, just until the edges begin to brown. Cool cookies on a wire rack.

· ·

Cornstarch is added to the recipe to keep the cookies soft and tender when cooled.

> "We're not worthy."
>
> —Wayne's World

[ACKNOWLEDGMENTS]

WE THANK

We worship Robert McCullough. He is the Wizard of Publishing (brilliant and funny and kind, oh my!) and a true friend; without him we never would have made it to Oz. There's no place like Appetite.

We adore the teams at Appetite and Penguin Random House Canada. Lindsay "LindsPat" Paterson has held our hands every happy step along the yellow brick road and has expertly minded our p's and q's. Thanks also go out to Susan Burns and Laura Cameron, and future thanks go to the raring-to-go publicity and sales teams that include Trish Bunnett, Lindsey Reeder, Cathy Paine and Jennifer Herman.

We respect and revere Scott Richardson. He's a truth-telling designer who delivered us from the '80s with his modern, clean and beautiful vision.

We cherish our Eye Candy Dream Team. Ryan Szulc, a photographer with extreme talent, who led us shot by shot—we're so lucky to work with you and your super-skilled sidekick Matt "Matty Boy" Gibson. Food was expertly styled by Nicole Young, a captain of cuisine and woman with *the* magic touch. Huge thanks also to Matt Kimura for his sick food styling and to superb stylist Catherine Doherty for serving up cool, creative props and awesome ideas.

We idolize Ben Wiseman, an illustrator whose mad skills inspired us every step of the way in creating the look for *Lick Your Plate*.

We applaud and appreciate Michael Levine of Westwood Creative Artists. His door opening abilities and salesmanship are legendary.

We treasure those who continue to support us in our quest. Yes, that means you, Heather Reisman, Meryl Witkin, Dara Willow, Big3 Video, Cheryl Louvelle, Mark Stein of Kick 10 Sports & Entertainment, Julia and Julia Beauty, Métier Creative, Pure Leaf Tea, Sassan Jahan, Lourdes Seminario, Marnie Sugarman, the Lustig family, Rachel Wexler, Jade Zylberberg, Susan Sacchi, Bonnie Levy, Nancy Duckman, Penny Offman, Melissa Yung, and of course, our big bro Ken, sis-in-law Jen and our late and unbelievably great grandmother Alice Lieberman.

We love Larry and Judy Tanenbaum, parents who nourish us with all that's delicious—family, food and fun.

JULIE THANKS

I'm forever grateful to Kenny A., a man with boundless love, kindness and an insatiable appetite. My kids, Jamie, Perry and Benjy, are the butter to my bread. I also send xo's to my PB girls (in alpha order), Lisa Diamond, Miriam Elmaleh, Wendy Geller, Andrea Goldstein, Estelle Goldstein, Dahra Granovsky, Carolyn Offman, Joanna Sugar and Elise Teitler.

LISA THANKS

Thanks to Jordan, Emmy, Lauren and Alex, the best taste testers who know which side of the kitchen they belong on. Your love, support and suggestions fuel me at the stove. To Sophie, the twinkling one who lay at (and under) my feet, and to my friends, I thank you for all your love and encouragement.

[INDEX]